Mormons
and
Muslims

THE RELIGIOUS STUDIES
MONOGRAPH SERIES

Mormons and Muslims

Spiritual Foundations and Modern Manifestations

Edited with an Introduction by
SPENCER J. PALMER

VOLUME EIGHT
IN THE RELIGIOUS STUDIES MONOGRAPH SERIES

Religious Studies Center
Brigham Young University
Provo, Utah

Copyright © 1983 by
Religious Studies Center
Brigham Young University

Library of Congress Catalog Card Number: 83-60881
ISBN O-88494-483-2

4TH PRINTING, 1992

Produced and Distributed by
BOOKCRAFT, INC.
Salt Lake City, Utah

Lithographed in the United States of America
PUBLISHERS PRESS
Salt Lake City, Utah

To Robert J. Matthews
who suggested this conference on Islām

Acknowledgments

I am grateful to the directors and advisory board of the Religious Studies Center, as well as to the symposium arrangements committee, who also served as presenters and discussants, for their valuable assistance in preparing for the conference on Islām from which this book has been produced. It is also with heartfelt appreciation that I wish to acknowledge the services of Lillian Osborne, John Madsen, and Brett Stauffer in handling the details of the conference, and of Dilworth Parkinson and Lavina Fielding Anderson for helping bring the manuscript into publishable form. Hap Green of Publishers Press and George Bickerstaff of Bookcraft deserve special recognition for their encouragement, good judgment, and skill.

S.J.P.

Contents

Panel Discussion
Mormons and Muslims:
Values, Life-styles, and Faith

Introduction

Nearly one out of every six people on earth today is a Muslim. They are found in almost every nation, in hundreds of racial groups, speaking dozens of languages. Indonesia has the largest Muslim population with 150 million, South Africa has 3 million, the Soviet Union has 40 million, the People's Republic of China has 18 million. The largest Muslim ethnic group is the 120 million Arabs. There are 800,000 Muslims in the United States, and even Taiwan has 20,000.

Islām, the religion of the Muslim peoples, makes up the second largest religious group on earth, next to Christianity. Islām is known as a "biblical faith" in part because Muhammad (570-632 A.D.), the Arabian prophet of Islām, revered the teachings of Abraham and Moses and eighteen other major prophets of the Bible. But Islām makes a special revelatory claim for the teachings and narratives of the Qur'ān, the sacred book of scripture of the Muslim world.

Although the largest concentrations of the world's 750 million Muslims today appear in nonindustrial third-world states which are not generally regarded as leaders in scientific, intellectual, economic, or even cultural development, they can lay claim to a brilliant history of achievement in these fields. "No people in the early Middle Ages," Philip K. Hitti concludes, "contributed to human progress so much as did the Arabs, a term which in our usage would comprise all Arabic-speaking peoples, including the Arabians, that is, the inhabitants of the Arabian peninsula. . . . For centuries in the Middle Ages Arabic was the language of learning, culture and progress throughout the civilized world. Between the ninth and twelfth centuries more works—philosophical, medical, historical, religious, astronomical, geographical—were produced through the medium of Arabic than through any other tongue."[1]

For five hundred years Islām dominated the world by its power, its learning, and its superior civilization.[2] Heirs to the scientific and philosophical treasures of the Greeks, Islām passed on its treasure, after enriching it, to Western Europe. Together with astronomy, mathematics was the science which the Arabs favored most. Many basic principles of arithmetic, geometry, and algebra were discovered by Muslim scholars. Western arithmetic still uses the numerals and methods of counting invented by the Arabs. The Muslims perfected the Chinese compass and made practical application of it in navigation.

Among their most beneficial inventions has been the manufacture of paper from cotton, linen, and rags. Upon this single invention depended the subsequent diffusion of cheap books and the popularization of learning, a social revolution bottlenecked by the expensive parchment of the ancient world and the silk paper of the Chinese. Furthermore, Arab doctors have played a decisive role in Western medical science, particularly in the field of surgery. As early as the eleventh century, Muslim physicians treated cataracts, practiced cauterization, knew about anesthetics—generally considered a modern discovery—and pioneered ophthalmology.

Although Muslims have excelled in many branches of science, some of their most significant and lasting contributions have been in the realms of language, literature, architecture, and the visual arts. The West is indebted to the Arabs for a heritage of scientific terms—*alchemy, alcohol, algebra, borax, cipher, elixir,* and *zenith*—and only the comparative isolation of the two cultures has hampered a fuller appreciation of Islām's written aesthetics. An Arab proverb says, "God gave three great things to the world: The brain of the Frank, the hands of the Chinese, and the tongue of the Arab." That distinctive union of intellectual qualities and powerful poetics may best be illustrated by the Qur'ān itself, which was meant to be heard as it was chanted, not analyzed for its historical and narrative values. Visually, its verses decorate mosques and sacred buildings throughout the world—not only in Mecca and Jerusalem. In a religion that prohibits the image and icon, Arabic calligraphy has assumed the stature of artistic and religious expression, while Muslim architecture continues to be admired wherever Muslim culture has flourished. Examples today are the Mosque of

Sultan Hasan in Cairo, the Mosque of Omar in Jerusalem, and the Taj Mahal of India.

Mormon interest in the lands and peoples of the Near East is deep-seated. Mormons recognize that the Arabs are literal descendants of Abraham through his son, Ishmael—therefore entitled to the promises pronounced upon the seed of Abraham in the Bible. Like Muhammad and the Muslims, Mormons also regard their religion as a restoration of the covenant which father Abraham and the ancient patriarchs made with God. However, the intense historical Mormon involvement in the geographical region of Islām's roots has sometimes emphasized certain traditions and regions at the expense of a more complete picture, and Mormons have not been immune from the general Western tendency to accept stereotypical pictures of Islamic faith and practice.

The pages which follow record the discussions, lectures, and papers of a conference on "Islām: Spiritual Foundations and Modern Manifestations," which was held on the campus of Brigham Young University under the sponsorship of BYU's Religious Studies Center in cooperation with the university's Near Eastern Studies Program of the David M. Kennedy Center for International and Area Studies. The meetings included some of the ablest exponents and finest interpreters of Islām's relationships with Christianity.

The discussions of this conference provided a diversified, realistic, and appreciative view. The analogies and associations between Christianity and Islām became vividly apparent through contrasts in the development of Islām in different cultural settings. For example, Islām in Indonesia's peasant society has been conditioned by its productive rice cultivation, inwardness, patience, and self-effacement, while in Morocco it has assumed some of the restless, aggressive, extroverted tribal qualities of that society. Theological distinctions between the larger Sunni community and the smaller but sometimes highly vocal Shicites, with their interpretations of the *Mahdi* (the Directed One), a redemptive figure to come, provided an image of active theological diversity to replace the monolithic stereotype sometimes held.

Mormons in attendance expressed keen interest in several cultural and historical points of contact—a view of a theology of responsibility, of judgment, and a cultural matrix which produced pre-Islamic prophets. A keener curiosity and a greater sense of maturing commitment to fellowship with the people of Islām were fully realized hopes of the symposium. A unique dimension developed as participants focused on parallels, similarities, and contrasts with Mormonism in its emergence as a world faith. It was an underlying theme of the conference that authentic interchange and deepening understanding are prerequisite for "crossing the divides" between Mormons and Muslims in today's world.

One aspect of that hope is expressed in the visual symbol of the conference program, and the design which appears on the dust jacket of this book. It is an excerpt from "Thunder," a *Sūra*, or chapter, of the Qur'ān, in the original Maghribi script, a script developed in Spain and North Africa in Western Islām in the Middle Ages. Its translation runs "And those who ward off evil with good, these shall have a blissful end. They shall enter the gardens of Eden together with the righteous among their fathers."

We at Brigham Young University were gratified by the cordiality and friendship that mutually prevailed. Attendance at the sessions of the symposium was large, interested, and respectful. A considerable number of Muslim students who attended from Logan and Salt Lake City joined with other conference visitors at the customary afternoon hour of prayer in a private room. The schedule was arranged to accommodate this ceremony. Speakers frequently expressed appreciation for the opportunity to explain and amplify aspects of their own scholarly interests but which also touched closely upon matters of their personal faith.

David M. Kennedy, former Secretary of the Treasury of the United States and currently Special Representative for the First Presidency of The Church of Jesus Christ of Latter-day Saints, recounted his experiences in Indonesia and his personal acquaintance with Haji Alamsjah, the Minister of Religion of that country. Minister Alamsjah's keynote message, read by Haji Anton Timur Djaelani, Director General for Islamic Institutional Development in the Ministry of Religion, explained *pancasila*, the five principles of state philosophy that have governed Indonesia's transformation into an actively religious country without a state religion. He explained that the overwhelming majority of Indonesians are Muslims; and that Indonesia has been energetically developing and expanding a progressive strain of Islamic thought that deals with the modern world, not by capitulating to it or by withdrawing from it but by finding acceptable theological and cultural ways of acquiring and enjoying its fruits in a context of Islamic values.

A panel on "Mormons and Muslims: Values, Life-styles, and Faith," was carried out by people with wide experience in both religion and academics—scholars who have studied Islām and found it not entirely foreign. David C. Montgomery, professor of history and coordinator of Near Eastern studies at Brigham Young University, moderated the discussions. I attempted the task of pointing out some of the teachings and beliefs that make for common ground between Mormons and Muslims, even while acknowledging significant differences that exist.

Orin D. Parker, president of AMIDEAST based in Washington, D.C., commented on observations of family closeness and reverence for God that had particularly struck him during his many years of living among the peoples of the Near East. Robert L. Staab, assistant director of the Middle East Center at the University of Utah, who spent two years in a Turkish village, described his detailed observation of how the "five pillars of Islām"—the creedal belief in God and the prophet Muhammad, prayer, almsgiving, fasting, and pilgrimage—affected village and individual life day by day.

Omar Kader, assistant to the dean of the College of Family, Home, and Social Sciences at Brigham Young University, had grown up Muslim in a very Mormon Provo and remembers his father's insistence on sharing Muslim holidays with gifts of food to their neighbors during the feast following *Ramadān*. He reminded the audience of a point that was becoming clearer—one cultural image is inadequate to express the extensity of Islām. Kader discussed both realities and misperceptions of Islām among Americans in general as well as Mormons.

Of special interest to Latter-day Saints was a paper by Arnold H. Green, associate professor of modern Near Eastern history at American University in Cairo. He traced historic and literary comparisons between Joseph Smith and Muhammad that began in Joseph Smith's lifetime, concluding that no serious attempt had yet been made to examine the comparison in the context of the

sociology of religions and posing the intriguing possibilities of what
might happen if the differences and similarities could thus be
examined. Green observes that the comparison has sometimes been
pursued for questionable reasons and with questionable methods,
but Mormons at least should use it as a metaphor to help them view
Muhammad "not as a fraud and a heretic but rather as a great and
good man who was instrumental in the establishment of an
important world religion belonging to the Judeo-Christian
tradition."

William Hamblin, a doctoral candidate in Near Eastern studies
at the University of Michigan, also dealt with prophets and
prophethood in the Islamic tradition. With the use of slides, he
examined two of six non-biblical prophets described in the Qur'ān,
focusing particularly on one called Hūd in the southern part of the
Arabian peninsula. Although he warned that no causal link can be
established between Hūd and the pre-Islamic Book of Mormon
Lehi, who traveled in Arabia, the parallels are at least intriguing.
His research confirms that, according to the Qur'ān, God has
inspired not only Hebrew and Christian prophets but nonbiblical
prophets as well.

Mahmoud Mustafa Ayoub, associate professor in the Centre for
Religious Studies at the University of Toronto, delivered a lecture
on the idea of redemption in Islām. He observed that to understand
it one must first understand Western Christianity's idea of
redemption through suffering and death and the Eastern (Greek
Orthodox) idea of redemption through the victorious conquering of
death. Though Islām has its martyrs and the role of Muhammad as
mediator is central, it draws primarily on the rich Eastern image of
the cross as a throne of glory, one that grows out of the Muslim
concept of man's nature as essentially good, not burdened by
original sin. Ayoub concludes that in the idea of the *Mahdi*, Islām
and Christianity meet. Jesus will come to restore the world to its
purity, but Muslim piety affirms that Jesus and the *Mahdi* will work
together.

In a panel on "Women and Worship: Islām in the Mosque and in
the Home," four scholars who lived among and studied women in
Muslim societies examined the responses of Muslim women to discriminatory Qur'anic injunctions and authoritative male practices.

Jane I. Smith, associate dean for academic affairs and lecturer in comparative religion at Harvard, described how Egyptian women, faced with impersonal rites in a mosque, where women are physically separated from the service, tend to meet their religious needs in a creative variety of informal ways—particularly through participation in quasi-healing rituals that have remained the province of women. In so doing, Smith concludes, Muslim women in Egypt have found ways to establish and exercise power separately from designated male authority.

Anne H. Betteridge, a doctoral candidate in the Department of Anthropology at the University of Chicago, presented some of the results of her research on the "informal" aspects of women's religion, particularly on their visits to local shrines in Iran. Betteridge explained that the formalized structured activities of the mosque are more often for men; women are kept in the role of spectators and on the ceremonial sidelines. But women frequent local shrines dedicated to Muslim saints. Such pilgrimages seem particularly suited to expressing the feminine side of human nature with its spontaneous life-giving elements.

Donna Lee Bowen, assistant professor of political science at Brigham Young University, has done extensive surveys on family planning among Moroccan women. Her data showed that although Islām thoroughly safeguarded the welfare of the family, no dogma existed on family planning; instead, whatever would be best for the family at a given time period was considered to be Islamically correct. In Bowen's view, discriminatory laws and practices in Islām, when understood within the total social context, can make good sense.

Frederick M. Denny, associate professor of religious studies at the University of Colorado, challenged the stereotype of Muslim women—that of the veil and the cloister—by explaining that Indonesia not only fosters progressive education for its women— including specific instruction in the Qur'ān—but also is the home of a proudly matrilineal and matrilocal ethnic group that is also Islamic.

Umar F. Abd-Allāh, chairman of the Islamic Studies Division of the Department of Near Eastern Studies at the University of Michigan, followed the twin concepts of the perceptible and the

unseen through the Qur'ān and into the beliefs and practices of
Islām, contrasting them with the practices of pre-Islamic and polytheistic Arabs, and expanding almost poetically upon their role in
developing a sense of God's greatness, man's moral responsibility,
and man's innately good nature. He argued that to fully appreciate
Islām one must see it as a courageous redefinition of prophethood;
that unlike the shamans, diviners, spirits, and oracular figures of the
folk religion of pre-Islamic Arabia, a prophet in the Islamic view has
no independent knowledge of the unseen. He has true knowledge
only through the revelation of God, which he must obey. In the
Muslim view, prophetic revelation is man's only means of gaining
explicit and definite knowledge of the great realities of the unseen
that affect his destiny.

Elder Carlos E. Asay of the Presidency of the First Quorum of
the Seventy of The Church of Jesus Christ of Latter-day Saints not
only brought the personal greetings of the leadership of the Church
to the conference but shared his own experiences during his years in
Lebanon and Syria. He reported that his life among the Muslims
had a sanctifying influence and stimulated a spiritual renewal. He
emphasized ways in which Mormon consideration of Islām must
acknowledge the hand of God. In these remarks, he echoed the
welcoming tone that had been provided on behalf of Brigham
Young University President Jeffrey R. Holland by Noel B.
Reynolds, associate academic vice-president for religious
instruction. Reynolds told the Muslims in attendance that "there are
many important elements of Mormon thought in which we would
feel closer to the followers of Muhammad than to the contemporary
Christian culture in which we have been located since our
beginnings."

In addition to the information provided by the participants at
this symposium, another message was given: In an atmosphere of
good will in an educational setting, the old magic of human
sympathy was working. For those who may have thought that
Islām was imponderable and distant, this was an experience among
Mormons, Muslims, and others that was both enlightening and
reassuring.

SPENCER J. PALMER

NOTES

1. Philip K. Hitti, *The Arabs: A Short History* (New York: St. Martin's Press, 1968), pp. 2, 5.

2. For a more detailed survey see Haidar Bammate, *Muslim Contributions to Civilization* (Takoma Park, Md.; Crescent Publications, 1962).

1
Brigham Young University: A Special Commitment to Faith

Noel B. Reynolds

It is an honor to represent our university president, Jeffrey R. Holland, in welcoming all of you to this important symposium today. As President Holland had to be out of the country this week and next, he asked me to greet you and to read his personal statement to you:

I am delighted *in absentia* to welcome all of our symposium participants and guests to Brigham Young University. I

Noel B. Reynolds, associate academic vice-president and professor of government at Brigham Young University, received his M.A. and Ph.D. from Harvard in political and legal theory and has done post-doctoral work at Harvard in law and legal and political philosophy. During the past ten years of teaching at BYU he has served as chairman of the Philosophy Department, associate director of the Honors Program, and director of General Education.

apologize for my absence, but I know all of my colleagues will put forth every effort to make your BYU visit a pleasant and rewarding one.

I especially wish to commend Dr. Spencer J. Palmer and his committee members for organizing and sponsoring this discussion of "Islām: Spiritual Foundations and Modern Manifestations." I fear we in the Western world have been unconscionably negligent in addressing this very important topic. I am delighted that BYU, including its Religious Studies Center and Near Eastern Studies Program, can play some role today in expanding our understanding of and appreciation for Islām's traditional beliefs and contemporary significance.

Those conference participants whom I personally invited to join us, I thank warmly for their response. I do hope that the future will hold many opportunities for me to meet you personally and enjoy your personal and professional friendship. Once again, I wish you well for a stimulating symposium in an atmosphere of faith, fellowship and genuine goodwill.

I especially want to add my own greeting and expression of gratitude for those of our participants who have traveled so far for this meeting. We recognize in your participation a gesture of extraordinary generosity and goodwill. We hope that you will feel welcomed here in that same spirit.

BYU's interest in such a symposium merits some attention. BYU differs from every other university in the world in that it owes its existence to the appearance of a modern prophet. Joseph Smith was called by God in 1820 to bear a special message to the world and to counteract the forces of evil and disbelief that were mounting on all sides. Joseph Smith was told that his call had come because the people of the earth had strayed from the ordinances and covenants of God; that they no longer respected the teachings of the prophets, but that "every man walketh in his own way, and after the image of his own god, whose image is in the likeness of the world, and whose substance is that of an idol."

Joseph Smith was instructed to teach faith and repentance to all people and was promised that "inasmuch as they were humble they might be made strong, and blessed from on high, and receive knowledge from time to time" (Doctrine and Covenants 1:15-16, 28).

Because of their adherence to this nineteenth-century prophet, the early Mormons were driven from one community to another and were finally expelled from the heart of Christian America out into the great western desert, where they began to build their own society. Freed from the dogmatism and intolerance of a nineteenth-century Christianity which could not conceive of a new prophet, the Mormons began to flourish.

Learning was especially important to these people and they established schools wherever they settled. Amazing and pretentious though it may have seemed, they determined at a very early stage to establish a university. Evidence of this early and continuing commitment to education is seen in the fact that even though Utah still has a relatively small population, it supports four universities and has an average level of education that has led the nation for many years.

To understand the Mormon commitment to education, however, one must see that for us it is a sacred charge. In the revelations received by Joseph Smith, the Latter-day Saints were instructed to "seek learning, even by study and also by faith"; to "seek . . . out of the best books words of wisdom," and to study all peoples and nations, both near and far. (Doctrine and Covenants 88:79, 118.) Furthermore, we have been taught in our own scriptures to look for the inspired teachings of God that have come to men in all nations; "For behold, the Lord doth grant unto all nations, of their own nation and tongue, to teach his word, yea, in wisdom, all that he seeth fit that they should have" (Alma 29:8), and in the words of Joseph Smith himself, "We should gather all the good and true principles in the world and treasure them up, or we shall not come out true 'Mormons'."[1]

But assessing our own achievements as a university, it is painfully obvious that only a handful of our scholars here have carefully studied the history and culture of Islām—one of the great religions of the world. We earnestly hope that this conference will increase the awareness of and active interest in these subjects on this campus. I have to confess a serious weakness in my own studies of this area. Of all the literature produced in the culture and history of Islām, I have read only in the Qur'ān and in the works of a handful of medieval philosophers, such as Avicenna, Averroes, and Alfarabi. Because of its special commitments, Brigham Young University should prepare to lead the way among American universities in more extensive studies in such areas as this.

I am sure there will be many opportunities in this symposium to make some comparisons between Islamic and Mormon beliefs. It may come as some surprise to our visitors to learn that there are many important elements of Mormon thought in which we would feel closer to the followers of Muhammad than to the contemporary Christian culture in which we have been located since our beginnings. This point was emphasized for me a few years ago as I observed a map of the world indicating country by country the relative ease with which abortions might be obtained. Mormons today are increasingly uncomfortable in a greater Christian society which has rapidly moved to an extremely liberal approach to abortion. I was impressed to see that it is the Muslim countries of the world that have most successfully resisted this alarming trend. But this is only one of many such issues which might be mentioned.

The secularization of belief is a challenge of the contemporary world which is vigorously resisted by Mormons and Muslims alike. To the extent that the secular studies which comprise the bulk of the offerings in modern universities seek to develop a view of the world in which the will and power of God is of no relevance, our scholars are confronted with the special task of seeking out what is good and true in those studies as a means of enhancing and enriching faith without compromising it.

Although many religions find exposure to the learning of the world extremely threatening, such need not be the case here. Our confidence in God and in the teachings of his prophets is such that we feel quite free to examine the findings and theories of all fields of scholarly endeavor with openness and genuine interest. Because of our faith we have no ultimate commitment to academic theories, and we are, therefore, in an important way much freer than others to consider the weakness of such theories at the same time that we admire the strengths.

Finally, as Latter-day Saints we firmly believe that the pursuit of knowledge and truth will be of most value to those who have learned first to submit themselves to God in all things. The character of the seeker affects both his ability to find enlightenment and his ability to use it wisely. For us, as with Plato of old, knowledge without virtue is nothing, and the better understanding we can get of this world, the better will be our understanding of God who made it. The better our understanding of man becomes, the better will be our understanding of his Creator.

NOTES

1. Joseph Smith, Jr., *History of the Church,* ed., B. H. Roberts, 7 vols. (Salt Lake City: Deseret Book, 1971), 5:517.

2
A Context of Brotherhood

David M. Kennedy

It is a great pleasure for me to be at this symposium, an effective means in bringing understanding to all of us in an area where understanding is too often lacking. I am honored to introduce our distinguished visitor for the keynote address, Mr. Haji Anton Timur Djaelani, who will be reading the speech of Mr. Haji Alamsjah Ratu

---

David M. Kennedy received a B.A. degree from Weber State College and M.A. and LL.B. degrees from George Washington University, and also graduated from the Stonier Graduate School of Banking, Rutgers University. He was president of Continental Illinois Bank of Chicago, 1966-1969, then served as United States Secretary of the Treasury, 1969-1971, followed by service as United States ambassador to the North Atlantic Treaty Organization (NATO) in Europe and United States ambassador at large, 1971-1973. Ambassador Kennedy is now Special Representative of the First Presidency of The Church of Jesus Christ of Latter-day Saints.

Perwiranegara, Indonesia's Minister of Religion. I wish to do so in the context of brotherhood and understanding.

I have been in most areas of the world, and in many of the countries of the world. I have seen people from all over the world in many walks of life with various views and different cultural backgrounds. It impressed me early that all of us are seeking a common end—an increase in happiness and a better way of life. I have found that even the leaders of nations are interested in the same things that we're interested in—home, family, our children and grandchildren, and in economic and social progress that will make life better for all of us.

Despite our common interests, however, there are different views about how to seek these ends. In some way, we must come to an understanding so that our means will be as peaceful as our ends are desirable. I've been impressed over the years with the lack of understanding in our country—the United States of America—of the Islamic world. It is time indeed for gatherings such as these here.

Our debt to Dr. Palmer is great. My personal debt is equally profound. I met Dr. Palmer years ago for the first time in Korea. I found him very much interested in the people of Korea, knowledgeable about their culture, their history—even their folk music. He gave me records of Korean music that have been an important part of my understanding of those fine people and their national spirit.

At the same time, we talked about other areas. I found that Dr. Palmer was interested in all of Asia—in the various religions, cultures, history, and background of the peoples. He had a great interest in Buddhism and Islām. Since I have been serving as ambassador at large for the Church, I have had many discussions with Dr. Palmer; and he has been most helpful in providing information and counsel. He has also been kind enough to introduce me and others to scholars who can give in-depth views of various nations and their characteristics.

Another participant in this symposium, Orin Parker, is a friend whom I met for the first time in Lebanon. We found we had a common friend in Lebanon—Dr. Adam Malik—who welcomed us to his beautiful home, which I hope has not been destroyed. He took us to his political and religious libraries on the third and fourth floors. I was very much impressed—the room was perhaps twenty feet by twenty feet, covered on four sides with bookshelves full of books. When I asked, "Do you have anything on Mormonism?" he took me to a bookcase where he had two shelves at least six feet long filled with books on Mormonism. I asked him why he was so interested in Mormonism. He had been to Utah, knew a great deal about the Mormon Church, and had several Mormon friends. But more than that, he was very much interested in all religions and their influence on people, economics, and political conditions.

I have also visited Indonesia many times, the first time, I think, as Secretary of the Treasury of the United States. President Kemusu Suharto, after the revolution, had accepted the national and international debts of the Sukarno administration. It was a very large debt owed to the United States, to Europe, and to Russia. We had Dr. Herman Apps of the Duchi Bank make a very careful study to see what terms and conditions would be necessary for Indonesia to meet its obligations. I was amazed at the tremendous wealth of Indonesia's natural resources—their oil, their timber, their minerals, and other resources. We rescheduled the debt, giving a longer period for payment, reducing the rate of interest, and so on, we had talks with the other creditor nations in a conference in Paris to secure Soviet agreement that United States aid to Indonesia would not be liable in payment on the debt due Russia, and also secured the approval of the Congress of the United States. Mrs. Kennedy and I then flew to the island of Bali for a few days' rest in that beautiful place, then went to Djakarta, where we were received in a most friendly way by President Suharto, by Adam Malik, then foreign minister and now vice president, and by my counterpart, Ali Wardana, minister of finance of Indonesia. We signed the treaty rescheduling the Indonesia debt.

I have also gone to Indonesia for the Mormon Church on several occasions, and in so doing I have had the privilege of meeting Minister Alamsjah, minister of religion of Indonesia. He kindly invited us to his home for dinner, where we had a very helpful discussion. On one of these journeys I carried a copy of a letter that President Jeffrey Holland had written inviting Minister Alamsjah to this conference. Dr. Palmer and I felt that a representative from Indonesia would be an ideal person to give the keynote address. It is a country of some 147 million people, largely of the Muslim faith, where people are able to pursue their religious desires in open freedom. There is no discrimination in their country because Indonesia has no state religion, although Islām is very important there.

Minister Alamsjah was tremendously interested to learn that a university here in the United States wanted a discussion of this kind to exchange views and to publish a report. He considers this conference very important, but the pressure of current political activities made it impossible for him to attend. The university and the symposium committee were willing and pleased to have Mr. H. Anton Timur Djaelani represent the minister.

Mr. Djaelani, Director General for Islamic Institutional Development in Indonesia's Department of Religion, has an impressive background in Islām's history, teachings, and principles. In our meetings with our distinguished visitor we have found him not only well informed but a delightful person to know, a human being that you could learn to love. May we give his presentation not only our gracious attention but our open hearts.

3
Islām and
Modern Trends

Haji Alamsjah Ratu Perwiranegara

Paper read by Haji Anton Timur Djaelani, Director General for Islamic Institutional Development, Department of Religion, Republic of Indonesia.

Mr. Djaelani: Mr. Kennedy, whom I thank for that introduction, is a close friend of our Minister of Religion of the Republic of Indonesia. The minister's name is Mr. Haji Alamsjah Perwiranegara, but we call him bapak (father) Alamsjah. All the prominent leaders and high-ranking government officials in Indonesia call him father. This is important to know, I think,

Haji Alamsjah Ratu Perwiranegara is Minister of Religion of the Republic of Indonesia. Haji is an honorific title bestowed upon Muslims who have made a pilgrimage to Mecca, a duty enjoined upon all believers at least once during their lifetime.

because what I have seen here among the Mormons leads me to believe that family life and family relations are very important for you as well as in the Indonesian culture.

Let me express Mr. Alamsjah's personal regrets that pressing activities in connection with the May 1982 elections in Indonesia keep him from this very important symposium. Let me also express his appreciation for the opportunity to explain a unique aspect of our country in this setting.

Indonesia is not a secular state. It is also not a state with a particular state religion. But it is a national state based on the five principles of state philosophy called *pancasila*, a Hindu term. *Panca* means five and *sila* means principles. What follows is bapak's message.

Islām, the world religion which has the greatest number of converts annually, is still commonly referred to by many European writers as Muhammadanism. The latter term is derived by analogy with Christianity, taken from its founder, Jesus Christ; or Buddhism, taken from the name of its founder, Gautama Buddha. The term is not known or accepted in the Muslim world. It appears in neither the Qur'ān nor the *hadīth* (traditional sayings or teachings of Muhammad).

The religion of Muhammad (peace be upon him), which is properly called Islām, is the religion neither of any particular people nor of any particular society nor of any particular place. Islām is a universal religion.

The Muslims use the Arabic word *Islām* (to submit oneself, submission, or obedience to Allāh, the Almighty) to refer to their religion, as this word is found in the holy Qur'ān. Those who confess the religion of Islām are called Muslim (those who submit to God's will).

Submission and obedience is not exacted by force. Submission is stimulated by one's intention to gain eternal happiness, happiness that can be obtained only when one has the guidance of religion. For the Muslims' religion is based on the doctrine that "there is no God but Allāh, and Muhammad is his messenger."

Islām also means to "be at peace" in the sense that every Muslim should be obedient and submissive to his God, and peace also means that every Muslim is both obliged to restrain himself from doing evil to others and to exert himself to do good to all mankind. It is stated in the Qur'ān, *Sūrat al-Baqara*, which would be interpreted: "Nay, whoever submits his whole self to God and is a doer of good, he will get this reward with his Lord. On such shall be no fear, nor shall they grieve." (Qur'ān 2:112.)

Thus, built into the very name of Islām is its character as a religion of peace. Its principal doctrine is the belief that God is only one and that unity in fraternity is, for mankind, a necessity. It is on this basis that Islām constitutes a guidance for the Muslims in spreading Islām throughout the earth. The battles in earlier periods of Islamic history were self-defense from external threats and attacks by non-Muslim people who did not want Islām to be glorious in the world.

Islām is the last religion which has permanently changed the history of the world. Its doctrines retain the elements of Allāh's previous revelations and oblige Muslims to believe in Allāh's prophets and messengers to older revealed religions. This is a major difference between Islām and other religions whose believers are obliged to believe exclusively their own prophet and doctrines. A Jew believes only in the prophets for the Israelites; a Christian believes only in Jesus Christ and some prophets of the Israelites, and so forth.

Islām is not a religion which should be accepted to obtain happiness. Islām is a revelation which constitutes reliable bases of conduct for mankind, because the doctrines are in accordance with human need, not contradictory to human nature. Accordingly, Islām is concerned not only with the hereafter but also with the demands of daily life. A good life today, Muslims believe, will lead to a happy life in the hereafter. In addition to teaching duties toward God such as prayer and fasting, Islām requires believers to deal justly in social interaction among people. Islām has the aim of integrating every aspect of life, making each aspect whole and significant. And only religion can provide such integration and significance.

To gain such a life, Islām points out two things that Muslims must be aware of, the proper relationship between humankind and God and the proper relationship between humankind and the universe. The consciousness that man has been created by Allāh the

Almighty, the Most Merciful, the Most Righteous, instills in the believer the desire to reflect Allāh's attributes in himself. For that reason, prayer, fasting, and other spiritual disciplines are designed for bodily, mental, and spiritual training. *Salāt* (prayer), for instance, begins with *takfīr*—saying *Allāhu akbar* (Allāh is the Greatest) and ending with *salām* (peace and Allāh's blessing be upon you all), thus extending benevolence to all mankind and even to all the world of creatures and universe. Such a prayer, sincerely spoken and pondered, fosters a consciousness of the greatness of Allāh. This consciousness will save one from vanity, yet it will also preserve him from despair, for a believer also understands Allāh as most merciful and most beneficent. Similarly, desiring peace and blessing for all humankind means that every Muslim should become a means of blessing. Such are just a few meanings of *salāt*.

The second aspect of the integrated life is a consciousness of the proper relation between man and his universe. According to Islām, the universe is a reality which should be faced. Appreciating and applying religious teachings should result in harmonious relations between human beings and the universe. Human good, within the framework of devotion to Allāh, the Almighty, should be the criterion for developing and using new technologies. An individual who is fully aware of being created by God to whom everything will return will surely live an integrated and significant life.

The history of Islām has known many great philosophers and scholars dedicated to the study of Islām. Their works have greatly influenced the development of the Muslim world. Their unity of basic principles, however, is not always reflected in the area of detailed proscriptions, rules, and laws known as *furūʿīyah*. The most influential schools of thought in the field of Islamic law are based on the teachings of four great *imāms* (spiritual teachers): Shāfiʿi, Maliki, Hanafi, and Hanbali. The differences need not concern us today except to note that Islām can accommodate great diversity of philosophy on its foundation of unity in principle.

As another example, Muslims are usually classified as traditionalists or modernists. The traditionalists are generally reluctant to accept new ideas from the West. A traditional educational system stresses the teaching of religious subjects, not the secular subjects associated with the West. Modernists or reformists are generally more open to innovation and willing to adopt the Western educational system with some adaptation to Islamic doctrines. Good Muslims can be associated with either position.

Underlying differences, however, are certain principles held in common. One is that humankind's mission toward the universe is to acknowledge its reality, not deal with it as an illusion or avoid it. "The Almighty adds to creation as He pleases" (Qur'ān 35:1); it is not a fixed and unchanging thing. From God's creation of a waterfall, for example, humankind has derived electricity and irrigation. We have the duty to think and work for the interests of humankind itself. It is also our duty to make tame and comfortable the seemingly wild and terrible universe. In other words, we have the obligation to civilize the universe. By so doing, we can make a better use of it so that we can increase our living standard and devotion to God.

To know the benefits of the universe we need to explore and investigate it. The obligation to equip oneself with knowledge, skill, and intelligence is not only a duty to one's fellow creatures but a duty to God.

According to Islām, human life should be directed by guidance from God. Because the main sources of Islamic precepts are the holy Qur'ān and the *hadīth,* these two sources have become the compass for Muslims. Islamic teachings take on new life in new social contexts as they meet the living reality of the country where Islām develops.

The holy Qur'ān and the *hadīth* are not scriptures that shackle the mind. On the contrary, they have materially altered for the better the history of the Islamic world from the eighth to the eighteenth centuries, when Europe then was still in the dark age. A Muslim engaged in religious duties encounters forces which encourage the growth and development of science, as indicated by the history of such centers of Islamic civilization as Baghdad and Cordova.

The holy Qur'ān and the Traditions teach a respect for the human mind. Our responsibility is not only to use our intelligence to attain our needs but to use our intelligence properly, in harmony with the way of Allāh. As the holy Qur'ān records: "They will further say: Had we but listened or used our intelligence, we should not now be among the companions of the blazing fire!" (Qur'ān 67:10.)

Thus in deciding how to employ his efforts, a Muslim should properly consider what will be beneficial to himself and the society around him. If he is successful, he will create a proper balance between physical and spiritual needs. One *hadīth* from the prophet Muhammad tells us: "Religion is logic: no religion for those without logic." Perhaps Islām is the only religion that makes the power of thinking the yardstick for truth. In cases of conflict, when reason can no longer distinguish between good and evil, a Muslim, using his logic, will undoubtedly accept the guidance given by religion. In such conflict, God's revelations will serve as restraint so as to avoid further deviation. With independent judgment (*ijtihād*), Muslims have tried to overcome the problems brought about by the progress and development which are the products of man's mind.

Islām also places an obligation on believers to acquire knowledge. This concept is related to the believer's responsibility to understand this seemingly wild and terrible universe and, through knowledge, to make it tame and comfortable for humankind. This goal can be achieved only after we have understood the purposes and benefits of the elements found in the universe. As the Traditions state: "To acquire knowledge is an obligation of every Muslim, man and woman."

To that end, the prophet Muhammad has also proclaimed that acquiring knowledge cannot be limited by time and place: "Pursue knowledge from the cradle to the grave. . . . Pursue knowledge even to China."

Fulfilling this obligation once made such Muslims as Averroes (ibn Rushd), Avicenna (ibn Sina) and Razes (al-Rāzy) masters of science between the eighth and eighteenth centuries.

The Islamic teachings requiring individuals to perform their religious obligations and to understand the natural world are demanding, but the rewards are mighty indeed: "He granteth wisdom to whom he pleaseth: and he to whom wisdom is granted receiveth indeed a benefit overflowing; but none will grasp the message but men of understanding." (Qur'ān 2:69.)

In view of humankind's urgent need of knowledge, every Muslim prayer should be: "O my Lord! advance me in knowledge."

With this kind of prayer on their lips, Muslim scholars made Islamic Spain the stepping-stone to Western Europe for such new ideas as philosophy and medicine which brought an end to the Dark Ages.

The good life for a Muslim is one that brings happiness in the present life and the life hereafter. These two parts of life are inseparable. The life one will receive in the hereafter is the result of the life one has led in the present world. The life that puts too much stress on materialism actually violates man's own nature. Ignoring spiritual matters threatens all of one's well-being. Islām demands that Muslims pay equal attention to both sides of life, as revealed in *Sūrat al-Qasas:* "But seek, with the wealth which God has bestowed on thee, the home of the hereafter, nor forget thy portion in this world." (Qur'ān 28:77.)

As this verse requires, a Muslim should be equally prepared for life in this world and life in the hereafter, a concept reinforced in the Traditions: "Work for your worldly life as though you lived forever, and for the Hereafter, as though you died tomorrow."

This concept has encouraged Muslims to think about ways by which they can improve daily conditions to increase their happiness both here and hereafter. For all Muslims, the best way is to perform good deeds and exercise *ijtihād* (independent judgment). As the Traditions state: "For those who pioneer a good way is the reward of it and the reward of those who follow it; for those who pioneer an evil way is the sin of it and the sin of those who follow it."

This Tradition has clearly indicated that each Muslim should always try to do something beneficial to himself and to others. To that end, it is necessary for him to interpret Islamic teachings by means of *ijtihād.*

The Islamic teachings that deal with the vertical relationship between the Creator and the created have inspired Muslims to create effective systems and organizations by which individuals do their duties in accordance with their respective abilities. This is a process that obligates an individual to value planning, organization, and efficiency. In the matter of the teachings that deal with the horizontal relationship between individuals, Islām demands that each Muslim pay attention to the application of religious guidance in such a relationship. Such an orientation will strengthen the unity and fraternity among individuals in society.

In the Islamic view, mankind originates from the first human couple, Adam and Eve, as revealed in the holy Qur'ān, *Sūrat an-Nisā'*: "O mankind! reverence your guardian-Lord, who created you from a single person, created, of like nature, his mate, and from them twain scattered like seeds countless men and women." (Qur'ān 4:1.)

Based on the belief that humankind has sprung from a common origin, Islām asserts that human dignity cannot be measured by race, color, language, physique, social status, occupation, and so forth. One's dignity comes from one's humanity itself and must not be denied on distinctions of race, sex, kinship, or wealth. An Arab does not rank higher than a non-Arab.

The contents of the holy Qur'ān and Traditions are not limited to one race. They are meant for all of mankind, regardless of distinctions. On the five continents in more than 160 countries live thousands of different ethnic groups, more than four billion people, all equal in the sight of God, the Almighty. As stated in the holy Qur'ān, *Sūrat al-Anbiyā'*, "We sent thee not but as a Mercy for all creatures." (Qur'ān 21:107.)

From this verse we can conclude that Islām brings mercy and blessing for the universe, good news and fresh water for the spiritual thirst of any nation. Islām is the liberator of mankind from suffering and uselessness. To retain equilibrium and order in social and national life and to preserve peace, individuals have definite social obligations to help each other in righteousness, to avoid conflicts and division, and to avoid scolding, mocking, and despising each other.

According to Islām, individuals have equal rights and opportunity in conformity with their natures. Islām does not, however, approve of deviation of artificial equalities—or as put by a contemporary scholar, Maududi, in *The Islamic Way of Life*, "replacing limited natural inequalities by artificial equalities."

To measure the degree of one's dignity, Islām sets spiritual values as the standard. As stated in the holy Qur'ān, *Sūrat al-Hujurāt*: "Verily the most honored of you in the sight of God is the most righteous of you." (Qur'ān 49:13.)

As a religion, Islām's teachings direct all fields of human life: material, mental, and spiritual. Islām provides guidance so that an

individual, as a good citizen, functions as an energetic and responsible element in the society; and as a spouse and parent, relates to
members of the family in the manner appropriate to the guidance of
God. Thus, as the servant of God, country, society, and family, a
good Muslim is able to spread God's blessing on earth, promote
social justice and a healthy economy, and increase knowledge, all of
which will increase the happiness of mankind. No area of life's
activity is left untouched by Islamic teachings. The light of Islām
guides and directs all activities of Muslims in building a prosperous
and peaceful life.

The comprehensiveness of Islamic teachings is proof that in
Islām there is no place for poverty, ignorance, backwardness, and
fanaticism. On the contrary, Islām gives effective answers to the
challenge of the modern world based on concepts which can make
this life more meaningful without disregarding the reality of moral
and spiritual aspects of the human personality. Unlike the Christian
dictum, "Render . . . unto Caesar the things which are Caesar's; and
unto God the things that are God's" (Matthew 22:21), Islām does
not compartmentalize but instead provides a proper balance
between material and spiritual life.

To achieve this balance is to redress an unfortunate overemphasis on other worldly matters that led to weakness in the
Muslim world after the eighteenth century. Such recent Muslim
scholars as al-Maududi, al-Banna, and al-Hudaibi were motivated
to restructure Muslim life more holistically to show the relevance of
Islām to the challenges of modern life. While this phase of Islamic
development continues, Muslim solidarity requires cooperation
even at the expense of some limitation on individual freedoms.
Muslims must develop the social aspects of Islamic values so that
Islām will remain a vital element in the reality of national life in each
country where it develops.

Such a challenge is great. Our technological culture has a great
and sometimes negative impact upon religious values. Can religion
survive modern life? The phenomenon of increasingly secularized
Western societies with little or no interest in religious values has
made the question more urgent.

Islām stands at the crux of a paradox. As a Muslim, I have a
strong belief that Islām is the last religion, the religion for all

mankind. The Qur'ān, I believe, is the one and the only most original holy book containing guidance for earthly life and for life hereafter. Yet the historical fact remains that Islām fell into a deep slumber while the Western world was developing rapidly. Moreover, after Westerners conquered the Islamic world, the condition of the Muslim adherents became worse. How can a dynamic and true religion produce backward peoples?

A number of Muslim thinkers and reformers have described various aspects of the problem, some blaming it on Muslim politics, others on orthodoxy, and others on the secularism of adapting Islamic teachings over-readily to meet changing conditions.

I would like to summarize the points of view of prominent modern Muslim thinkers on the cause and treatment of the backwardness of the Muslims.

According to Muhammad ʿAbd ul-Wahhāb, the backwardness of Islām arose because the door of *ijtihād* (independent judgment) was closed, the *ʿaqīda* (creed) was polluted as a result of thirteenth-century *tarīqāt* (mysticism), and further weakened by animism and *khurafāt* (superstition). He urged Muslims not to worship tombs, stones, or saints, but to worship only Allāh. He strongly felt that a Muslim should be guided only by the Qur'ān and by the Traditions, that *taqlīd* (indiscriminate adoption of traditional religious interpretations) by the *ʿulamā'* (Islamic scholars) must be avoided, and that the *ijtihād* is open, not closed.

But perhaps his greatest contribution was to firmly declare the necessity of reopening the door of *ijtihād* after Ibnu Taimiyah had declared that after the deaths of the four *imāms,* Maliki, Hanafi, Shāfiʿi and Hanbali, the door of *ijtihād* was closed.

Rifāʿah Badawi Rafīʿ al-Tahtawi (1801-1873) was born in Egypt. As part of the Mediterranean community with its lively interchange of cultures, he fearlessly suggested learning from the West, especially stressing the primacy of literacy as the key to accelerated improvement. In addition, he also rejected the overemphasis on submitting to the will of Allāh that had become fatalistic and had brought the Muslims toward backwardness. In his *Road for Egyptians towards Understanding Modern Literature* he described the importance of achieving progress for the Muslims.

Sayyid Jamāluddīn al-Afghāni (1839-1897) felt that the backwardness of Islām was not caused by Islām itself or the orthodoxy of its teachings but because the Muslims left its true teachings and followed outside teachings, particularly those from the West.

As he outlined matters in politics, the backwardness of Islām was caused by factions in the Muslim communities, absolute governments, entrusting the leadership of the *umma* (Islamic community) to unreliable persons, neglecting defense, entrusting state administration to incompetent leaders, and allowing foreign intervention. Therefore, if the Muslims longed for the rebirth of the glory of Islām, they must first free themselves or their countries from Western domination.

Obviously a related symptom was the weakened condition of Muslim brotherhood. Accordingly Jamāluddīn al-Afghāni urged that Pan-Islamism should be revived, since through unity and close cooperation the Muslim world would be able to win independence and improve itself.

Muhammad ʿAbdu (1849-1905) was the pupil of Jamāluddīn al-Afghāni. Carrying further the ideas of his teacher, he elaborated the causes of the weaknesses of the Islamic community. The faith and worship of the Muslim had been tainted by nonreligious teachings, or *bidʿa*. They had seized and burdened the Muslim's life through ritual feasts that had never been taught by the Messenger. He therefore urged freeing themselves from the bounds and burdens of *bidʿa* and returning to the purity and simplicity of Islām. Further, the Muslims had become enmeshed in regulations which had been applicable for the Islamic community a thousand years earlier; thus, he urged the *ʿulamā'* to reform Islamic laws to meet problems of the present age, as long as they did not touch creed and ritual.

He also argued that the shortage of Muslim scholars and scientists could be corrected by a balanced educational system, but a Muslim one—not a Western one. He also urged that Islām break the political hold of the West and stop being Western colonies.

Muhammad ʿAbdu's search of the Qur'ān and the Traditions found many teachings which could be applied to social problems. Obviously these principles could be made relevant to the conditions existing in each age, but new interpretations would be required. Of necessity the door of *ijtihād* should be opened. Also, because Muslims need science to develop their community, he took the initiative in establishing a more modern educational system and encouraged not only his students but all Muslims to avoid fatalism.

Some of Abdu's prominent followers and pupils are Rashīd Rida, Haykal, Mustafā ʿAbd al-Rāzik, Taha Husain, and ʿAli ʿAbd al-Rāzik. In the Muslim world, the influence of Jamāluddīn and ʿAbdu is considerable, especially in Indonesia.

Like other Muslim thinkers, Sir Muhammad Iqbāl (1876-1938) grappled with the question of why Muslim countries were backward in every aspect of civilization. His well-known book, *The Reconstruction of Religious Thought in Islam*, argued emphatically and repeatedly that "Islām must be rethought in modern terms." He too urged that the gate of *ijtihād* be open.

Iqbāl rejected Western society as a model for modern Islām because its emphasis on materialism had alienated it from religious values. He urged the Muslim world to take technology and science from the West without abandoning the religion of Islām. He also rejected capitalism but accepted socialism because of some similarities between Islām and socialism.

Mustafā Kemāl (1881-1938), a Turkish thinker who is also known as Kemāl Ataturk, the founding father of modern Turkey, is a pioneer of secularization in the Muslim world. His controversial plan called for following the West and adopting its civilization and culture. Westernization, secularization, and nationalism were the foundation of his plan to modernize the Muslim world. He failed, however, and the spirit of Islām continues its search to modernize Turkey on its own terms.

Like some other Muslim thinkers, Sir Sayyid Ahmad Khan (1817-1898) of India held that the Muslim should master science and technology and adapt the norms and values of the West. India's Aligarh movement embodies this philosophy.

Sayyid Amir Ali (1849-1923), also an Indian Muslim thinker, blamed Islām's backwardness on its history of devotion to ritual and life hereafter. Because closing the gate of *ijtihād* produced the defeat of rationalism, the revival of rationalism would remedy the disease, he argued.

Indonesia, like other Muslim countries, also has had a colonial history. The Dutch alone occupied its archipelago for 350 years, leaving Muslims second-class citizens in their own land, feeling and experiencing inferiority in every sector of life: political, educational, socio-cultural, economic, and so forth.

In the nineteenth century a Dutch Calvinist student of Islām and advisor to the Dutch colonial government, Christiaán Snouck Hurgronje, recommended to the Dutch government that Islām as religion be differentiated from Islām as political power. Hurgronje advocated that Islām as a religion be tolerated, that a neutral attitude prevail on the governmental level. Islām as religion posed no threat to the colonial government. However, Islām as politics could not be tolerated. All demands of pan-Islamism should be regarded as foreign interference. He further recommended that the government assist in the construction of mosques and aid pilgrims, encouraging the cooperation of local Indonesian elites, the *adat* (common-law traditional leaders), and *priyayi* (Indonesian court functionaries).

Balancing these public relations gestures, however, were efforts to paralyze the Indonesian Muslims by disseminating fatalism and antimodern attitudes. Typical false *hadīths* or traditional sayings were: "The worldly life is for those who do not believe in Islām, the hereafter is for Muslims"; and "The bad fate undergone by Muslims is natural, since they will attain happiness hereafter."

Hurgronje also urged that local common-law traditions (*adat*), which have the force of law, should be accepted in a clash with Islamic law. Furthermore, the Dutch colonial government created a dual system of education: Islamic education and secular education.

In reaction to these colonial policies, several Muslim movements appeared with a variety of emphases but all working to revive the spirit of Islām and reconstruct religious thoughts.

Sarekat Islām was the first political movement in Indonesia before independence. Born in reaction to the Dutch economic system, which weakened the economic role of the Muslim majority by making it difficult to leave the peasant class, Sarekat Islām's aim was to modernize the Indonesian people through fraternity, unity, and cooperation among the Muslims.

In his report to the Dutch colonial government, Dr. Hazeu, adviser for native affairs, called Sarekat Islām a reflection of the people's consciousness seen through the way the people talked and dressed, their attitudes, and so on.

Muhammadiyah, a Muslim reform organization, was founded in Java in 1912 by K. H. Ahmad Dahlan, following the example of reform movements in Egypt and India. It lays special emphasis on education, social welfare, and Islamic propagation. It advocated opening the gate of *ijtihād*.

Nahdlatul Ulama was founded by K. H. Hasyim Asy'ari of Jombang, East Java, in 1926, originally in protest against Turkey's abolition of the caliphate but soon expanding its aims to strengthen unity among the *ʿulamā'* to spread Islām, to assist mosques, and care for orphans and the poor. By holding firmly to the doctrines of the *ahl is-sunna wa-l-jamāʿa* (the traditional "orthodox" majority) it succeeded in fostering unity among the Muslims. When Japan occupied the archipelago in 1942 many of the *ʿulamā'* were empowered to deal with religious affairs.

Many other modernist Muslim organizations were born during the preindependence period: Persyarikatan Ulama (the Union of Ulama), founded by K. H. Abdul Halim in Majalengka, West Java; the Paderi Movement in West Sumatra; Sheikh Ahmad Chatib's movement, also in West Sumatra; Persatuan Islām (the Moslem Union) in Bandung, West Java; and Alwashliyah, founded in Medan, North Sumatra.

When independence was achieved after World War II, religion was integrated into the social fabric. Indonesia has a population of more than 140 million; 99 percent believe in one religion or else subscribe to the *pancasila*, the five philosophic principles of the state:

1. Belief in the one and only God;
2. Humanism;
3. Indonesian unity;
4. Democracy based on the wisdom through consultation with the people;
5. Social justice for all Indonesians.

These five principles have inspired all Indonesian political, economic, and socio-cultural systems.

The first principle is, in reality, a reiteration that Indonesian people believe in God the Almighty; accordingly, there is no room for atheism and secularism.

Indonesians are fully aware that our independence, as stated in the 1945 constitution, is a blessing from God the Almighty; this is further stipulated in Article 29, where the state fully guarantees the freedom of each citizen to confess his respective religion (e.g., Islām, Protestant, Catholic, Hinduism, Buddhism) and to practice it.

The state gives active support in building places of worship, providing holy scriptures, and managing religious education from elementary to university levels. At the university level, for instance, we have fourteen state institutes for Islamic studies scattered throughout Indonesia. At the elementary and secondary levels there are thousands of religious schools, both government run and privately run. In jurisprudence, Islamic civil laws have been authorized by the government in the Islamic court of law, and Islamic marriage offices have also been set up throughout Indonesia.

As a nation with very strong religious beliefs, it is our wish that the universal values of religion be manifested in the nation's life towards a peaceful, just, and prosperous society; because spiritual and material prosperity are so closely linked, we recognize no separation between religion and state—we do not consider them two separate worlds. Our state's philosophy, *pancasila*, and religion are so closely interwoven that each strengthens the other. That is why secularism has no place in our national life.

It should be noted that *pancasila*, in its present form, as the state's principles, was endorsed by the four well-known Muslim leaders, Ki Bagus Hadikusumo, K. H. Wahid Hasjim, Kasman Singodimedjo, and Teuka Hasan on 18 August 1945. With the new spirit of national unity and tolerance, they willingly agreed to omit seven words attached to the first principle which made it obligatory for the Muslims to practice their religious teachings. With that historic agreement, Muslims have a sense of belonging and a sense of responsibility towards *pancasila*. It is our belief that without the broad-mindedness of these four unselfish Muslim leaders, Indonesia would not be a unified state today. This unity is further strengthened by the fact that we as a nation have five things in common that guard us against dispute and conflict: one national language, one nation, one country, one government, and one state ideology, *pancasila*.

In conclusion, then, Islamic beliefs and their application in Indonesia might be summarized thus:

1. Islām is the religion revealed by God for the whole universe through his messenger, the prophet Muhammad, for the guidance of life in this world and hereafter.

2. Islamic teachings describe the means to achieve happiness not only in the present life but also in the life hereafter.

3. As the result of long oppression and colonization, Islām's teachings have been misunderstood and misinterpreted, resulting in backwardness in the Muslim world.

4. Islām has the most complete and authentic source of teachings—the Qur'ān and *hadīth*.

5. Muslims have shown considerable tolerance and broadmindedness for the sake of Indonesian national unity in sacrificing a political monopoly to accept *pancasila* as the ideology of the state, in spite of the fact that Muslims make up 90 percent of the population.

6. Islām cannot be judged fairly from the fanatical practices of individuals but should be judged by its pure and universal precepts.

7. Scientific and technological advancements have encouraged Muslims to understand and follow their religious teachings.

Those are some clarifications on the issues relating to Islām's basic teachings. It is hoped that they give a clearer picture and understanding of Islām.

4
In Search of Understanding

David C. Montgomery

I have had the opportunity of spending two years in the Near East—one year in Turkey and another in Soviet Turkestan, both areas of large Muslim populations. Though the political orientations and experiences in both instances were quite different, I was very positively impressed with the cultural strength and individual

David C. Montgomery, professor of history at Brigham Young University, coordinates the Near Eastern Studies Program and teaches survey courses on Near Eastern history covering the ancient, medieval, and modern periods. His main research and writing is centered on Soviet Central Asia, in particular on the twentieth-century cultural history of the Uzbeks, a Turkic-speaking people. Professor Montgomery lived in Turkey in 1966-67 on a Fulbright grant and has a year's experience in Soviet Uzbekistan on three separate grants (1969, 1977-1978, 1982) from the International Research and Exchange Board. He is author of a book and several articles and conference papers about the peoples of Central Asia.

goodness of the Muslim people with whom I became acquainted. In Turkey, after the end of my year there, my landlord asked me if I could not stay longer because he would like me to become a Muslim. I was extremely flattered.

The second experience was in Soviet Central Asia, where despite a half-century attempt by the Soviet government to discourage religious practice, Islām persists as the majority population. Students from Egypt asked me to come with them on Friday, the *jumah* day (day of common prayer), to the large mosque in Tashkent to observe prayers with them. I had not been in a house of worship for almost five months before this experience. As I observed the prayer rituals and listened to the sermon, I felt very moved by the sincerity of this religious expression and, even though I was not of their faith, I sensed a common good spirit which we all shared. I hope that one of the results of this conference will be an expression of this spirit.

5
Comments on
Common Ground

Spencer J. Palmer

Today I have been thinking about my first visit to Saudi Arabia. It was in 1954. One evening at dusk, a rapidly moving caravan of brightly painted Chevrolet cars came to a sudden stop at the side of a lonely road in the desert. A dozen young Arabs, dressed in the customary *kafia*, unrolled their prayer rugs, faced Mecca, then prostrated themselves in prayer. It was a quiet, orderly, and

Spencer J. Palmer is director of world religions in the Religious Studies Center at Brigham Young University and is the associate director of BYU's David M. Kennedy Center for International and Area Studies. Professor Palmer graduated from Eastern Arizona Junior College, received his B.A. from Brigham Young University, and his M.A. and Ph.D. degrees from the University of California at Berkeley in East Asian studies and history. His research and publications include numerous books and articles on history and comparative religion, as well as on Mormon subjects. His latest study deals with the cult of Confucius in East Asian countries.

respectful exercise. And it seemed for a moment that all nature had paused, sharing that meaningful act of devotion. I was deeply touched.

Then last year, I was privileged to be on holy ground in Jerusalem, between the Mosque of Omar and the al-Aksa Mosque, on Friday at noon. I had been invited to attend this special day of prayer where hundreds of men and boys faced al-Aksa Mosque, while a like number of women and girls faced the Mosque of Omar, to acknowledge the presence of Almighty God. My spirit was quickened; I was stirred by feelings of appreciation and love.

Now we are here at BYU to explore relationships between Mormonism and Islām. I cannot help but approach our meetings with positive and appreciative feelings, drawn by the belief that these two great faiths have much in common. Of course, I realize there are important differences, but I feel certain that many who are assembled here will be impressed by common ground.

The idea that resemblances between Mormonism and Islām deserve careful comparative study is not new. Numerous books and articles have been printed on the subject, but not always with a constructive purpose in mind. Eduard Meyer, the great German scholar, was more positive than most:

> Of the many new religious movements originating in our time, Mormonism very early awakened my interest, especially because of its surprising and close resemblances to the historical development of Islam.
>
> Without the least exaggeration, we may designate the Mormons as the Mohammedans of the New World according to their origins and their manner of thinking. There is hardly a historical parallel which is so instructive as this one; and through comparative analysis both receive so much light that a scientific study of the one through the other is indispensable.[1]

At the outset I want to say that although analogies in world religions can rather easily be drawn, we must be cautious in doing so. And we must be careful in our interpretations and conclusions. It is easy to oversimplify. Especially, we must resist the human tendency to force the faith and practice of others into ideological compartments or stereotypes familiar only to ourselves—or to compare the "best" within our religious traditions with what is least appealing in others. Now having said this, let me suggest a few rather obvious parallels between Mormonism and Islām.

1. Neither of them is merely a creedal faith. Rather, they represent ways of life. To belong to either community requires an almost total commitment in customs, values, and life-style. For both, religion is more than a recitation of creed or articles of faith; it includes prohibitions against the drinking of alcohol or the use of drugs; a commitment to fasting and prayer; modesty in dress; the payment of alms and tithing; emphasis on the family, obedience to parents; concern for the elderly and the poor; and many other social concerns.

2. In both, obedience to a living God is at the core of all faith and practice. God is the supreme deity and he demands strict moral adherence to divine law, with retribution and judgment for the sinner. In both Islām and Mormonism, God is a revelator, he is revealed. Man's opportunity and obligation is to testify of him. But within the purview of this similarity there are differences: In Islām, God is not only absolutely unique and all-powerful, he is unapproachable. Neither Muhammad nor any man can withstand his immediate presence and live. Muhammad received God's revelations at the hands of an angelic messenger, Gabriel; whereas Joseph Smith stood in the immediate presence of Almighty God just as Moses and others before him also claimed to have done. Joseph Smith not only reported receiving visitations from the angel Moroni, but he said he talked with God face to face as a man might communicate with his friend.

3. Closely tied to this belief in the omnipotence of a living God is the common belief in the physical resurrection of the dead. In a day when religious people in the world are increasingly skeptical about such things, Mormons and Muslims hold tenaciously to this belief, which originally may have appeared strange to some of the people of Mecca when it was first revealed to them. Muhammad argued that if a perfectly formed person can be created from a clot of blood, God can then also perform other miracles, such as restoring the dead and calling them to accountability for their acts.

4. Both Mormons and Muslims, perhaps more than any other two peoples in the religious world today, greatly emphasize the importance of prophets. Twenty-eight prophets are mentioned in the Qur'ān. Eighteen of these are prophets mentioned in the Old Testament of the Bible, all of whom are accepted as authoritative exponents of God's mind and will by the Mormon people. Yet even

in this basic similarity there is an important difference. In orthodox Islamic belief, Muhammad was the last of the prophets of God — "the seal" of the prophets; whereas in Mormon belief, not only was Joseph Smith, the historical founder of the faith, a legitimate prophet of God in a continuing line of Old and New Testament prophets, but his successors down to the present president of the Church are also bona fide messengers of God. But again, as Professor Ayoub explains in his discussion of the doctrine of the *Mahdi* in Islām, the discrepancy and difference on this latter point of doctrine are not as critical in some Islamic traditions as in others.

5. Both Muhammad and Joseph Smith are regarded as instruments in the hands of God in revealing new scriptures — the Qur'ān and the Book of Mormon. Both men reported they were directed by angels in bringing forth these new volumes of scripture.

6. Both Joseph Smith and Muhammad believed they were divinely called to restore the patriarchal religion of father Abraham; both not only taught that their disciples were literal blood descendants of father Abraham (the Arabs are lineal descendants of Ishmael, Abraham's firstborn son), but that the God of Abraham was also their God.

7. Both Mormonism and Islām are strongly opposed to idolatry, and to the use of idols and images and mystical symbols in their daily prayers and in their places of worship. Simplicity of form in architecture, art, and worship characterize both. The Mormon view on this matter was first given in 1855 by one of the apostles of the Church in a public discourse in Salt Lake City, when he said: "Now this man [Muhammad] descended from Abraham and was no doubt raised up by God on purpose to scourge the world for their idolatry."[2]

8. There are passages in the Qur'ān that have special doctrinal interest to Mormons, and which may not strike a responsive chord among others in such a meaningful way. For example, there is the incident of the fallen angel *Iblīs* who, according to the Qur'ān, (*Sūra* 7:10-20; 38:65-88) refused to bow down and take instruction from Adam at the time of creation and thus was cast out of heaven for rebellion before the world was ever made. This episode is well known in Mormon theology, wherein Satan rebelled in the premortal life and was cast out. (2 Nephi 24:12-16, Abraham 3:27-28; Moses 4:1-4.)

I have just referred to the books of Abraham and Moses, two important texts not found in the Christian Bible but included in the scriptures of the Mormon people, having been translated from ancient papyrus by Joseph Smith. The Qur'ān quotes from the book of Abraham and the book of Moses in *Sūras* 53 and 87, although there is no explanation in the text as to exactly what these books are.[3]

Muslim-Mormon comparisons are wide-ranging. The investigation of the subject by Mormons has just begun. I want to say frankly that this symposium is not a naive or misguided effort to establish sameness of some kind between Mormonism and Islām. That would be foolhardy. That would ignore obvious differences, such as the Mormon acceptance of Jesus as someone much more than a prophet, which Muslims would generally deny. But still, our meetings here mark a significant and meaningful milestone, a first effort by representatives of these two religious groups to join in a common endeavor to seek understanding.

We of the Religious Studies Center are grateful to have others on our campus, whether Mormon, Muslim, or belonging to neither group. We are impressed by the large and enthusiastic number of people in attendance today. For me, this is not only a positive sign of Mormon interest in the people of Islām but in reaching out to all peoples, nations, and religious communities heretofore largely neglected by us. All this bodes well for religious studies at Brigham Young University, and perhaps also for the direction of the Church which is its primary motivating force.

NOTES

1. Eduard Meyer, *The Origin and History of the Mormons: With Reflections on the Beginnings of Islam and Christianity* (Salt Lake City: University of Utah Press, 1961), translated from the original German by Heinz F. Rahde and Eugene Seaich, pp. 1, 44.

2. George A. Smith, *Journal of Discourses*, vol. III (Liverpool: B. James, 1856), p. 32.

3. In quotations from the Qur'ān, I have relied on the translations and commentary of A. Yusef Ali, *The Holy Quran* (New York: Hafner Publishing Company, 1946), vols. I and II, and N. J. Dawood, *The Koran* (Baltimore: Penguin Books, 1970).

6
Personal
Reflections

Orin D. Parker

For fourteen of the past twenty-three years, my wife, Rita, and I and our five children have lived and worked in Muslim communities of the Middle East, developing close and lasting friendships among these sensitive and loving people. We have found that we have much in common with them and a great deal indeed to learn from them. I've read Islamic philosophy and some Islamic history

Orin D. Parker is president of America-Mideast Educational and Training Services, Inc. (AMIDEAST). He received his B.A. from Brigham Young University and did graduate work at Stanford University, American University in Cairo, and the University of Baghdad in Iraq. Associated with AMIDEAST for twenty years, Mr. Parker has served as director of programs in Iraq, and Vice-President of Overseas Operations in Beirut from 1971-1979. His publications include a study of the educational system of Iraq and cultural aspects of Middle Eastern students.

and, of course, the Qur'ān. But it is really in studying the Muslim himself that we learn about this remarkable faith.

We have found our Muslim friends especially interested in the Mormon concept of family and family government, and the codes of conduct and rules of diet and health similar to their own. We, in turn, have been extremely interested in their customs, particularly those pertaining to the family. We're impressed by their use of religious language in all of their greetings. We're impressed by the way in which Muslim families ask God to bless them as they go about their daily business. Meetings that we attended in Iraq, gatherings such as this, also would be opened with a prayer: "In the name of God, the munificent and merciful." This prayer is also said before a Muslim family sits down to eat, as well as on many other occasions. It is even inscribed at the top of government stationery and included in the formalities of government, at least in those countries with which I am familiar.

Many of their greetings invoke Allāh, and their thanks are always expressed to Allāh. Though it is an unstructured religion in the Western sense, Islām is a living religion, an all-pervasive way of life. Its philosophy guides the thought and action of the true Muslim at all times. The true Muslim lives face to face with God. His house of God is wherever he may spread his prayer rug. It is a wonderful experience in the Middle East to see, five times during the day's business, all activity stop and people spread their rugs and address themselves to their God. It's a marvelous experience to visit Muslim friends in their homes at the time of prayer and watch as they excuse themselves and withdraw to another room to pray. I was highly complimented once when a Muslim neighbor asked me if I would care to join him.

The Muslim thanks God for everything because he believes that God provides everything; when God does not provide, we must accept doing without. When you give a devout Muslim a gift, he will thank not you but God, because it was God who moved you to be kind and generous.

Islām has developed as a paternalistic society. Within the family the parents' word is final. Great respect for parents and elders is expected, and it is given. In *The Arab World Today*, Morroe Berger compares the reaction of Muslims and Christians to the parable in

Matthew 21:28-30. In this parable, you'll remember, a man asks his two sons to work in the vineyard. The one says, "Yes, father," but then does not. The other says, "No, father, I cannot," but later relents and works. Now, in the Western mind and in the interpretation as given by Christ, the one who actually did the work is the one we should emulate. But the Muslim would follow the one who said "Yes, father," thereby showing respect to his father.

This paternalistic family pattern extends through the society to create a generally authoritarian structure. In my field, education, we find that students learn primarily through memorization and imitation rather than independent research or original work. Moreover, the individual student's academic field of study often reflects his father's or his family's desires more than his own wishes or capabilities. This, again, is an indication of how much the family dominates, and the respect the individual Muslim feels for his family. The family comes first. We have sometimes invited Muslim friends to our home for a special occasion, and then, at the last minute, they have not been able to come because a brother who lived down the street had come for a visit.

Education is as highly revered by Muslims as it is by Mormons. Muhammad said, "The pursuit of knowledge is an act of worship," and enjoined Muslims to "seek knowledge from the cradle to the grave." Another time, in a more humorous vein, he said, "Seek knowledge even if it be in China." Many of you may believe the oil-rich states of the Middle East provide unlimited education for their subjects as part of a modern welfare-state concept. In fact, education has been free throughout Islamic history.

The Muslims have a very deep faith which is sometimes misconstrued in the West as fatalism. I had a memorable experience with this kind of faith soon after first arriving in the Middle East. I was sent to Baghdad to take over an office which had been somewhat neglected for a couple of years. A young American, I was determined to go in there and get the office operating efficiently. As I proceeded to give the necessary directions and orders to my Muslim staff, I found that I was constantly receiving the answer, *"Insha' Allāh,"* which means, "God willing." I tended to interpret it as meaning something like "mañana," or "maybe," or "if I get around to it." So I decided one day that I'd had enough of *"Insha'Allāh"* and called the *farrāsh*, Zeydan, into my office. (A *farrāsh* is a combination messenger/janitor/concierge.)

Zeydan taught me something that day that I will never forget. First I gave him a little lecture on the necessity in an office for the boss to know that when something needed to be done, it would in fact be done. When I had finished talking to him in my best Arabic, he then proceeded to lecture me on faith. He explained to me that all that is done must be in accordance with the will of God, that nothing is done without or in spite of that will, and that I should always expect him to answer *"Insha'Allāh,"* because it would be wrong for him to say that he could do something on his own. He was not expressing unwillingness to work but his realistic humility that the results lay in God's hands. I finally understood.

This kind of faith was exemplified as well, I believe, by the late President Anwar Sadat. He had said several times that he knew he would live until the very day that God had planned for him to be finished with his work on earth. I do believe that his faith was unfeigned.

Muslims share with Mormons a strong belief in salvation and the hereafter. Muhammad said, "Life is a bridge. Pass over it to paradise, but do not build your houses upon it." We had a visit in Washington recently from a family that lived across from us in Beirut during the difficult times and who had constantly offered help and hospitality to me after I had sent my wife and children back to the States for safety. Hajj Abdullah, the head of this family, often told me things which seemed to come directly out of the Doctrine and Covenants, such as: "He who doeth the works of righteousness shall receive his reward, even peace in this world, and eternal life in the world to come" (59:23).

As someone who has received Muslim hospitality with gratitude, I have noticed with sadness that the Muslim coming into Western society is always surprised and disappointed at the ignorance of Islām which he finds around him, especially when he finds himself considered an unbeliever. The religion of Islām has dominated the Eastern world for centuries and continues to do so today. Any attempt to define culture in that area must recognize Islām as its foundation. And even those who no longer observe all its tenets remain loyal to its basic concepts and give Islām its proper respect. Within Islām, Christians and Jews have held from the beginning a special place of respect as "people of the book," the Old Testament. The term in Arabic is *"ahl al-kitāb,"* which can also be interpreted as "family of the book." In the view of Islām, Jews, Christians, and Muslims share the same God and the same early religious heritage. Muslims see their religion as the culmination of a process stretching from Judaism to Christianity in Islām. Prophets of the Old Testament are recognized as second only to Muhammad. Thus, it is surprising and culturally disturbing for a Middle Eastern Muslim to find himself considered outside the Judeo-Christian tradition. I make an appeal to the Church and to its members: If we seek to know and to interact with Muslims, we must understand and appreciate their belief, their philosophy, and their culture. We must know them before we can successfully reach their hearts.

Mormons and Muslims
(*Continued*)

7
Religion in
Village Life

Robert L. Staab

As I thought about comparing Islām and Mormonism, I decided to focus on a small village where examining religion may be easier because it is less heavily influenced by technology or so-called Westernization. When you live in a small town of 350 people, which I did for two years in Turkey, you get to know not only almost everyone in the town but also their life-styles.

One of the first things you will find in any Islamic Middle Eastern community or village—not only in Turkey—is a small

Robert L. Staab is assistant director of the Middle East Center at the University of Utah. A graduate of Texas Tech University in history, he received his M.A. and Ph.D. in Middle East studies/Turkish from the University of Utah. Professor Staab conducted research in Turkey on a Fulbright-Hays program in 1974-1975.

town square. And the dominating feature of that square is usually the mosque or the place of worship. Sometimes it will have a minaret, sometimes not, depending on the financial status of the village and whether they had a skilled individual who could do the brickwork or stonework.

The mosque is the focal point of the village. Many times it will be used as an assembly house for community or political meetings, especially if the back or side has smaller rooms in addition to the open meeting space. Here Muslims come and pray five times a day. Deaths, weddings, blessings of babies — the core events of human life — are linked to the mosque.

The religious leader of the mosque, the *imām*, is not necessarily a priest in a Western sense, but usually guides the prayer. In a village, you very seldom have someone trained in a theological college in, for instance, Cairo. A very pious person, or someone who has gone on a pilgrimage, may lead the prayer. But he is usually the community leader as well — the mayor of the village, or the only literate person in the village, or the village "doctor," who knows something about medicine. Obviously there is not the separation of church and state which Westerners may feel is essential. A Muslim villager would not necessarily perceive such a separation as necessary or even as desirable.

Dr. Palmer mentioned the five pillars of Islām. The first pillar is the *shahāda*. It simply states that one believes in God as a single being and Muhammad as his prophet. This is the ultimate Muslim belief — so intensely personal and so fundamental that I will concentrate on the last four pillars, because I feel that they are more ritualistic and play more of a role in village life. This is especially true of *salāt*, or prayer, the second pillar of Islām. Muslims pray five times a day facing always in one direction only, i.e., towards Mecca. (I visited an elementary school yesterday, and a fifth grader asked me, "If you live in Mecca, which direction do you pray in?" It was a good question. I said, "It really depends on what side of town you live in, because the focus of Islām is on the *ka'ba*, which is in the court of the Great Mosque in Mecca.") Praying towards Mecca and praying five times a day unites the Islamic community and gives its members an intense feeling of cohesiveness.

Some idea of the role given to the community, the *umma*, is indicated in the fact that it, the *umma*, is the third pillar. Before

Islām, the tribes tended to have ties within a tribe or possibly ties through confederations with other tribes. Muhammad expanded kinship as the only basis of loyalty and made Islām the major tie. Ideally, all Muslims are regarded as brothers and sisters. And in a small village you see a general gathering five times a day as a reinforcement of the idea of the community.

The next pillar of Islām is the *zakāt*, almsgiving or tithing. Its original purpose was to provide general income, and it has now developed into a kind of income tax. In a village, we have something that is more important than collecting money. Village members take care of one another. Taking care of the elderly is very important—that's part of it. It is also a matter of sharing whatever wealth you have, even a small piece of bread. When you're sitting on a curb eating in a small town and someone comes up to you, you automatically ask him if he would like some. You automatically invite a stranger into your home in the evening if he really does not have a place to stay. The particular village that I stayed in had a guest house for unexpected travelers and guests. It's very much a part of their creed to take in strangers. Obviously, they took me in for two years, an American living in a small village. They never could really figure out why I was there, but the hospitality they provided for the entire two years is the important thing I remember.

The idea of community strengthens the idea of almsgiving. For example, on one particular Islamic holiday the wealthy of the village collect a number of lambs, slaughter them, and provide meat for those who cannot afford to share in the holiday rituals. I thought of our own Thanksgiving. When we share, do we really share with our neighbors on the street or the neighbor next door, or the lady who is eighty-five years old? Do we actually share with these people? Sometimes I doubt that we do.

Another important activity of the village is *Ramadān*, a month of fasting and the fourth pillar of Islām. The people abstain from food from dawn to sunset for the health of the body and of the spirit. But at the same time, it was something shared by everyone in the village, including myself. No food or drink was allowed in the village during the daylight hours. The coffeehouses and teahouses literally closed up during the entire month of *Ramadān*. This period of fasting was the cause of some agitation, because people were obviously easily irritated, but it was also a time for very interesting discussions about life, politics, and, of course, religion. It was a time of sharing. The idea of equality among Muslims and the idea of the community played such an overwhelming role for the two years I was in Turkey that I still look back on them as the basic values in the Islamic religion. Remember, a Muslim is one who surrenders himself to God; Islām is the religion of surrendering oneself to God. Everyone participates equally, whether it's in prayer or in fasting, or whether it is in the last of the five pillars of Islām, the *hajj*.

The *hajj* is the pilgrimage. I am sure you have seen photographs of the pilgrimage, of men, women, and children arriving in Mecca, all wearing white as a sign of purity and equality. In the pilgrimage you cannot tell who is rich or who is poor. People from Africa, from Asia, and from Europe all wear the same garb. Hence, the idea of equality before God once again becomes evident in Islām.

Restrictions against the use of pork and alcoholic beverages appear in the Qur'ān, so we see that religion affects the dietary habits of the Muslim people as well. There are also customary restrictions dealing with dress. Village women by the time they were married (usually between twelve and sixteen) wore a black veil around their heads and shoulders and covered their faces, especially their mouths, when they were approached by a man. Underneath their black veil, they wore beautifully colored dresses and bodices. There was such a stark contrast between the drab outer garment and the bright inner dress that it was very hard to understand it sometimes. But it was their tradition, a protection from the eyes of men, a guarantee of purity. The men in the village traditionally wore a hat, a very important tradition because in the mosque you must wear something on your head. Ataturk, the first president of Turkey, tried to ban the fez and substitute a hat like a fedora, but the village men substituted a smaller hat with a bill in the front. When they prayed they turned the hat around and could touch the floor with their foreheads, part of the ritual performed in the mosque.

I think the most encouraging aspect of what I saw in the village was the role of women. Even in 1965, 1966, and 1967, when the idea of equality between sexes was barely emerging, the role of women in a Turkish village was stronger than you can ever find in a text-book. Women played very dominant roles, especially in raising their families and running their households. This recognition of women's prominence in their own spheres results directly from Muhammad's attempts to equalize the sexes. Equality in Islām is vividly expressed in many forms.

I looked at every facet of village life, from birth, with the *imām* coming and blessing the baby, to death, when the body was put into the ground and words from the Qur'ān were spoken by the *imām*, from circumcision when a young boy became a young man, to weddings, which were probably the high points of individual and group life. I was married in that village. I went through a typical village ceremony, including all the Islamic prayers that were whispered by our *imām*. And I feel that it was probably the ultimate experience that one could have in living in an Islamic community. It drew just about everything that I have talked about into a focal point. I shared their meals, and they shared their lives with me. Because of my effort to understand Muslim feelings and rituals, I feel I understand more about what is happening to me in my own community.

8
Thoughts on Islām

Omar Kader

Can we really make authentic comparisons, or are we only wishing to reach across our cultural barriers to find Mormons and Muslims similar? We both take prayer very seriously, but in the act of ablution the Muslim prepares for prayer quite differently than does the Mormon. Raised in Provo, Utah, as a Muslim, I wondered why the Mormon people were manifesting shame by bowing their

---

Omar Kader received his undergraduate education at Brigham Young University, did graduate work at the Middle East Center of the University of Utah, and received his M.A. and Ph.D. degrees at the University of Southern California in international relations. He presently teaches at BYU and has taught extensively courses on the U.S. and the Third World, with particular focus on the Middle East and the Muslim world. He has traveled in the Middle East, particularly the West Bank in Israel, studying conditions there. He was born in Provo, Utah, to Palestinian Muslim immigrant parents, in which place he currently serves as a Mormon bishop.

heads during prayer and closing their eyes and folding their arms in a very defensive prenatal position. What were they hiding from? Both groups, of course, fast. Mormons fast a couple of meals each month. Muslims experience a month of daily fasting and self-control. Are these experiences really comparable?

Both conservative religions are experiencing some pain in adjusting to the modern society that we live in. Mormons are admonished to be in the world but not of the world, and at times we are confused in sorting the two out—especially with our fine graduate degrees in business, teaching us to measure our success in secular terms in contrast to our traditional value of measuring success in family terms.

There are other points of comparison between the two groups: polygamy, the transition from rural to urban, the impact of industrialization on family structure, and so on. Let me make some specific observations.

In thinking of Dr. Palmer's comparisons, we should clarify one point. Although Islām is not only a creedal religion, it certainly has a creed: "There is no God but Allāh, and Muhammad is his prophet." If you've been in any Muslim community more than five minutes, you've heard that creed.

In regard to Orin Parker's presentation, I would stress the difference between cultural and doctrinal comparisons. For example, often we view Islām as Arabic and assume that all Muslims are Arab. In fact, I think Indonesia is the most populous Muslim country. About 80 million Muslims live in Russia. Pakistan, before Bangladesh was created, had one of the largest Muslim populations of any country in the world. Naturally we tend to see the Muslim world in terms of current events: the Arab-Israeli conflict, the oil situation, and so forth. Yet Arabia is not the center of major Islamic populations. How much of Islām is culture, how much of it is custom, and how much of it is doctrine and folklore? We must make those critical observations before our generalizations will be valid.

A related mistake is perceiving Islām as a monolithic and threatening world power. Rather we need to think of it as a series of diverse interests manifested through nationalistic policies.

Dr. Staab's descriptions of the Islām community were most interesting. Hospitality is a major characteristic of Islām. (Of course, horsemanship at one time was also—one's ability to translate his masculinity into some kind of stature in the community.) Dr. Staab's mention of *Ramadān* reminded me of our family celebrations here in Provo. My father would go downtown and buy twenty or thirty sacks of flour, and then he'd say, "Okay, now distribute this to all the neighbors, a sack apiece," even though all of our neighbors were quite well-to-do Mormons where we lived. We'd take a sack of flour up to a house and explain, "Dad said to drop this off." "What's it for?" "We're celebrating *Ramadān*." "Well, that's nice. But what's *Ramadān*?" He always had us dropping fruit off at the police station and the fire station as well. It was his idea of giving to the poor.

The *hajj,* or pilgrimage, is an interesting parallel with Mormonism in the clothing and the covenants that are made. I think my mother is the only Utahn ever to make a pilgrimage to Mecca from Provo, Utah. She went last fall. And as she explains it to me, on a pilgrimage everyone dresses alike, rich or poor. We Mormons also have our own covenants in the temple that have similarities to the covenants made on the pilgrimage.

One other matter that interests me is the *umma,* the community, the believers. I'm not convinced that we can see all of Islām as one monolithic community. Often we tend to see the Islamic world as involved in a *jihād,* a holy war, against Western modernization. I think it is a false conception of the Islamic community to see it as one gigantic threat to modern society. During the Iranian hostage situation we were beginning to hear commentators make observations like: "This is the beginning of the assault on the West.... This world is too small for these two guns in this little town. They've got to go or we've got to go." Many times we talk in such terms because we're spectator-analysts. We have to have winners and losers, good guys and bad guys. There isn't very much gray in the community we live in, and that stems primarily from our own belief that we are absolutely right. If this is the true church, others are not only a little wrong but totally wrong. This attitude makes our ability to tolerate others probably less than Joseph Smith himself had advocated or hoped for.

I'm a social scientist. By training I make observations about the things around me and then begin to try to explain those things, check them out further, and find out how accurate I am.

To begin with, the realities of Islām are not well known. Americans know more myth than truth regarding this religion. We understand Islām so very little in the United States. We think about its uniqueness—its role in the lives of its adherents, and the policies that direct its governments—but seldom do we think what it may mean to us in our small world. We tend to think of Islām as so large there is no real way to understand it.

A common misperception of Islām held in the West is that it's impossible for less-developed Islamic countries to move out of eighteenth- or nineteenth-century patterns into a twentieth- or twenty-first-century modern world. Maxim Rodinson, a French scholar on Islām, has challenged the traditional view which also assumes that religion in general somehow retards economic, political, and social progress. Rodinson suggests instead that Islām serves as an instrument in the hands of economists and politicians whose successes or failures are ascribed to Islām, not to themselves. It is interesting to realize that almost every third-world country is headed by Western-educated individuals. What may be said about policies in Islamic nations which are being implemented by leaders educated in Western institutions? What may be said about the successes and failures of those policies? Is failure a function of Islām? Are Western notions possibly preventing leaders from translating progress into terms that are harmonious with the culture within each country?

Westerners in general are products of an empirical tradition: computers, calculators, bottom lines, bookkeeping. The good society is measured in GNPs, per-capita income, acres of cultivation, miles of roads, doctors per thousand, etc. The number of miles per GNP equals a country's development. Or will it? This is hardly a soul-searching method. It does not talk about the value of that road. Materialism, secularism, and behavioralism, by necessity of method, relegate the good, the bad, the ought, the ought not, and the ethical to another realm, the realm of the irrelevant, the domestic—or worse, the mystic—religionist. In almost every major textbook in America on development, religion is seen as an obstacle, a retardant. It's no wonder that Americans specifically and Westerners generally have a difficult time imagining religion as aiding progress. Ataturk in the twenties had to eliminate the religious leaders, move them out of his system. An areligious model for development was his plan. And should we be glad or sorry that he failed?

Is the current return to Islamic fundamentalism a return to cultural authenticity more than it is a rejection of the modern West? We have decided that it is a threat to the West and treat it as a threat to progress rather than a return to authentic values. Yet the view of the West in most Muslim countries derives from the first representatives of the West in their countries—from the construction crews. And what do construction crews bring with them? Chaplains? Chapels? Rituals? No, they bring beer, brothels, and bars—some of the finest examples of decadence that the West has to offer. What do Muslims believe we stand for?

Now, our task in this conference is to reduce spots of ignorance within our own thinking. BYU campus is a good place to start because we hold a fairly typical range of American ideas, but have the advantage of being a bit more sensitive here about religion. Where do we begin? How do we tear down barriers? How do we expand the contacts? Is it through cultural exchange, visitors, residence tours, interesting exchanges such as this symposium?

Let me tell you what I think might help. The image of Islām in this country is completely dependent on our access to indigenous Islamic culture. An open exchange will reduce the crude inaccuracies and the crude images in the West of Muslim people and of nations. And the same is true of Mormons reaching out. BYU as a major institution of higher learning can invite students from all over the world to come here for a valid spiritual education and a valuable secular education. They can go back having preserved their traditions and their values, maintaining their sense of the sacred but having expanded it to include an understanding of Mormonism as well. They can return home and say, "Look what America did for me." That's our unique role. And of course, we will be gracious guests as well as hospitable hosts on our own campus. But to complete the process, we must have access to Muslim communities— and through them to the values of Islām. Part of the burden is on the shoulders of Muslim leaders throughout the world. They need us as much as we need them if we are to reach a common understanding.

9
The Muhammad-Joseph Smith Comparison: Subjective Metaphor or a Sociology of Prophethood

Arnold H. Green

The comparison of one individual to another can occur in a variety of literary or social contexts. It is in an essentially historical vein, for example, that a number of authors have attributed to Lafayette the aspiration to become the George Washington of France. By contrast, it reflected the rough and tumble (not to say the crudeness) of partisan politics when former Vice President Spiro

Arnold H. Green is associate professor of modern Near Eastern history at American University in Cairo. A graduate of California State College, Los Angeles, in American studies, he received his M.A. in history from Brigham Young University and his Ph.D. in Near Eastern history from the University of California at Los Angeles. Professor Green's scholarly work includes Tunisia, Yemen, Egypt, Turkey, Jordan, and Syria, with doctoral and postdoctoral research on the Ulama and the state in Egypt and Tunisia.

Agnew referred to Senator Charles Goodell of New York, a conservative turned liberal, as "the Christine Jorgenson of the
Republican Party." Comparisons can also represent attempts at
humor, as for example when Wilhelm Wyl, in an irreverent biog-
raphy of Joseph Smith, entitled his chapter on the Illinois period
"The Don Juan of Nauvoo." Of course references of this sort are
often superficial and are usually fleeting, although a few of
them—like Lafayette as a George Washington—occasionally do
manage to get passed on from one generation to the next. Rarely
does a comparison receive the supreme tribute of being taken
seriously; whereupon it is elevated from a rhetorical to an academic
level and may even come to be regarded as the demonstration of a
scientific principle. One of the few comparisons in this class is that
which depicts Joseph Smith as an American Muhammad. What
follows is an attempt to determine how and why this analogy
developed and whether it belongs to the realm of metaphor or to
that of science.

Metaphors and Polemics

The comparison of Joseph Smith to Muhammad—and of
Mormonism to Islām—seems to have entered the literary record as
an example of what psychologists call transference. In his lectures
on Islām, the Dutch Calvinist scholar Christiaán Snouck Hurgronje
mentioned a polemical tactic which he called "cryptomoham-
medanism. . . . The Roman Catholics," he explained, "often vilified
Protestantism by comparing the Reformed doctrine to that of
Mohammedanism."[1] Having endured the accusation themselves for
a century or two in Europe, the Protestants directed it in America
against the Mormons. Thus Joseph Smith's "extreme ignorance and
apparent stupidity" were identified by the Reverend E. D. Howe in
1834 as well-worn cloaks in the "wardrobe of imposters. They were
thrown upon the shoulders of the great prince of deceivers,
Mohammed, in order to carry in his train the host of ignorant and
superstitious of his time."[2] Writing two decades later at the request
of the Anglican Young Men's Society, W. S. Simpson observed that
Mormonism "bears in many respects a striking resemblance to

Mahometanism, especially as to its sensual character, its founder, and its pretended revelations."[3] By then, Joseph Smith had been identified in various Protestant publications as a "Yankee Mahomet" and as a "backwoods Mahomet."[4]

The tactic became sufficiently common that ex-Mormons also employed it. In 1838 Thomas B. Marsh testified that he had over-heard Joseph Smith boast that "he would yet tread down his enemies, and walk over their dead bodies; and if he was not let alone, he would be a second Mohammed to this generation, and that it would be one gore of blood from the Rocky Mountains to the Atlantic Ocean; that like Mohammed, whose motto in treating for peace was, 'the Alcoran or the sword,' so should it be eventually with us, Joseph Smith or the sword."[5] Similarly, in 1873 T. B. H. Stenhouse promised that "the student of Mormonism will be struck with the similarity of experience and claims of Joseph Smith and Mohammed."[6] Also in the Protestant cryptomuhammadan tradition there appeared, after the turn of the century, Jennie Fowler Willing's *Mormonism: The Mohammedanism of the West* (Louisville, Ky: Pickett Publishing Co., 1906) and Bruce Kinney's *Mormonism: The Islam of America* (New York: Revell, 1912).

In the context of cryptomuhammadanism, the Muhammad-Joseph comparison functions essentially as a figure of speech in the rhetoric of sectarian polemics. Christianity had long regarded Muhammad's claims to prophethood as fraudulent and his teachings as heretical.[7] A metaphor-loving cleric might consequently refer to someone claiming divine guidance for a departure from prevailing Christian norms as a Muhammad just as a politician might refer to an ex-supporter as a Benedict Arnold. Figurative references of this sort have less to do with objective historical realities than with subjective linguistic symbols. That is, a notorious person's name is used in lieu of words denoting the qualities attributed to him by a certain group. Since another group might attribute different qualities to the same person, the connotations of his name are subjective or are associated with a particular state of mind. Benedict Arnold might imply a traitor to Americans but a loyalist to Englishmen, just as George Washington might stand for an opportunistic rebel in eighteenth-century England but a nation-founding hero in the United States.

Cryptomuhammadan references to Joseph Smith by nineteenth-century Protestant writers as a rule were pejorative and connoted the qualities—such as deceitfulness, sensuousness, and potential violence—that Christianity then attributed to Muhammad. Such metaphorical connotations can of course change as the group's historical perception of the person becomes modified. Just as George Washington may now imply a nation-founder to many Englishmen, a Muhammad may convey positive rather than negative implications to certain Christians. In this regard, in 1842 the *New York Herald* editorialized that Joseph Smith "indicates as much talent, originality, and moral courage as Mahomet, Odin, or any of the great spirits that have hitherto produced the revolutions of the past ages."[8]

ORIENTALISM AND THE STUDY OF PROXIES

Well before the end of the nineteenth-century, the Muhammad-Joseph Smith comparison was transplanted from the domain of American clergymen to that of European orientalists: specialists in the languages, history, and religions of the Orient. The first agent of this transplant possibly was Richard Francis Burton, who is well known for his attempts to discover the source of the Nile, for his translation of *1001 Nights*, and for his visit to Mecca disguised as a Muslim notable. Burton traveled through Utah to California in 1860 and then published his *The City of the Saints* the following year. Having discovered the Muhammad-Joseph Smith comparison while reading up on Mormonism but familiar with Islām as none of the American clergymen were, Burton agreed that there were indeed a number of bona fide similarities. "Mormonism claims," he observed, "like El Islām, to be a restoration by revelation of the pure and primaeval religion of the world." He proceeded to suggest that, as an eclectic sect—a "spontaneous agglomeration of tenets"—Mormons "are Muslims" in their belief in a literal resurrection, in their practice of polygamy, and "in their views of the inferior status of womenkind." Brigham Young's title "Lion of the Lord," he added, "was literally borrowed from El Islām."[9]

Burton, who was inclined to show off his erudition by name-dropping exotic terms, went on to allege that other Mormon beliefs and practices were borrowed from other sources, including Arianism and Epicureanism. He thus hints, somewhat in accordance with the diffusionist methodology of the historian of ideas, that Joseph Smith had knowledge of many religions from which he indiscriminately plagiarized his dogmas and rituals. At least two researchers[10] subsequently followed up this suggestion but concluded that no direct link could be established between Joseph Smith's limited education and any work containing specific information about Islām. For our purposes, therefore, Burton's significance was in transplanting the Muhammad-Joseph Smith comparison from its native habitat of American religious polemics into the realm of European orientalism.

It was perhaps via Burton that the comparison came to the attention of a less adventurist, more bookish orientalist: D. S. Margoliouth of the University of London. In his widely read and much reprinted *Mohammed and the Rise of Islam* (3rd. ed., London: Putnam's, 1906), Margoliouth made two specific points of comparison: first, that Muhammad's initial religious experience, like Joseph Smith's, followed a period of perplexity engendered in part by observing the differences between rival sects; and, second, that in each case revelations were given piecemeal as circumstances required divine guidance. Margoliouth did not take the comparison beyond these two points, however.

The orientalist who took it well beyond these points was the German historian of ancient Near Eastern religions, Eduard Meyer. Having published his celebrated *Geschichte des Altertums* (History of Antiquity), in 1911 Meyer visited Salt Lake City and the following year published his *Ursprung und Geschichte der Mormonen* (Origin and History of the Mormons). He found numerous specific points of comparison, and his work became the main source for virtually all those who subsequently became interested in the Muhammad-Joseph Smith comparison.

The many points of similarity Meyer itemized include: "Neither Joseph Smith nor Mohammed were towering personalities." As they aspired to knowledge and experience of the deity, both figures went through a phase of withdrawal and perplexity. In the initial divine manifestation, the visit of angels to Muhammad "is very similar to the first vision of Joseph Smith." Why did God reveal books specifically to the Jews and the Christians while leaving the Arabs and the Americans without their own special scriptures? "The solution was the same in both cases. . . . Joseph Smith brought forth a Bible for America; a Bible for the Arabs is what Mohammed longed for and received bit by bit." Both prophets received abrogative revelations yet remained essentially consistent: "As often as Smith—like Mohammed—was ready to reinterpret or set aside older revelations when circumstances were altered, there could none the less [sic] be no compromise for him (or the Arabian prophet) regarding the basic issues at stake." Each, according to Meyer, experienced a decline and corruption of his revelatory powers: "One may follow in the case of both prophets a progressive degeneration, a transition from a stage of genuine vision to a later stage of purely fictional inspiration." And in each case, according to Meyer, the failure to "recognize the distinction between truth and independent invention was 'carried out unconsciously'." Also, "in the cases of both Mohammed and Joseph Smith, the sensuality of their lives grew continually stronger, and the means for satisfying it actually appeared as divine commands." Both men sought first a national territorial base and then world domination: "Just as Arabia was to be the inheritance of the Moslems, so was America to become the inheritance of the Mormons, but later on the whole world as well." Finally, with regard to revenue, "Like Mohammed he [Joseph Smith] demanded alms from the faithful."[11]

Even if we disregard such negative and questionable points of Meyer's comparison as the "later stage of purely fictional inspiration" and the notion of increasing sensuality, there remain a few intriguing aspects, including the structural parallels of a period of dissatisfaction and of searching, which led to a profound initial religious experience entailing the visit of divine messengers, which eventually resulted in a new book of scripture, and the acquisition and exercise of a political dimension to prophetic authority. It is perhaps understandable that, henceforth, Meyer became the main source of those inclined, for whatever reason, to pursue the comparison between Muhammad and Joseph Smith.

But although some of the substance of Meyer's comparison is plausible, his purpose and method are questionable. Meyer was at once a German Hegelian historian and a nineteenth-century

European orientalist; the weaknesses and follies of these two scholarly traditions manifest themselves clearly in his comparison of Mormonism with Islām. As a Hegelian, Meyer believed that the *Zeitgeist* (the spirit of the time) moved through history determining the course of events. When conditions were comparable, the *Zeitgeist* created comparable movements and institutions. As a "B.C. orientalist,"[12] Meyer became interested in Islām and the Arabs because Arabic was regarded as the purest of the Semitic languages although it was the last to emerge. The B.C. orientalists, who were interested mainly in the Old Testament but who felt that the study of Hebrew alone (because it was no longer a living language) was insufficient, studied Arabic to learn more about the language and culture of the Old Testament peoples.[13] Arabic and Islām were thus not studied for their own sake but as proxies for the language and religion of the Jews.

Eduard Meyer, whose primary interest was ancient Near Eastern religions, took this study of proxies a step further. Because the revealed religion of Islām was underdocumented, he would study Mormonism instead. Meyer's purpose and method can be seen in the following passages from his introduction and from his "Excursion" on the origin of Islām:

> Of the many new religious movements originating in our time, Mormonism very early awakened my interest, especially because of its surprising and close resemblance to the historical development of Islām. The basic impulses and forms under which it appeared gave reason to hope for important conclusions regarding the understanding of Muhammad and his religion.
>
> This new religion grew up during the nineteenth century, so that we can pursue its origin and history by means of the rich contemporary tradition, handed down by adherents and foes, and a body of well-dated documents which have grown in number with every passing day. Therefore, that which is generally unavailable to students of other revealed religions, is directly and reliably documented. The origin and growth of Mormonism have become of great value to the religious historians; this value is further increased by the fact that among revealed religions, it is one of the most unsophisticated and least intellectual.
>
> Without the least exaggeration, we may designate the Mormons as the Mohammedans of the New World according to their origins and their manner of thinking. There is hardly a historical parallel which is

so instructive as this one; and through comparative analysis both
receive so much light that a scientific study of one through the other is
indispensable.[14]

Given his Hegelian and orientalist assumptions, Meyer could
not legitimize his generalizations without making Muhammad and
Joseph Smith appear to be shaped by the *Zeitgeist* out of similar
conditions. This is why he insisted that they were not "towering
personalities," thereby suggesting a sort of malleability, and that
"for this very reason we are able to recognize more clearly the
driving forces behind the prophet's life."[15] This, in turn, is why he
intimated that nineteenth-century frontier America closely resem-
bled seventh-century Arabia. "The historical development and the
present condition of North America (1912) show the existence, side
by side, of refinement, intellectual and ethical culture, [and] a
downright primitive semi-barbarism," he explained. Thus Mormonism's origin "will be comprehensible only if the reader keeps in mind
the picture of very primitive ways of thinking in the midst of a
culture which is highly developed in many of its other forms."[16] The
academic stock of Meyer's Hegelian assumptions (two weak-willed
prophets were created by unseen "driving forces" out of identical
primitive circumstances) and of his orientalist method (studying as a
proxy a nineteenth-century religious movement to make generalizations about a seventh-century one whose origins are not well
documented) declined sharply after World War I when Hegelianism
and orientalism lost stock with the emergence of the modern
disciplines. Consequently, although subsequent commentators
acknowledge borrowing Meyer's information, they tend to remain
silent about or to disavow his methodology.

SOCIOLOGY OF RELIGION
AND THE NEMESIS OF ULTERIOR MOTIVES

Having been conceptualized by the end of the nineteenth
century, the social sciences were identifying their specialized subject
matters and developing their respective methodologies. A group of
such historians as Montesquieu, de Tocqueville, Comte, and
Marx—disgruntled at the tendency of traditional historians to
narrate political-military or religious developments without pro-

viding adequate explanations as to why they happened as they did—had pioneered the new science of sociology.[17] The sociologists pledged themselves to the task of examining all significant social institutions and phenomena: society's fundamental structures and processes which lay beneath the course of superficial events recorded by historians. They would accomplish this by using the method of observation and experiment with which Newton and Bacon had revolutionized the physical sciences and also by using the comparative method with which Lamarck and Darwin had revolutionized biology. Equipped with new interests and methods, the sociologists proceeded to explain various kinds of social phenomena by sorting them into categories and by suggesting cause-and-effect relationships between them.

Religion was a social phenomenon to which some first-generation theorists like Karl Marx gave little serious attention. Yet a few second-generation sociologists like Emile Durkheim, Vilfredo Pareto, and Max Weber become particularly interested in religion and, in effect, pioneered the sociology of religion. These pioneers were careful to stipulate that the process whereby committed believers acquire information about and provide explanations for religious phenomena, a process involving unobservable inner feelings and credulous respect for authority, was different from the ideal method of the sociologists, who ought to remain emotionally detached in their efforts to document and to explain those religious institutions and developments the outward manifestations of which can be witnessed by impartial observers. One of the principal obstacles to this development lies in the fact that the sociology of religion is a field in which sociological thinking and religious thinking are not always distinguished clearly.

One aspect of this obstacle is the problem of means and ends. According to the founding fathers of their discipline, sociologists ought to employ the comparative method as a means to the end of categorizing and explaining social phenomena. A religious partisan could employ it instead as a means to the end of, say, pinning a label of heresy on a rival sect. When sociology hived off from history, it thus did not leave behind it the problem of ulterior motives that had long plagued historical writing—a problem which is seen, for example, in Macaulay's progress-oriented essays on

English history, which were written to promote the passage of the Reform Act, and in Carlyle's glorification of Oliver Cromwell, the invader of Ireland, which reveals the historian's virulent anti-Catholic bias.[18]

Following World War I, at least two scholars, Hans Thimme, a German, and Georges-Henri Bousquet, a Frenchman, pursued the Muhammad-Joseph Smith comparison from the fresh perspective of sociology of religion. Both relied extensively on Eduard Meyer for their information and neither contributed any substantially new points of comparison. Rather, according to them, their originality consisted of their sociological methodology and framework.

Writing in 1934, Thimme, an amateur sociologist who was mainly a Protestant clergyman, begins in a tone of scientific detachment by denying that his purpose is polemical or that he seeks to criticize Mormonism "from the point of view of Christian doctrine." Rather, he reassures, "my purpose is that of comparative religion. I wish to describe this cult in so far as it shows parallels to another great religion of world history, Islām—parallels not only in its outward appearance but also in its inner essence." He promises to discuss "the question of the system or type of religion; whether perhaps Mormonism and Islām belong together as one peculiar type."[19]

Thimme's application of the comparative method of the sociology of religion is rather disappointing, however. In his initial point of comparison, the visit of divine messengers to the two prophets, he relates that Joseph Smith experienced his first vision after he had "roamed about in the forests" and because, "on account of his low intellectual standard, he united the wildest superstitions with his Christian belief." Afterwards, according to Thimme, Joseph Smith "continued his former life, dirty, shy and idle, as he is described by his neighbors, using his visual powers for seeking hidden treasures with a so-called 'peep-stone.'" Thimme's second point of comparison is that the subjective honesty of each prophet was accompanied by objective error: "That appears, for instance, in this, that both acknowledge the Old Testament and the New Testament as divine revelation, but they both, on account of their imperfect knowledge, alter the teaching of the Bible by subjective additions and arbitrary changes." To explain how subjective honesty can coexist with objective error, Thimme quotes Meyer to the effect that primitives like Muhammad and Joseph Smith "do not make a clear distinction between reality and hallucination" and "have no real consciousness of the difference between truth and deception." According to Thimme, "The most striking point of parallelism between Mormonism and Islām" consists of their political objectives and of their means of attaining them: "Their propaganda, therefore, has not only religious but political aims, and uses not only peaceful means of missionary preaching but also holy war."

Thimme concludes that "both religions are representatives of the same type of religion" and that, "as representatives of the same principle, Mormonism and Islām belong together." How does Thimme characterize this "theocratic-autocratic" type of religion? First, the founders were persuaded that "God needs human beings for carrying on His will and for helping to establish the kingdom" (read: "advocated works in addition to grace"). "This misunderstanding of the Kingdom of God," he continues, "leads them to undervalue human sinfulness and divine sovereignty" (read: "leads them to deny original sin"). Thus, according to Thimme, "Mormonism and Islām both lack this message of the cross" (read: "are not genuinely Christian"). It is noteworthy that Thimme's article appeared in *The Moslem World,* a journal published by a seminary then devoted in part to training missionaries for the conversion of Muslims to Protestant Christianity.

But, in any case, it has now become clear that it is Thimme's partisan religious commitment rather than his impartial sociological observations which govern the formulation of his typologies and of his conclusions. That is, from Thimme's own Protestant perspective, which emphasizes the utter hopelessness of man's sinful nature and the absolute sufficiency of God's grace, both Islām and Mormonism are Christian heresies. His purpose consequently appears to be polemical after all. Notwithstanding his opening disclaimer, he does indeed criticize from the point of view of a particular Christian doctrine. What he calls comparative religion is essentially nineteenth-century cryptomuhammadanism masquerading as twentieth-century sociology of religion. The problem of ulterior motives—essentially using sociological methods as a means to the end of waging sectarian polemics—thus frustrated Thimme's effort to engage constructively in comparative religion.

Another sociologist of religion who took a keen interest in the Muhammad-Joseph Smith comparison, Georges-Henri Bousquet, appears to have been much better prepared for the task than Thimme was. He was a formally trained sociologist who congratulated himself on lacking a religious commitment.[20] The author of scores of works on Islām and on sociological theory and method, he also wrote at least three articles and one book on the Mormons.[21] While freely acknowledging his debt to Eduard Meyer (although not the extent to which he borrowed extensive passages verbatim from Meyer's book), Bousquet characteristically begins each of his works on Mormonism with a profession of his impartiality and of his intent to consider his subject from the scientific perspective of sociology.[22] He suggests, for example, that Mormonism is of "sociological interest" because it "shows, before our very eyes so to speak, how a revealed religion is born and expands." Thus, according to Bousquet, studying Mormonism may throw light on the emergence process not just of Islām but of all other revealed religions, although he does point out that "there are, in particular, remarkable analogies between Muhammad and Joseph Smith." Yet, in contrast to Thimme, who at least attempted to establish a typology (albeit for purposes other than contributing new insights to the sociology of religion), Bousquet does not attempt to say what the comparison means in sociological terms. His treatment of the Muhammad-Joseph Smith comparison is therefore equally disappointing, although for different reasons.

A weakness of Bousquet that becomes immediately apparent is that he relies very heavily on Meyer and makes little effort to apply to his comparisons the methods and categories of sociology. Although he occasionally adds a clarification (the Doctrine and Covenants, not the Book of Mormon, is Mormonism's functional equivalent of the Qur'ān),[23] Bousquet is ordinarily content to repeat Meyer's points of comparison while claiming that they are sociological phenomena but without associating them with any sociological terms or categories and without attributing to them any sociological significance. For example, he introduces his discussion of revelation in Mormonism by the observation that "it is most

interesting to compare the role of revelation in Mormonism and in
Islām from the sociological point of view." But then he simply
quotes Meyer's account more or less verbatim.[24] Similarly,
Bousquet broaches the question of the Book of Mormon's origin by
saying that "the genesis of the work can be explained, more or less,
by psychological and sociological considerations." But then he
merely repeats Meyer's allegation that neither Muhammad nor
Joseph Smith could distinguish between truth and invention, and he
concludes that "it is not any more astonishing that a young farmer
from Vermont, steeped in biblical phraseology, believed himself
chosen to promulgate the Book of Mormon than it was for an Arab
caravaneer [to believe himself] designated to reveal the Qur'ān."[25]

Bousquet's failure to use all the tools of the sociology of religion
may be explained in part by the orientations and prejudices of his
teachers. As a Frenchman, Bousquet naturally came under the
influence of Durkheim, whose school of sociology was essentially
grounded in the theory of evolution. Durkheim's sociology of
religion thus postulated that complex religions merely possess
complicated versions of institutions of which simple religions
possess uncomplicated versions. The corollary is that a sociologist
can understand the essence of religion per se by studying the
simplest forms of it; Durkheim himself studied totemism among the
Australian aborigines. Bousquet also came under the influence of
the Italian-born, French-educated Vilfredo Pareto, who is the
subject of Bousquet's half-dozen books on sociological method.[26]
According to Raymond Aron, Pareto was something of a cynic. In
Pareto's view, society is held together by feelings, especially
religious ones, "which are not true but which are effective. If the
sociologist shows people the wrong side of the embroidery or what
goes on behind the scenes, he runs the risk of destroying indispensable illusions."[27] Bousquet was aware of Max Weber, the third
major pioneer of the sociology of religion, and even quotes from
him occasionally. But compared to the French-born Durkheim and
the French-educated Pareto, the German-born and -educated Weber
seems to have had little influence on Bousquet. And yet the
sociology of religion after World War I was essentially Weberian in
its basic concepts and categories, the influences of Durkheim and
Pareto having greatly declined.

But is this the most we can say of Bousquet: that, perhaps because of his teachers' shortcomings, he failed to live up to sociology's potential in his treatment of the Muhammad-Joseph Smith comparison? No, for Bousquet was French not only in the slant of his sociological training but also in his biases toward France's colonial territories and subjects—particularly the Muslims of Algeria, where Bousquet taught sociology at the University of Algiers. In 1950 Edouard Bremond published his *Berberes et Arabes: La Barbarie est un pays europeen* (Berbers and Arabs: Barbary is a European Country), which advocated France's Berber policy: to treat Berber customs as the essential North African culture and, concomitantly, to treat Arabic and Islamic institutions as being foreign, superficially imposed, and inconsequential to facilitate France's *"conquete morale"* (moral conquest) of North Africa and cultural supremacy there.[28] At about the same time Bousquet also published two books on the Berbers[29] via which he joined Bremond and other prominent French scholars of his generation in legitimizing and perpetuating the Berber policy. As a teacher in the French school system of Algeria, Bousquet was advised—and advised others—to tolerate Islām where it was entrenched but not to treat it as a "higher religion."[30] For North Africa, where French civilization competed for primacy with Arabic-Islamic civilization, could become truly French only if the Arabic and Islamic character of the region could be undermined. Thus, according to Bousquet, knowledge of Islām is important "for we Frenchmen, who aspire, like Islām does, to make our civilization triumph here."[31]

It thus appears that Bousquet, the student of Durkheim, pursues this anti-Islamic national objective by insisting on the archaic rudimentariness of Islām, which, he asserts, differs from Catholicism "principally by its extreme simplicity. The comparison evokes an impression of remarkable sterility."[32] And Bousquet, the student of Pareto, delves into Islām's most intimate matters—such as its rituals and its sexual mores[33]—perhaps deliberately to "show the other side of the embroidery" as a means of destroying the indispensable illusions of the competition. A number of passages could be excerpted from his many writings in order to illustrate Bousquet's attitudes, but one will do. It is a crude passage; Bousquet apologizes for composing it, and I apologize for reproducing it here. Yet it is too appropriate in another sense not to do so. Explaining why Islām does not treat theology, law, and ethics as separate and distinct categories as Christianity does, he points out that "In mammals we find a urinary bladder, a vagina, [and] a rectum, whereas birds and reptiles have only a single, undifferentiated organ: the cloaca, which corresponds to an earlier stage of evolution. Similarly, Islamic law, the Shari'a, remained at a more primitive stage of evolution than did Christianity."[34]

Bousquet's crude metaphor is symbolic not only of the evolutionary framework which he inherited from Durkheim but also of his contemptuous attitude towards Islām, an attitude associated with French national policy in colonial North Africa. It was this ulterior motive, along with other factors, which prevented Bousquet from realizing the full potential of the sociology of religion and, consequently, from treating the Muhammad-Joseph Smith comparison in a meaningful and instructive way.

A SOCIOLOGY OF PROPHETHOOD

This intriguing comparison, which has existed in the literature for nearly 150 years, has thus been pursued for questionable reasons and with questionable methods: to discredit Mormonism by equating its founder with Muhammad, who was presumed to be a fraud and a heretic, to study one religion as a proxy to reach fundamental conclusions about another, or to pay lip service to sociology as a means of attaining the ends of sectarianism or of colonialism. Seemingly paid the tribute of being taken seriously and of being elevated from a rhetorical to an academic level, it instead has been used cynically and has received the insult of continuing to be employed rhetorically to realize partisan objectives.

But if no one has thus far pursued the comparison with impartiality, genuinely using sociological concepts and methods, does that mean that it cannot be done or that it is not worth doing? Could we do it ourselves if we wanted to? There are, on the one hand, hopes of possibilities that such a task could be done properly. We should first have to select an appropriate conceptual framework, preferably one derived from Weber rather than from Durkheim or Pareto, and then proceed to reexamine the comparison in its light. An example of an appropriate conceptual framework might be the section on prophets in *The Sociology of Religion* by Joachim Wach, a leading Weberian sociologist of religion.[35]

In the tradition of Weber, who distinguished between the functions of founders of religion, prophets, and priests, Wach conceptualized a number of types of religious figures, including founder, reformer, prophet, seer, magician, diviner, saint, and priest, each category typified by a few distinctive characteristics. In his section on prophets, Wach explicitly disagrees with certain earlier writers who deny the title of prophet to all but the Hebrew personalities of the Old Testament. For example, in his article on prophecy for Hastings' 1925 *Encyclopedia of Religion and Ethics*, E. Konig argued that the Hebrew figures of the Old Testament were the only genuine prophets. Rejecting the suggestion that personalities like Muhammad be included in the same category, Konig pointed out that Muhammad "falls far below the true Hebrew prophets": and that, "when compared with Muhammad, the prophets of Israel still maintain their distinctive place in the history of religion." Konig does not mention Joseph Smith.[36] In his category of prophets, by contrast, Wach includes Zoroaster, Muhammad, Joseph Smith, and other nonbiblical religious figures. He then proceeds to discuss the observable characteristics of typical prophets.

Most notably, according to Wach, a prophet is charismatic (charisma being a concept which Weber borrowed from the New Testament account of Peter being filled with the Holy Ghost). That is, as the recipient of a distinct religious "call," the prophet enjoys direct communication with Deity and is conscious of being the instrument or spokesman of the divine will. As in the case of the founder (whose tendency to become the object of worship distinguishes him from the prophet, whom he otherwise resembles), most of the prophet's other traits are related to or derived from his charisma. In his precall phase, the prophet is typically of humble origins rather than from among the elite or the learned, yet is spiritually sensitive, has a natural disposition to receive and to interpret divine manifestations. As a rule, these manifestations are not induced, as in the case of the diviner or medium. Like the founder, the prophet enjoys a number of charismatic gifts or tendencies: he is a renewer of contacts with supernatural forces; he possesses extraordinary powers and performs miracles; he is the recipient and dispenser of vital, God-given knowledge; he feels the obligation to make universal the message of Deity among all men; and he is concerned with a special liturgy or with holy ordinances, often in connection with a sacred place.

The prophet shares at least two qualities with the seer. Frequently he possesses the ability to transcend limitations of time, thereby to illuminate the past and to foretell the future—or to prophesy. He is also eschatological, perceiving the conditions and developments of the world in the light of its ultimate destiny. In a final set of traits, the prophet resembles the reformer: he is given to blunt expressions of moral judgment; he is uncompromising in his insistence on basic principles; he tends to make vigorous declarations that are sometimes cryptic and often innovative; he displays a critical or "protestant" attitude toward prevailing beliefs and forms of worship as falsified or otherwise illegitimate (an attitude which typically results in conflict with established religious institutions and leaders); and these criticisms result in a general reintegration of principles under the prophet or his successors and the formation of an independent cultic unit. He sometimes goes beyond his role as the community's conscience to become a political-military leader and social reformer with the task of establishing a new political and socio-economic order.

Someone pursuing the Muhammad-Joseph Smith comparison in accordance with this or another framework might then proceed to discover that Muhammad and Joseph Smith shared many of these prophetic characteristics. Most notably, each was of humble birth, each displayed a predisposition to spirituality, each had a profound initial religious experience involving heavenly messengers, each articulated the concept of restoring a primeval religion, each founded a religion without becoming an object of its worship, each was a medium for the issuing of new scriptures, each established new rituals, each directed a community of believers continuously via revelation, and each extended prophetic authority into the political realm.

On the other hand, there are at least two reasons for suggesting caution to someone inclined to pursue the comparison beyond this point. The first of these is that, alongside the similarities, there exist a number of significant differences between Muhammad and Joseph Smith. Even those who pursued the comparison most zealously acknowledged some important dissimilarities. For example, Burton observed that Joseph Smith endowed Mormonism with a hieratic priesthood whereas Muhammad left Islām without any priesthood at all; and Bousquet pointed out that, in Islām, revelation ended with Muhammad, whereas it continued in Mormonism after the death of Joseph Smith.[37] Other significant differences could also be mentioned. For example, Muhammad transformed an essentially pagan and polytheistic community into a strictly monotheistic one, whereas Joseph Smith introduced among Christians a "restored" version of Christianity having pluralistic tendencies. Also, in a sociological sense Muhammad was vastly more successful than Joseph Smith in both the religious and the political roles. Within Muhammad's own lifetime virtually all the Arabs were reconstituted into an Islamic state under his leadership, whereas Joseph Smith, at the time of his death, had merely created a comparatively small religious movement ignored or despised by most Americans, and although he aspired to national political leadership he died as mayor of Nauvoo.

Thus, as Bousquet put it, "Mormonism differs from Islām, because the latter appeared in a land where the state was unknown and therefore rapidly transformed itself into a theocratic state [whereas] sixty years after its appearance, Mormonism had already been vanquished by the state."[38] Meyer's allegation notwithstanding, nineteenth-century America appears to have been rather dissimilar from seventh-century Arabia after all; and the role of a prophet in the one time and place consequently differed considerably from the role of a prophet in the other. That is, the two prophets' similarities lay in their having performed prophetic roles as other prophets did; while their differences lay in their distinctive environments and in their distinctive personalities. By and large, the same could be said for all prophets.

Second, once a sociological category of prophets is conceptualized in Wach's framework and Muhammad and Joseph Smith are included in it along with the others who shared the same general characteristics, are there grounds for insisting that one particular prophet resembles another any more than he resembles all the others? If so, do we need to conceptualize subcategories of prophets, and do Muhammad and Joseph Smith belong in a special subcategory of their own that is separate and distinct from, say, Abraham, Moses, Isaiah, Lehi, and Brigham Young? If so, what does it mean? What cause-and-effect relationships can we discover to explain the conditions and factors which produce prophets of this particular subcategory? And if we regard certain types of prophets as being mere effects of certain environmental causes, shall we fall into the deterministic trap of treating religion as being no more than a particular kind of response to socio-economic stimuli and not a stimulus in its own right? In other words, it might be more reasonable to say that Muhammad and Joseph Smith both belong in the larger category of prophets and let the matter rest there.

CONCLUSIONS

Having questioned the motives and methods of the American Protestants, the European orientalists, and the sociologists of religion in their use of the Muhammad-Joseph Smith comparison, it might be interesting and appropriate, by way of a conclusion, to wonder why *we* are interested in it. It does make a nice bibliographic essay to trace the development of this alleged parallelism from E. D. Howe to Bousquet and beyond, much as scholars have traced the history of such issues as Max Weber's Protestant ethic thesis.[39] That is, it makes for an intriguing conference paper and for fascinating reading. But our interest, at this conference and at this university, surely goes deeper than that.

If we do pursue the analogy further, we shall have to establish a good working relationship with the department of sociology. For, in addition to demonstrating that the similarities outweigh the differences (rather a formidable task in itself), we shall need assistance in working out the characteristics of the subgroup inhabited by Muhammad and Joseph Smith to the exclusion of all other prophets; and we shall need assistance in seeking to discover and to isolate the cause-and-effect relationships which produced the two prophets of that particular little subgroup. Moreover, we shall need support and critical collegial scrutiny lest we imitate those we have criticized for pursuing the comparison simply as a means to the end of vindicating their own theological tenets and advancing their own ulterior motives.

It may be, coming full circle, that the Muhammad-Joseph Smith comparison can be no more than a subjective metaphor for us. If so, let it be a constructive one, used for the purpose of communicating to our own people and to others that Latter-day Saints, unlike most Christians of the nineteenth century and before *and* since, regard Muhammad not as a fraud and a heretic but rather as a great and good man who was instrumental in the establishment of an important world religion belonging to the Judeo-Christian tradition. And let it be used not to promote polemics of one sort or another but rather to promote understanding and friendship. Although we may not consider the analogy to be the demonstration of a scientific principle, we are able—and we ought—to consider it in its most positive metaphorical light.

NOTES

1. *Mohammedanism: Lectures on Its Origin, Its Religious and Political Growth, and Its Present State* (New York: Putnam's, 1916), p. 18. Snouck Hurgronje was a Calvinist in the sense that his father served as a minister in the Dutch Reformed Church and that he himself also studied for the ministry. Ultimately, however, Snouck Hurgronje, who masqueraded as a Muslim for a long period of study in Mecca, came to consider himself agnostic. See Georges-Henri Bousquet, "C. Snouck Hurgronje (1857-1936)," *Revue algerienne* 1: 183-85.

2. E. D. Howe, *History of Mormonism* (Painesville, New York, published by the author, 1834), p. 12.

3. William Sparrow Simpson, *Mormonism: Its History, Doctrines, and Practices* (London: A. M. Pigott, 1853), p. 57.

4. "The Yankee Mahomet," *American Whig Review* 13 (1851): 554-64.

5. Joseph Smith, Jr., *History of the Church of Jesus Christ of Latter-day Saints*, ed. B. H. Roberts, 7 vols. (Salt Lake City, Utah: Deseret News Press, 1948), 3:167n.

6. T. B. H. Stenhouse, *The Rocky Mountain Saints* (New York: Appleton, 1873), pp. 2-3.

7. See Norman Daniel, *Islam and the West: The Making of an Image* (Edinburg: Edinburg University Press, 1960); P. M. Hold, "The Treatment of Arab History by Prideaux, Ockley and Sale," in B. Lewis and P. M. Hold, eds., *Historians of the Middle East* (London: Oxford University Press, 1962), pp. 290-302; Jacques Waardenburg, *L'Islam dans le miroir de l'Occident* (The Hague: Mouton, 1963); James Kritzeck, *Peter the Venerable and Islam* (Princeton: Princeton University Press, 1964); W. Montgomery Watt, "Muhammad in the Eyes of the West," *Boston University Journal* 22 (1974): 61-69.

8. Smith, *History of the Church*, 4:477-78. Upon reading this editorial to the Nauvoo City Council, Joseph Smith proposed "that we recommend our fellow citizens to subscribe for the *New York Weekly Herald*."

9. Richard Francis Burton, *The City of the Saints and Across the Rocky Mountains to California* (1861; reprint ed. by Fawn M. Brodie, New York: Knopf, 1963), p. 428.

10. Hans Thimme, "Mormonism and Islam," *Moslem World* 24 (1934): 166; Georges-Henri Bousquet, "L'eglise mormonne et ses livres sacres," *Revue de l'histoire des religions* 130 (1936): 219.

11. Eduard Meyer, *Ursprung and Geschichte der Mormonen* (Halle: Verlag von Max Niemeyer, 1912); the discussion which follows is drawn from its English translation by H. F. Rahde and E. Seaich, *The Origin and History of the Mormons, with Reflections on the Beginnings of Islam and Christianity* (Salt Lake City: University of Utah Press, 1961), pp. i, 1, 31, 37, 44-48, 52, 56, 61, 100.

12. According to Harry Elder Barnes, *A History of Historical Writing* (New York: Dover Publications, 1962), p. 249, "By far the greatest orientalist who has ever lived was Eduard Meyer, who dealt in magisterial fashion with the history of antiquity from the Stone Age to the rise of Christianity."

13. See William R. Polk, "Sir Hamilton Gibb between Orientalism and History," *International Journal of Middle East Studies* 6 (1975): 132.

14. Meyer, *Origin and History of the Mormons*, pp. i, 44.

15. Ibid, p. ii.

16. Ibid, p. v.

17. See Raymond Aron, *Main Currents of Sociological Thought, vol 1: Montesquieu, Comte, Marx, Tocqueville* (New York: Anchor Books, 1965).

18. See Pieter Geyl, *Debates with Historians* (Cleveland, Ohio: World Publishing Co., 1958), pp. 30-69; W. H. Walsh, "Can History Be Objective?" in Hans Meyerhoff, ed., *The Philosophy of History in Our Time* (Garden City, New York: Doubleday, 1959), pp. 216-24; Morton White, "Can History Be Objective?" in Meyerhoff, *Philosophy of History*, pp. 188-202.

19. Thimme, "Mormonism and Islam," p. 155; the discussion following is drawn from pp. 156-57, 161, 163-64, 166-67.

20. Georges-Henri Bousquet, *Les Mormons: histoire et institutions* (Paris: Presses universitaires de France), p. 5.

21. His Mormon works, besides the book cited in n. 20, are "Le Mormonisme contemporain," *Outre-mer* 7 (1935): 150-71; "Une theocratie economique," *Revue d'economie politique* 50 (1936): 145-66; "L'eglise mormonne et ses livres sacres," cited n. 10.

22. Bousquet, *Les Mormons: histoire et institutions*, op. cit.

23. Bousquet, "L'eglise mormonne et ses livres sacres," p. 232.

24. Ibid., pp. 24-25.

25. Ibid., p. 16.

26. Georges-Henri Bousquet, *Vilfredo Pareto: le developpement et la signification de son oeuvre*, 2 vols. (Paris: Riviere, 1924); *Precis de sociologie d'apres*

Vilfredo Pareto (Paris: Payot, 1925); *Introduction aux systemes socialistes de Vilfredo Pareto* (Paris: Giard, 1926); *Essai sur l'evolution de la pensee economique* (Paris: Giard, 1927); *Introduction a l'etude du manuel de V. Pareto* (Paris: Giard, 1927); *Bibliographie methodique des ecrits de Vilfredo Pareto connus a ce jour* (Genoa: Universita degli Studi di Genova, 1959); *Pareto (1848-1923): le savant et l'homme* (Lausanne: Librarie de l'Universite, (1960); *Vilfredo Pareto: oevres completes* (Geneva: Droz, 1964).

27. Raymond Aron, *Main Currents of Sociological Thought*, vol. 2: *Durkheim, Pareto, Weber* (New York: Penguin Books, 1967), p. 13.

28. See Robert Ageron, "La France a-t-elle eu une politique Kabyle?" *Revue historique* 223 (1960): 311-52; "La politique berbere du protectorat marocain de 1913 a 1934," *Revue d'histoire moderne et contemporaine* 18 (1971); 50-90.

29. Georges-Henri Bousquet, *Justice Francaise et coutumes kabyles* (Algiers: Imprimerie Nord-africaine, 1950); *Les Berberes: histoire et institutions* (Paris: Presses universitaires de France, 1957).

30. Robin Bidwell, *Morocco under Colonial Rule* (London: Frank Cass, 1973), pp. 237-57.

31. Georges-Henri Bousquet, *L'Islam maghrebin: introduction a l'etude generale de l'Islam* (Algiers, Maison des livres, 1941), p. 19.

32. Bousquet, *L'Islam maghrebin*, p. 204.

33. See Georges-Henri Bousquet, *Les grandes pratiques rituelles de l'Islam* (Paris: Presses universitaires de France, 1949); *La morale de l'Islam et son ethique sexuelle* (Paris: Maisonneuve, 1953).

34. Bousquet, *La morale d'Islam*, p. 12.

35. Joachim Wach, *Sociology of Religion* (Chicago: University of Chicago Press, 1944), pp. 346-51.

36. E. Konig, *Encyclopedia of Religion and Ethics*, 1925, s.v. "Prophecy."

37. Burton, *City of the Saints*, p. 445.

38. Bousquet, *Les Mormons: historie et institutions*, p. 25.

39. See S. N. Eisenstadt, "The Protestant Ethic Thesis," in Roland Robertson, ed., *Sociology of Religion* (Harmondsworth, England: Penguin Books, 1969), pp. 297-317.

10
Pre-Islamic
Arabian Prophets
William J. Hamblin

O ne of the most important concepts in Islamic theology is that the message of Islām is of universal significance for mankind.[1] This principle is inherent in a number of Muslim doctrines and grows directly out of the revelations of the prophet Muhammad. According to Muslim theology, whereas all prophets previous to Muhammad had been sent to only one people, the message revealed

---

William J. Hamblin is a Ph.D. candidate in the Department of History at the University of Michigan. A graduate of Brigham Young University in history, he received his M.A. in history and Near Eastern studies at the University of Michigan. His dissertation topic is "Fatimid Military Organization During the Period of the Crusades." A Sterling Scholar from the state of Utah, he was also a University Scholar with highest honors from BYU.

to Muhammad in the Qur'ān is a message for every nation on earth. In the Qur'ān (7:158) God commands Muhammad: "Proclaim: O Mankind, verily I am God's Messenger for all of you." In another passage Muhammad is called the "seal of the prophets" (*khātim an-nabiyīn*, Qur'ān 33:40), which is generally interpreted by Muslim commentators as meaning that he is the last of the prophets, his message a confirmation and fulfillment of the messages of all former prophets.[2]

God's revelations and the religion of Islām also are considered to have universal significance historically, that is, all true forms of past religion have been Islamic. Likewise, all true prophets of the past are believed to have preached the same Islamic faith, although it did not receive its fullest expression until the revelations of Muhammad. Thus, the Qur'ān contains numerous accounts of many biblical prophets, including Jesus, all of whom Muslims accepted as having been true prophets of God.[3] According to Muslim theology, however, the Bible is not a fully reliable source on religious matters nor are its accounts of the prophets necessarily accurate, because the Bible has been changed from its original form by later deletions or additions. *Sūra* 2:80, often interpreted as referring to Jews and Christians, states: "Wo unto those who write the book [Bible] with their own hands and then say, This is from God." Likewise *Sūra* 5:13, 15, states: "They twist the words from their proper place and have forgotten a part of that which was given to them . . . O People of the book [Jews and Christians], our prophet has come to you to make clear much of the book which you have forgotten."

Thus, Muslims have interpreted various biblical passages as actually being prophetic references to Muhammad. For instance, Haggai 2:7-9, reads in part: "The desire [Hebrew *hem^edath*] of all nations shall come. . . . and in this place I will give peace [Hebrew *shalōm*]." The triliteral Semitic root of the Hebrew word for desire, *hem^edath*, is equivalent to the Arabic root *hamada*, which is also the basis for the name Muhammad. Likewise, *shalōm* is the equivalent of the Arabic *salam*, which is the root of the word *islām*. Some Muslims therefore interpret this verse as reading, "the desire of all nations [Muhammad] will come . . . and in this place I will give peace [Islām]."[4]

The revelations of God, however, were not limited only to those given to the Israelites and Christians in the Bible. God has offered many nations an opportunity to accept his revelations by sending to them various nonbiblical pre-Islamic prophets. For example: "For every nation there is a messenger" (Qur'ān 10:47); and "We [God] have sent to every nation a messenger" (Qur'ān 16:36). In other words, God has revealed his word not only to those prophets mentioned in the Hebrew and Christian scriptures but to numerous others as well.

Perhaps the most intriguing of these nonbiblical prophetic figures are six prophets whom the Qur'ān identifies as God's messengers to pre-Islamic Arabia: Hūd, Sālih, Abraham, Ishmael, Shuʿayb, and Muhammad. Muhammad is, of course, the last and greatest of the Arabian prophets and the historical founder of Islām. Abraham and Ishmael are the Islamic counterparts of the biblical figures, although the Muslim interpretation of these figures differs radically from the biblical.[5] According to the Qur'ān, it is Ishmael, not Isaac, who receives the birthright from Abraham and whom God asks Abraham to sacrifice as a test.[6] Shuʿayb may well be a nonbiblical prophet, but later Muslims tended to associate him closely with the biblical Jethro, Moses' father-in-law.[7]

The stories of Hūd and Sālih, who have no traditional associations with biblical prophets, are related on three occasions in the Qur'ān and by numerous later Muslim theologians and historians.[8] One of ancient Arabia's powerful tribes was called ʿĀd.[9] The ʿĀdites, polytheists and idol worshippers, were renowned for elaborate buildings which reportedly imitated the glories of Paradise and in which the ʿĀdites thought they could live forever.[10] It is said that no other structures created by the hand of man were as magnificent as those of the ʿĀdites. Because of their pride and polytheism, God sent the prophet Hūd to them, calling them to repentance and monotheism. Most of the ʿĀdites rejected Hūd's message, for which God cursed the tribe with a three-year drought. The ʿĀdites then sent a delegation to pray for rain at Mecca. In response to their prayers, God sent three clouds, one white, one red, and one black, and had the leader of the delegation, Qayl, pick the cloud which would be sent to the ʿĀdites. Qayl chose the black cloud, thinking it would bring rain. Instead it brought a devastating desert storm from which the ʿĀdites sought refuge in their great buildings. But the entire tribe along with its magnificent buildings were destroyed and buried in the desert sands. Only Hūd and his few followers escaped.

The prophet Sālih was sent to Thamūd,[11] a tribe to whom God had granted great prosperity after the destruction of ʿĀd. The Thamūdites also lived in great buildings and cut houses out of the rocks in the sides of mountains. Sālih called the Thamūdites to repentance, telling them to act justly and worship only God. God granted the Thamūdites a sacred she-camel as a sign that Sālih was a true prophet. (The traditions say variously that God caused this camel to spring from a rock or that it gave amazing amounts of milk.) Sālih warned the Thamūdites not to harm this sacred beast. When some members of the tribe hamstrung the camel to show their defiance, God destroyed them with a great earthquake.[12]

A number of historical questions surround these traditions, not the least of which involves the sources. Scholars have generally taken one of three approaches. First, some assume that the Qur'anic versions of the story accurately describe actual historic events, the position taken by most faithful Muslims. Second, the Qur'anic accounts can be seen as representing Muhammad's version of pre-Islamic tales which reflect, however dimly, actual historical events. Third, some scholars dismiss them as fabrications by either Muhammad or by some pre-Islamic storyteller.

This study assumes some historical basis for the traditions and examines some possible interpretations of the origin and significance of these traditions by using seven types of evidence.

First, archeological and pre-Islamic epigraphic evidence represents one of the most important types of historical data available, since no contemporary histories from pre-Islamic Arabia have survived. There are, of course, a number of difficulties involved in trying to correctly interpret such evidence. Second, non-Arabian historians and geographers often provide useful clues concerning events in pre-Islamic Arabia. Third, the large body of pre-Islamic poetry occasionally deals with some aspects of the traditions of Hūd and Sālih. Fourth, the Qur'ān, one of the earliest written records in classical Arabic and one of the most important links between pagan and Islamic Arabia, refers to Hūd and Sālih. The Qur'ān exerted a tremendous influence on all subsequent Islamic versions of the traditions. Fifth, there is a large body of *hadīth* literature (traditional sayings of Muhammad), some of which has some bearing on the question at hand. Sixth, Qur'anic *tafsīr* (commentaries) deal with Hūd and Sālih.[13] Finally, later Muslim works such as histories, literature, and geographies, give the fully developed Islamic versions of the Hūd and Sālih stories, but apparently also occasionally refer to nonreligious pre-Islamic Arabian traditions.[14]

The main historical questions surrounding the traditions of these pre-Islamic prophets are: Can the traditions be traced to the pre-Islamic period? If the traditions have a pre-Islamic origin, how far back can that origin be potentially traced? Can geographical boundaries for the traditions be established? What facts, if any, can be learned concerning the prophetic figures themselves? And finally, do these stories have any general significance to pre-Islamic society?

Archeological evidence supports a pre-Islamic origin for the Hūd traditions. In Hadramawt, near the border between Oman and South Yemen on the southern coast of the Arabian peninsula, is the most important Islamic shrine of southern Arabia—the Tomb of Hūd. R. B. Serjeant, by correlating a number of literary texts with the geography of the current tomb, concludes that it is the same site frequently mentioned by Muslim historians and geographers.[15] He has also found evidence that the site was a pre-Islamic cult center. Merchants arriving on the monsoon winds from the east would congregate at Shirh, near Hūd's Tomb, to meet and exchange goods with traders and Bedouins from the interior regions at an annual trade fair. The Tomb of Hūd would thus have served as a regional shrine much as Mecca was the shrine center for the more famous Fairs of 'Ukāz.[16] Such fairs, the major cultural, religious, and economic events of the year, caused a month's truce from the otherwise continual strife and have consistently been held in Hadramawt from pre-Islamic times well into this century.

The traditions of Sālih are linked to al-Hijr in central Arabia, also known as Madā'in Sālih, or "Sālih's cities."[17] Its ruins, Nabataean tombs dating from about the first century A.D., may be

Muhammad's "houses cut in the mountains" (Qur'ān 7:74). It is impossible to determine whether this connection was made by pre-Islamic Arabs or later Muslims.

Some pre-Islamic inscriptional evidence refers to Hūd, one particular inscription in a religious invocation, even though what is definitely known about these inscriptions is too fragmentary to allow generalization about their relationship to Hūd.[18] I am unaware of any inscriptional evidence relating to Sālih.

Some pre-Islamic poetry shows that pagan Arabs knew the general outline of traditions relating to the destruction of the tribes of ᶜĀd and Thamūd and the city of Irām.[19] The poet Umayya tells the story of Sālih and the camel.[20] Although Umayya lived until a few years after the Hijra, he never converted to Islām and indeed was somewhat antagonistic to Muhammad. It would seem strange for him to compose a poem concerning Sālih if Sālih had been a creation of Muhammad rather than a figure of pre-Islamic tradition. References to Hūd are less definite, since almost the entire corpus of surviving pre-Islamic poetry is from the north,[21] and Hūd was a prophet of southern Arabia.

An Islamic tradition which, if authentic, would indicate that Hūd was known to pre-Islamic Arabs, relates that during the reign of the first Caliph Abū Bakr, a man from Hadramawt came to ᶜAlī bin Abī Tālib, Muhammad's cousin and son-in-law, to discuss religion and convert to Islām. During their discussion the man from Hadramawt said that Hūd was considered an important prophet by many of the Hadramī Arabs.[22]

The medieval historian and theologian At-Tabarī reports that the Jews questioned the validity of the Hūd traditions by claiming that he was not mentioned in the Bible. At-Tabarī replied:

> The Jews claim that the tribes of ᶜĀd and Thamūd and the prophets Hūd and Sālih are not mentioned in the Torah. Nonetheless, their fame among the pre-Islamic Arabs and Muslims today is like the fame of Abraham and his people.
>
> If I didn't hate lengthening books with irrelevant matters, I could recount poems of the pre-Islamic poets, which discuss the tribes of ᶜĀd and Thamūd which confirm what I have said.[23]

This combined evidence would seem to indicate that the Hūd and Sālih stories had a pre-Islamic origin. The tribes with which they are associated, ʿĀd and Thamūd, as well as the mythical city or tribe of Irām, appear in a large number of pre-Islamic poems. The Tomb of Hūd is a shrine dating from pre-Islamic times, possible pre-Islamic inscriptions mention his name, and later Muslim traditions claim that he was known to pagan Hadramī Arabs. Pre-Islamic poetry indicates that the Qurʾanic story of Sālih was also based on pre-Islamic traditions. It would seem, then, that the stories of these prophets were not fabrications of Muhammad.

This leads then to the next question: If the traditions did not originate with Muhammad, can chronological boundaries be set within which the origins of the traditions of Hūd and Sālih can be said to lie? Islamic versions of the story call Hūd and Sālih descendants of the biblical Noah in either the fourth or eighth generations (Hūd) or the eighth or tenth generations (Sālih). However, these genealogies seem to have essentially been borrowed verbatim from the biblical genealogies found in Genesis chapter 10.[24] Probably the medieval Muslim writers assigned Hūd and Sālih such great antiquity because in all three Qurʾanic versions the Hūd and Sālih stories directly follow that of Noah, and later Muslim commentators and historians apparently attributed a specific chronological meaning to the probably somewhat arbitrary ordering of the Qurʾanic stories. They thereupon grafted the figure of Hūd onto biblical genealogies to make him fit the apparent Qurʾanic dating.[25] Thus, the later Muslim accounts probably do not reflect pagan Arabian tradition. Likewise pre-Islamic poetry also offers no chronological clue.

It is possible, however, to attempt to develop a chronological frame of reference for the traditions by correlating non-Arabic sources with Arabian tradition. The tribe ʿĀd, to which Hūd was sent, has been linked by O. Loth to an historical Arabian tribe named Iyād, mentioned in a Palmyren inscription dating to the reign of Zenobia (A.D. 267-272). Another scholar, A. Sprenger, associates the ʿĀdites with an Arabian tribe mentioned by the classical geographer Ptolemy called the Oaditai, and D. Sidersky associates ʿĀd with the biblical city of Admah.[26] None of these explanations, however, has found general acceptance among scholars, and the historical questions relating to the tribe of ʿĀd remain essentially unanswered.

More light is available on the ᶜĀdites' sister tribe, Thamūd, to whom Sālih was sent. ᶜĀd and Thamūd are closely connected by both Islamic and pre-Islamic sources. Qur'anic accounts of Sālih always follow those of Hūd.[27] Both tribes are of great reputed antiquity, and according to traditional Arab genealogists, are two of the four *bāᶜida* or extinct tribes.[28] This genealogical relationship is further reflected in the theory that "the people of ᶜĀd were called Irām; when the ᶜĀdis were destroyed, the name Irām was transferred to Thamūd."[29] The way in which medieval Muslims linked ᶜĀd and Thamūd to biblical genealogies emphasizes the close relationship thought to exist between the two tribes.[30] They were also linked by pre-Islamic poets who "mention Thamūd with the ᶜĀd as examples of the transitoriness of worldly glory."[31] A chronology of Thamūd could therefore provide at least some parallels for ᶜĀd as well.

The tribe of Thamūd makes an excellent historical test case. Inscriptions in Thamūdic script date back to the fifth and sixth centuries A.D.[32] Nicholson claims that Byzantine sources refer to the *"equites Thamudeni"* in the fifth century, although I found no ancient authority which confirmed this.[33] A number of classical geographers writing around the time of Christ make reference to the *Thamudenoi,* and in an Assyrian inscription of circa 710 B.C. Sargon II describes his victory over an Arab tribe named *Thamud.*[34] These historical references demonstrate that the tribe of Thamūd existed as a functioning tribal unit from late pre-Islamic times to possibly as early as the eighth century B.C.

The historically verifiable chronological span of existence for the tribe of Thamūd offers us some indication of the possible antiquity of the Sālih and Hūd traditions. Examples of the oral transmission of traditions across a number of centuries are well known—the Jewish Mishna, Muslim *hadīth,* and, perhaps the most famous example, the case of Abraham. Depending on what dates are established for Abraham and when the stories are thought to have been written down, the Abraham stories can represent the transmission of an oral tradition for over a thousand years.[35] This does not mean that the Sālih and Hūd traditions necessarily originated in remote periods; they may have emerged a few centuries or even decades before the birth of Muhammad. But there is no reason to limit those origins to the period just before Muhammad.

Although the Hūd and Sālih traditions are chronologically vague, they are geographically precise. The Hūd traditions center in Hadramawt in southern Arabia around the Tomb of Hūd. All Arabic sources agree that the tribe of ᶜĀd, to whom Hūd was sent, inhabited the region of Hadramawt, and that the city of Irām dhāt al-Imād is to be found there. Likewise, the traditions of Sālih can be reasonably linked to northwestern Arabia, historically the geographical location of the tribe of Thamūd.[36]

Philological and literary approaches provide further information. Sālih means simply "virtuous or pious." Attempts to equate Sālih with the biblical Salah contradict Muslim genealogies. More probably, Sālih is a descriptive title rather than a personal name.[37]

The name Hūd is much more interesting. One interpretation sees him as an allegorical figure representing ancient prophets or religious teachers in general rather than being any definable historic figure, a view given some support by linguistic evidence related to the names ᶜĀd and Irām. J. Wellhausen points out that the Arabic phrase, "since the time of ᶜĀd" has an alternative form, "*min al-ᶜādi*," which means simply "from ᶜĀd." He speculates that ᶜĀd meant "ancient time" and that the tribe was invented because of a misinterpretation of the original meaning. *Irām's* adjectival form, *irāmī*, is used by one pre-Islamic poet to mean "a man of ancient race." According to this interpretation, the Qur'anic Hūd is an allegorical figure, only arbitrarily related to pre-Islamic tradition.[38]

On the other hand, the triliteral root for *hūd*, H-W-D, is used in a number of different ways in the Qur'ān. The basic meaning of the Arabic word relates to Jews or things Jewish, and several times in the Qur'ān, *hūd* means *Jew*, while the verbal form *hāda* in the Qur'ān means "to practice Judaism."[39] This Jewish connection is further emphasized by one of the two medieval versions of Hūd's genealogy, which equates him with the biblical Eber, the traditional ancestor of the Jews. Further, according to Hadramī traditions, Hūd had a son with the Jewish name Daniel.[40]

An objection might be that the Qur'ān specifically calls Hūd the "brother of the ᶜĀdites" (Qur'ān 7:65; 11:50). However, medieval

Muslim scholars could not agree on an interpretation for this phrase. Was Hūd an actual member of the tribe of ᶜĀd, a Semite, or simply a descendant of Adam? Medieval theologian Al-Qurtubī discusses the name Hūd and the Arabic root for *Jewishness*, concluding that such a connection might have some validity.[41]

The most obvious possibility that this theory presents is that if an actual historic figure existed whose activities formed the basis for the Hūd traditions, he may have been a Jew, who for some reason took to preaching in Arabia. His actual name could have been forgotten over the years, causing him to eventually become known simply as "the Jew," or Hūd.[42]

What were Jewish and Christian religious influences on pre-Islamic Arabia? The penetration of Judaism into the Arabian peninsula can be traced back possibly as early as the seventh century B.C., when Jewish traders may have established small colonies or trading outposts in different parts of Arabia.[43] There is also good evidence of strong Jewish influence in Arabia in the first century before Christ, when the Idumaeans, who were apparently semi-sedentary Arabs living in the deserts east of Judaea, were converted to Judaism and eventually formed the Idumaean dynasty to which the famous Herod of the Gospels belonged.[44] In the first century A.D. when the Jews were expelled from Judaea by the Romans, it seems that some fled into Arabia, forming the basis of important northern Arabian Jewish tribes such as the Banū An-Nādir and the Banū Quraiza. Other Arabs, such as the Jewish colony at Yathrib (Medina), which was to play an important role in the life of Muhammad, were possibly early converts to Judaism.[45] An important Jewish dynasty was also established in southern Arabia in the fifth century A.D., where for a time Judaism became the state religion.[46]

Christianity also had an important influence on early Arabia. It is possible that Christian missionaries first entered Arabia during the reign of the Roman Emperor Constantine II (334-361) from the recently converted kingdom of Aksum in the horn of Africa and possibly from Syria at the same time. In time the Orthodox, Monophysite, and Nestorian proselyters all found converts among the Arabs: the entire tribe of Banū Ghassān became Monophysite Christians, and mercenaries for the Byzantine emperors. A Christian dynasty from Abyssinia, aided by Justinian the Great, was established for a time in southern Arabia, and the Sassanian Persians established hegemony over parts of southern Arabia in the latter part of the sixth century, which lasted until the rise of Islām.[47]

The existence of important Jewish and Christian elements in pre-Islamic Arabian society has led many scholars to search for Jewish and Christian origins for many Islamic practices and doctrines, including attempts to link the Hūd and Sālih traditions with biblical or other Jewish sources. Heinrich Speyer, for example, associates the tale of the great windstorm which destroyed the tribe of ᶜĀd with similar stories from the apocryphal Book of Jubilees, and even Josephus's *Antiquities*. Likewise he tries to find biblical names, such as Ammihud and Abihud,[48] from which the name Hūd could have been drawn.

Pointing out such parallels can be useful, but there is also, however, the potential danger that the existence of a parallel will lead to an assumption of causality. Simply establishing that a certain concept existed before a later similar concept does not necessarily imply that the former caused or influenced the latter.[49]

Bearing in mind these dangers, it is interesting to examine some possible parallels between the traditions of Hūd and the Book of Mormon, a work which Latter-day Saints accept as an ancient scripture and which begins with the story of Lehi, a Jewish prophet in self-imposed exile from Jerusalem with his family. They wandered through the "wilderness" to the Red Sea, built a ship, and voyaged to the New World.

Although the Book of Mormon provides no specific information on the route, Latter-day Saints generally accept that Lehi and his party traveled through Arabia, ending their journey in Hadramawt,[50] the same region where Hūd is supposed to have preached. In a religious sense, Lehi was a Jew, which corresponds with the theory that the name Hūd could refer to a Jewish prophet.

A theoretical reconstruction of Lehi's stay in southern Arabia could run something like this. Lehi and his family eventually arrive in Hadramawt, at that time a highly populated region serving as one of the main trade routes of southern Arabia. There they would have necessarily made contact with the local inhabitants, if only because every well in the region would have been owned by some tribe or city, and strangers would not have been allowed to drink from the wells without permission. The Book of Mormon makes no mention of any contacts with local inhabitants, but Ishmael was buried "in the place which was called Nahom" (1 Nephi 16:34), implying that it was so called by local inhabitants, in contrast to Lehi's usual practice of giving a new name to each place where they stay. (See 1 Nephi 2:14, 16:13, 17:6.)[51] According to this theory, Lehi discusses religion with the local inhabitants of Arabia, possibly converting a few, but at least leaving the impression that a man of God had dwelt among them. The oral tradition eventually becomes the pre-Islamic and Qur'anic traditions of Hūd.

In view of this theory it is possible to examine some parallels between the literary images of Lehi's vision of the tree of life and some similar images in the story of Hūd, with the assumption, still speculative, that Lehi told the Arabians of his vision in Jerusalem, and its images became, in oral tradition, the activities of the prophet Hūd. Take the following examples:

1. According to the Islamic Hūd traditions, one of the chief sins of the tribe of ʿĀd was pride symbolized by magnificent buildings, an attempt to create an earthly replica of paradise. For this impious pride, God sent the prophet Hūd to call them to repentance. For the most part, the ʿĀdites failed to heed his call. This religious image of the building symbolizing man's pride correlates with the image of the "great and spacious building" of Lehi's vision, filled with mocking men and women representing "the pride of the world" (1 Nephi 8:26, 11:35-36).

2. The city of the ʿĀdites was built at a place "beneath which rivers flowed."[52] Likewise a prominent part of Lehi's vision is the "river of water" flowing between the "great and spacious building" and the "Tree of Life." (1 Nephi 8:13, 12:16.)

3. When the ʿĀdites reject Hūd's message, God sends a drought to chasten them. A delegation of ʿĀdites pray for rain at Mecca. In response to their prayer, God sends a black cloud and a great windstorm, which destroys them and their city. An important image in Lehi's vision is the "mist of darkness," which causes that men "perish and are lost."[53] The black cloud of the Hūd story and the "mist of darkness" of Lehi's vision are both religious images relating to the destruction of the wicked.

4. The final vindication of Hūd's prophetic calling comes when the magnificent buildings of the ᶜĀdites, in which they thought they could live forever, are destroyed by the storm. Likewise, in Lehi's vision, the triumph of God over the wickedness of the world is by the destruction of the great and spacious building: "and it fell, and the fall thereof was exceeding great."[54]

5. Salvation comes to Lehi and his party by partaking of the fruit of the tree of life. Hūd, on the other hand, and those few who believed in his message, are saved in a *hazīra*, "an enclosure for camels made of trees to protect them from the cold and wind."[55] To an Arab transmitter of oral traditions, it would have seemed strange for Hūd to be saved from the destroying winds because of a single tree; a barricade of trees would be more reasonable. Although this process of transmutation is hypothetical, it could account for the tree of life becoming a *hazīra*; certainly both images have the similar function of providing salvation from the wrath of God.

Although a number of remarkable parallels exist between the stories of Lehi and those of Hūd, we cannot conclude that Lehi is the basis of the Hūd traditions. The causal link is missing. We can, however, conclude that the record of Lehi, a pre-Islamic prophet of Arabia by Mormon belief, coincides with what Islamic traditions tell us about such prophets. In other words, Lehi fits the pattern of what we know concerning pre-Islamic Arabian prophets.

Similarly, the causal link is often missing from attempts to connect the Hūd and Sālih traditions with possible Jewish or Christian antecedents. Islām was indeed greatly influenced in its development by Judaism and Christianity, just as Christianity was greatly influenced by Judaism. But the attempt to link virtually every aspect of Islām to Jewish or Christian antecedents obscures Arabia's independent religious history, of which only traces have survived. Great Arabian religious leaders, whose stories have been lost, were undoubtedly a part of that history. I would maintain that rather than reflections of outside religious influences, the stories of Hūd and Sālih are important traces of an independent Arabian religious tradition, manifestations of the religious mentality of the pre-Islamic Arabs.

Such manifestations indicate that pagan Arabs, unlike almost all other religious groups of Southwest Asia at that time, believed in the possibility of prophethood. If a prophet like Muhammad had appeared in a Jewish or Christian community (or a later Muslim community), he would have been denounced as a false prophet because prophecy had ceased.

For most Christians, Christ was the ultimate and last revelation. For Jews, prophecy had ceased in favor of trying to discover the will of God in the Torah and Mishna. In fact, Muhammad was rejected by the Jews of Yathrib as a false prophet.

Pagan Arabs, however, did not reject Muhammad because they rejected outright any possibility of prophethood. They said first that they would accept Muhammad as a prophet upon receiving a visitation from an angel or a sign from God. They also objected that a true prophet should somehow be different from normal men, above mundane necessities such as eating. The Quraysh claimed that if God really had a message for mankind he would deliver it through one of the leaders of their community.[56] These objections are not against the idea of prophethood in general but only against the idea that Muhammad himself was such a prophet, a concept further reinforced by the great number of "false prophets" who appeared after Muhammad's death.

Pre-Islamic Arabia was filled with religious controversy and confusion. Nestorians, Monophysites, Christians, Jews, Zoroastrians, and pagans all practiced and preached in Arabia. Umayya ibn Abī As-Salt,[57] who died about A.D. 630, reflects such religious awareness. He was a *hanīf*, a member of an important religious group in pre-Islamic Arabia characterized by ascetic monotheism and rejection of idolatry. They sought to worship God in the manner of Abraham (known to the Arabs as "the *Hanīf*"),[58] while generally believing that neither Christianity nor Judaism had the full religious truth. Umayya "traveled in search of the true religion,"[59] visiting monasteries, interviewing religious leaders, and even learning to read so he could study religious books. Above all he was searching for an Arab prophet, and even hoped that he himself might one day receive a revelation from God. In one of his poems he says, "[We need] a prophet from among us to inform us of the afterlife."[60] Significantly, in Umayya's poetry, he recorded the story of the pre-Islamic prophet Sālih, and those of many other prophets.

It is in relation to this type of religious mentality that stories of Hūd and Sālih should be understood. They reflect the desire of many Arabs to find someone who could bring them closer to God. It is in such a religious environment that prophets can arise.

NOTES

1. I am dealing with these questions solely from the point of view of classical Islamic theology, without making any attempt to distill what may or may not have been the original Arab interpretations of the meaning of Muhammad's revelations. All Arabic translations are mine.

2. Abū Jaᶜfar Muhammad ibn Jartr At-Tabari (d. 922/3) *Jāmiᶜal-Qur'an* (The Collection of the Explanations of the Exegesis of the Verses of the Qur'ān), 30 vols. (Cairo: Mustafa al-Babi, 1954), 22:16.

3. For an excellent study of the Qur'anic view of Christ see Geoffrey Parrinder, *Jesus in the Qur'an* (London: Faber and Faber, 1965); for examinations of how the Qur'anic accounts of biblical prophets relate to the Bible, see Heinrich Speyer, *Die Biblischen Erzählungen im Qoran* (Hildeschein: Georg Olms, 1961), and D. Sidersky, *Les Origines des Legendes Musuemanes* (Paris: P. Geuthner, 1933).

4. For further similar examples see Abdu al-Ahad Dawud, *Muhammad in the Bible* (Kuala Lumpur: Pustaka Antara, 1979).

5. For a discussion of the Muslim and Israelite accounts of Abraham and Ishmael see the appropriate chapters of Speyer, *Biblischen Erzählungen;* Sidersky, *Origines des Legendes;* Josef Horovitz, *Koranische Untersuchungen* (Berlin: W. de Gruyter & Co., 1926), pp. 86-87, 91-92.

6. Qur'ān 37:99-109. Isaac was also considered an important prophet (Qur'ān 37:100-103).

7. Qur'ān 7:85-93, 11:84-95; F. Buhl, *Encyclopedia of Islam,* old ed., s.v. "Shuᶜaib"; Horovitz, *Koranische Untersuchungen,* pp. 119-20.

8. See Qur'ān 7:73-79, 11:61-68, 26:141-59; F. Buhl, *Encyclopedia of Islam,* old ed., s.v. "Sālih"; Horovitz, *Koranische Untersuchungen,* p. 123; Abū Jaᶜfar At-Tabari, *Tārīkh ar-Rusul wa-l-Mulūk,* ed. M. J. DeGoeje, 15 vols. (Leiden: Brill, 1879-1901), 1:244-52. An English summary of At-Tabari's accounts can be found in R. A. Nicholson, *A Literary History of the Arabs* (London: Cambridge University Press, 1969), pp. 1-3. In chronological order the three accounts of Hūd are Qur'ān 26:123-40, the *sūra* (chapter) of Hūd; 11:50-60, 7:65-72; Hūd is also mentioned in 46:21. These tales are developed in At-Tabari, *Tārīkh,* 1:231-44. Essentially the same story can be found in Abū Ishāq Ahmad ibn Muhammad Ath-Thaᵓlabi, (d. 1038), *Qisas al-Anibyā'* (Cairo, Maktaba al-Jumhariyaa al-Arabiyya, n.d.), pp. 66-71. Ath-Thaᵓlabi includes very complete *isnāds* which are important for a study of the origin and development of the Hūd traditions in Islamic times. The present study is limited to seeing what can be determined if we accept the latter Islamic accounts as faithful reflections of earlier traditions.

9. See F. Buhl, *Encyclopedia of Islam,* new ed., s.v. ᶜAd; Horovitz, *Koranische Untersuchungen,* pp. 125-27.

10. Medieval Muslims equated the buildings of ᶜAd with the mythical city of Irām dhāt al-ᶜImād. See Qurʾān 89:6; Yāqūt ibn ᶜAbdallāh al-Hamawi, *Muᶜajam al-Buldān*, 5 vols. (Beirut, Dār Sādir, 1955-1957); A. J. Wensinck, "Irām dhāt al-ᶜImād," *Encyclopedia of Islam*, old ed.; W. Montgomery Watt, "Irām," *Encyclopedia of Islam*, new ed. Medieval Muslims even attributed the building of the pyramids of Egypt to the ᶜAdites. Jamāl ad-Din Ibn Taghribardii, *An-Najūm az-Zahira fī Mulūk Misr wa-l-Qāhira*, 16 vols. (Cairo: Dār al-Kutub, 1929-1972), 1:38; Taqiad-Din Al-Maqrīzī, *Al-Mawāᶜiz wa-l-iᶜtibār bi Dhikr al-Khitāt wa-l-Athār*, 2 vols. (Beirut: Dār Sādir, n.d.; a reprint of the Bulāq edition), 1:111-12. On the ᶜAdites' belief that they could live forever in their buildings see Qurʾān 26:129.

11. H. H. Brau, *Encyclopedia of Islam*, old ed., s.v. "Thamūd."

12. F. V. Winnett and W. L. Reed, *Ancient Records from North Arabia* (Toronto: University of Toronto Press, 1970), p. 39, give a variation on this story from local traditions.

13. At-Tabari's monumental *tafsir, Jāmiᶜ al-Bayan*, is one of the most useful. One of the earliest extant *tafsir*, it is also relatively free from many of the polemical doctrinal questions which fill the *tafsir* of later schools and sects but which also may well contain some important additional relevant traditions.

14. Besides the history of At-Tabari and Ath-Thaᶜlabi's collection of stories mentioned above there is the important geographical study of southern Arabia by ibn al-Hasan Ahmad Al-Hamdani (d. 945), *al-Iklil*, ed., N. A. Faris (Princeton: University Press, 1940); Faris translated this work into English as *The Antiquities of South Arabia* (Princeton: University Press, 1938). There is also an important collection of south Arabian legends by scholar and antiquarian Wahb ibn Munabbih (d. 732), *At-Tijān fī Mulūk Himyār* (Hyderabad: Dāʾira al-Muᶜārif, al-ᶜUthmāniya, 1928); he relates some traditions of Hūd on pp. 325-56.

The important, difficult and controversial questions of the historicity of the entire corpus of early Muslim traditions and history fall outside this study. For recent conflicting opinions see the fascinating work by Patricia Crone and Michael Cook, *Hagarism: The Making of the Islamic World* (Cambridge: University Press, 1977), which attempts to completely reinterpret Islamic history by rejecting the Muslim historical tradition and relying solely on non-Arab sources. See also Patricia Crone, *Slaves on Horses* (Cambridge: University Press, 1980), pp. 3-17, for a summary of her views on the problems of early Islamic historiography. For a defense of the reliability of the early Islamic traditions based on the study of early Arabic papyri, see Nabia Abbott, *Studies in the Arabic Literary Papyri, vol. 2: Qurʾanic Commentary and Tradition* (Chicago: University of Chicago Press, 1967), pp. 5-83.

15. R. B. Serjeant, "Hūd and other Pre-Islamic Prophets of Hadramawt," *Le Museon* 67 (1954):121. See also Landberg, *Hadramout* (Leiden: Brill, 1901), pp. 152-60, which reviews some of the classical literature used by Serjeant.

16. Serjeant, "Hūd," pp. 123-31; F. Krenkow, "The Annual Fairs of the Ancient Arabs," *Islamic Culture* 21 (1947): 111-13, refers briefly to the fairs of Shihr; Philip Hitti, *History of the Arabs*, 10 ed. (New York: St. Martin's Press, 1974), pp. 93-94. Although almost all Arabic sources agree on the location, a few medieval writers say that the Tomb of Hūd is in either Mecca or Damascus. See A. J. Wensinck, *Encyclopedia of Islam*, old ed., s.v. "Hūd." On population in Hadramawt see Brian

Doe, *Southern Arabia* (London: Thames and Hudson, 1971), pp. 97-102, where he reviews the archeological and inscriptional evidence. On trade routes see Gus W. Van Beek, "The Rise and Fall of Arabia Felix," *Scientific American* vol. 221 (December 1969): 36 ff.

17. Winnett and Reed, *Ancient Records,* pp. 37-39, 42-54, 130-32.

18. Horovitz, *Koranische Untersuchungen,* gives a number of possible inscriptions, p. 149; A. Jaussen and R. Savignca, *Mission archeologique en Arabie* (Paris: E. Leroux 1909-1920), 2:348, give an inscription which is translated "By Hūd. Allahi."

19. Waraqah bin Nawfal, in *Bulūgh al-Arab fī Ma ʿrifa Ahwāl al-ʿArab,* ed. M. S. al-Ālūsi (Càiro: Maktaba Muhammad af-Tayyib, 1964), 2:271-72; At-Tabari, *Tārīkh,* 1:236, 241; Ath-Thaʿlabi, pp. 66, 71. Horovitz, *Koranische Untersuchungen,* pp. 89-90, 126-27, gives over a dozen other references to various pre-Islamic poets, and pp. 105-6 gives additional pre-Islamic references to Thamūd. On Irām, see *Diwān Labid,* (Leiden: Brill 1889), p. 8; *Diwān Zuhayr* (Cairo: Dār al-Qawmīyya li-t-Tibāʿa, 1964), p. 158. It is not necessarily clear from these passages that the Irām referred to is the same as the Irām dhāt al-Imād mentioned in the Qur'ān. Irām may also have been a tribe.

20. *Diwān Umayya,* ed. F. Schulthefz (Leipzig: Brill, 1911), p. 44. See also H. H. Brau, *Encyclopedia of Islam,* old ed., s.v. "Umaiya."

21. Hafiz Ghulam Mustafa, *Religious Trends in Pre-Islamic Arabic Poetry* (Bombay: Asia Publishing House, 1968), pp. xiii-xiv. Hūd is mentioned in two unidentified poems which At-Tabari seems to accept as being pre-Islamic (At-Tabari, *Tārīkh,* 1:237, 241). The same poems can be found in Ath-Thaʿlabi, pp. 66, 71. They may be forgeries. On the practice of forging pre-Islamic poetry in later times see K. A. Fariq, *History of Arabic Literature* (Delhi: Vikas Publications, 1972), pp. 29-32. The earliest confirmed reading seems to be Thābit (d. 674? at over 100 years old), *Diwān Thābit* (Gibb Memorial Series, vol. 13, ed. H. Hirschfeld (Leyden: Brill, 1910), poem 91, line 5 (Arabic p. 44-45, with English notes pp. 72-73). This poem, however, was apparently written after his conversion to Islām. I could find no other pre-Islamic references to Hūd.

22. Hamdani, *al-Iklīl,* pp. 132-33; English translation pp. 78-80.

23. At-Tabari, *Tārīkh,* 1:251-52.

24. For Hūd, ibid, 1:231; Ath-Thaʿlabi, pp. 66. For Sālih, see At-Tabari, 1:244; Ath-Thaʿlabi, p. 72. The same genealogies, with some variations, can be found in many *tafsir* dealing with the appropriate Qur'anic verses. Hūd's genealogy found in At-Tabari, 1:231, is compared to the Hebrew genealogies in Genesis 10; Sālih's genealogies follow much the same pattern.

Hūd genealogy 1:

Arabic	Biblical
Nūh	Noah
Sām	Shem
Irām	Aram
ʿUs	Uz
ʿAd—mythical, the ancestor of ʿAdites	

Al-Khulūd
Rabāh
ᶜAbd Allāh
Hūd

According to this tradition, then, Hūd is a member of the tribe of ᶜAd. Note also the genealogical relationship between Irām/Aram and ᶜAd.

Hūd genealogy 2:

Arabic	Biblical
Nūh	Noah
Sām	Shem
Arfakhshād	Arphaxad
Shālakh	Salah
ᶜAbir	Eber

According to this tradition, ᶜAbir is Hūd, which would make Hūd the ancestor of all Hebrews and Arabs.

25. The prophetic stories in the Qur'ān are essentially but not consistently chronological. *Sūra* 7 discusses Noah, Hūd, Sālih, Shuᶜayb, and Moses. *Sūra* 11 deals with Moses, Noah, Hūd, Sālih, Abraham, Lot, Shuᶜayb, and Moses again. *Sūra* 26 discusses Moses, Abraham, Noah, Hūd, Sālih, and Lot. Although Hūd consistently follows Noah, the ordering of the stories as a whole is too inconsistent to allow us to conclude that Muhammad or the pre-Islamic Arabs necessarily thought of Hūd as chronologically following directly after Noah.

26. O. Loth, "Tabari's korancommentar," *Zeitschrift der Deutschen Morsenlandischen Gesellschaft* 35 (1881): 628. He refers to a Palmyren inscription dating to the reign of Zenobia discussed in the same journal by O. Blau, "Altararabische Sprachstudien," 27 (1873): 342-43. Ptolemy, *Geography* 6: 7, 21; A. Sprenger, *Das Leben und die Lehre des Mohammad* (Berlin: A. Effert & L. Lindtner, 1869), 1:505-18. Buhl summarized his and Loth's views in *Encyclopedia of Islam,* s.v. "ᶜAd," along with some related archeological evidence. D. Sidersky, *Origines,* pp. 29-30; his biblical reference is Genesis 10:19; Horovitz, *Koranische Untersuchungen,* pp. 125-27; Speyer, *Biblischen Erzählungen,* pp. 116-19, explains the story of ᶜAd as being founded on an Arabian misunderstanding of Judaic scriptures and legends.

27. So do all accounts with which I have dealt, excepting isolated *hadīth.* See, for example, At-Tabarī, *Tārikh,* 1:244-52; Ath-Thaᶜlabī, 72-79.

28. Hitti, *History of the Arabs,* pp. 30-32. In the Qur'ān both Thamūd and ᶜAd are termed *buᶜdin* (7:60, 68).

29. A. J. Wensinck, *Encyclopedia of Islam,* new ed., s.v. "Irām."

30. See note 24 for references:

Ad	Thamūd
Nūd (Noah)	Nūh
Sām (Shem)	Sām
Irām (Aram)	Irām
ᶜUs (Uz)	Jathir (Gether)
ᶜAd	Thamūd

31. H. H. Brau, *Encyclopedia of Islam,* old ed., s.v. "Thamūd."

32. For complete references see Sidersky, *Origines*, pp. 29-30. Winnett and Reed, *Ancient Records*, pp. 67-164, also give a large number of references.

33. Nicholson, *Literary History*, p. 3.

34. "*Thamoudenoi*," Diodorus Siculus *Bibliotheca* 3:44; "Thamudeni," Pliny, *Natural History* 6:28:32; "Thamudenoi" or "Thamuditai," Ptolemy, *Geography* 6:7:4-21; for *Tamud* see D. D. Luckenbill, *Ancient Records of Assyria and Babylonia* (Chicago: University of Chicago Press, 1927), 2: number 17. In the Assyrian inscriptions possible philological links can be found also to the tribe of ᶜAd. The Sargon II inscription also refers to his victory over the Ibādi tribe. Later, circa 668 B.C., Sennacherib is said to have conquered "Adumu, the fortress of Arabia" (possibly linked with Admah of Genesis 10:19?). See Hitti, *History of the Arabs*, p. 38.

35. There is some question that the transmission of *hadīth* was fully oral. See Abbott, *Papyri*; E. A. Speiser, *The Anchor Bible Genesis* (New York: Doubleday, 1964), pp. xxii-xxiii. John Van Seters on Abraham in *History and Tradition* (New Haven: Yale University Press, 1975), pp. 7-9, while disagreeing with the conclusions, summarizes the views of various biblical scholars dating Abraham as early as the third millennium B.C.

36. Buhl, *Encyclopedia of Islam*, s.v. "ᶜAd"; Watt, *Encyclopedia of Islam*, s.v. "Iram." For Sālih see Winnett and Reed, *Ancient Records*, pp. 130-33.

37. Speyer, *Biblischen Erzählungen*, p. 119; Salah is found in Genesis 10:24; Winnett and Reed, *Ancient Records*, p. 44.

38. Hartwig Hirschfeld, *New Researches into the Composition of the Qoran* (London: Royal Asiatic Society, 1902); J. Wellhausen, *Gottinger Gelehrte Anzeigen* (1902), p. 596, summarized in Buhl, *Encyclopedia of Islam*, s.v. "ᶜAd"; Harith bin Hilza in his *Muᶜallaqa*, line 68, discussed by Watt, *Encyclopedia of Islam*, s.v. "Irām." It is possible, of course, that the tribe of Irām was of such renowned antiquity that it became synonymous with great age.

39. Edward W. Lane, *Arabic-English Lexicon*, 8 vols. (New York: F. Ungar Pub. Co. 1955-56), 8:2905-6. It is naturally related to the main word in Arabic for Jew, *yahūd*. See Horovitz, *Koranische Untersuchungen*, pp. 153-55; Qur'ān 2:62, 111, 135, 140; 4:46.

40. Serjeant, "Pre-Islamic Prophets," pp. 166-67.

41. Al-Qurtubī, *Al-Jāmiᶜ li-Ahkām al-Qur'ān* (Collection of the Wisdom of the Qur'ān) 20 vols. (Cairo: Dār at-kutub al-Misriyya 1935-1950), 7:235-36.

42. Winnett and Reed, *Ancient Records*, agrees with this possibility (p. 45).

43. Charles Cutler Torrey, *The Jewish Foundation of Islam* (New York: Ktav Publishing House, Inc., 1967), pp. 10-11. It is interesting for Latter-day Saints that his description of the expansion of Jewish traders into Arabia corresponds with Hugh Nibley's reconstruction of Lehi as a merchant. Hugh Nibley, *Lehi in the Desert* (Salt Lake City, Utah: Bookcraft, 1952).

44. DeLacy O'Leary, *Arabia Before Muhammad* (New York: E. P. Dutton, 1927), p. 172; Josephus, *Antiquities*, 13:9:1.

45. O'Leary, *Before Muhammad*, pp. 173-74.

46. H. StJ. B. Philby, *The Background of Islam* (Alexandria, 1947), pp. 116-20.

47. For a general study of the influence of Christianity in Arabia see Richard Bell, *The Origin of Islam in its Christian Environment* (1926; reprint ed. Frank Cass, 1965); O'Leary, *Before Muhammad*, pp. 125-49; Hitti, *History of the Arabs*, p. 78; Philby, *Background*, pp. 112-15, 121-26; J. S. Trimingham, *Christianity Among the Arabs in Pre-Islamic Times* (New York: Langman, 1979).

48. Torrey, *Jewish Foundation*; Bell, *Origin of Islam*; the extensive bibliography in Abraham I. Katsh, *Judaism and the Koran* (New York: A. S. Barnes and Co., 1962), pp. 229-45; Speyer, *Biblischen Erzählungen*, pp. 116-19.

49. David Hackett Fischer, *Historian's Fallacies: Toward a Logic of Historical Thought* (New York: Harper Torch book, 1970).

50. Nibley, *Lehi*, pp. 123-28.

51. Nibley, *Lehi*, pp. 72-77, 85-91.

52. Yāqūt, vol. 1, p. 155. In Arabic, *"allatī tajrī min tahtihā al-anhār."* This phrase is a direct quote from a Qur'anic description of paradise (Qur'ān 2:25).

53. At-Tabarī, p. 238; Ath-Thaʿlabī, p. 68; 1 Nephi 8:23, 12:17. No Hūd parallel to the important Book of Mormon image of the iron rod seems extant.

54. Qur'ān 26:129; At-Tabari, 1:239; Ath-Thaʿlabī, pp. 68-69; 1 Nephi 11:35-36.

55. 1 Nephi 8:10-11; 11:21-22. In the Qur'ān also salvation is symbolized by partaking of fruit in a garden by flowing rivers (Qur'ān 2:25). Lane, *Lexicon*, 2:596.

56. This analysis follows Mustafa, *Religious Trends*, pp. 56-59; Qur'ān 6:37, 25:7, 43:31.

57. See Mustafa, *Religious Trends*, pp. 40-41, 97-103; Brau, *Encyclopedia of Islam*, old ed., s.v. "Umaiya."

58. Qur'ān 3:67, 95; 10:105; 22:31.

59. Mustafa, *Religious Trends*, p. 97.

60. *Diwān Umayya*, p. 46.

11
The Idea of Redemption in Christianity and Islām

Mahmoud Mustafa Ayoub

*b*ism illāh irrahman irrahīm. assalāmu ʿalaykum. Peace be with you all. It is the Islamic greeting with which I greet you. May I also add my voice to the many voices which have spoken and not spoken of the appreciation which we all have as Muslims of your effort at a time when Islām is looked upon as a distortion of the truth, as a backward religion, and Muslims and their faith have

Mahmoud M. Ayoub is associate professor at the Centre for Religious Studies, University of Toronto, Canada. He graduated from the University of Beirut with a B.A. in philosophy, received his M.A. in religious thought from the University of Pennsylvania, and his Ph.D. from the Center for the Study of World Religions of Harvard University. Professor Ayoub specializes in comparisons between Islām and Christianity. He is presently engaged in translating the Qurʾān into modern English.

been, and still are, maligned in many circles in the West. To have people who are genuinely concerned and interested is a heartening event indeed. Let me then, as a Muslim, thank you for your efforts and wish for all of us the blessing of God and his guidance to the truth, whatever its source may be.

Among historians of religion, the approach has largely been to categorize a religion according to its concept of God. This approach, fruitful as it may be, has problems; and it may well be a more enlightening exercise if we begin not with the concept of God alone but with the way a religious tradition views human society or, in other words, man's relationship to the Divine.

From that starting point, it can be said that from the earliest beginnings of human civilization, it has been a matter of human awareness of the mysteries of suffering and death. From the earliest times, in China, in Egypt, and notably in Mesopotamia with the cults of Tammuz, we find that the main concern is to understand the purposes of life and of death. (I will resist a great temptation to retell the tale of Gilgamesh as a commentary on the human predicament on life and on death.)

We Muslims and, as I have been learning today, Mormons as well, believe that revelation is an ongoing process. For Islām, revelation began with Adam when he received words from his Lord, and God turned towards him. And while we believe that revelation reached its technical culmination in the prophet Muhammad through a long period of what we call progressive revelation, nonetheless it may be said that revelation continues, not in the form of *wahi* (revelation technically considered) but in the form of *ilham*, or inspiration which is open to the friends and worshipful servants of God. This mode of revelation will not end. It did not begin only after prophetic revelation had ended, but rather, in my view, it always coexisted with it. In other words, the beginnings of what I may call collective revelation are our rich heritage of mythology.

Unfortunately, we call anything which is not true, which cannot be taken seriously, mythical. But if we consider seriously that mythology has been the language of faith, that religious tradition has done far better in poetry than in prose, and that poetry is usually the language of myth, then we can see the crucial importance of myth in the development of human religious consciousness.

It is in mythology also that the idea of redemption was born. As the prophet Ezekiel put it, "And there sat women weeping for Tammuz" (Ezekiel 8:14). On the banks of the Tigris and the Euphrates sat women and men expressing their emotions of fear and hope, as they sang dirges for the God who died, in order to bring Him back to life. This really meant to bring the sap back into the date palm tree, the milk to the cow and hence to the milkskin, and the grain to the surface of the earth.[1]

If we look carefully, the ideas expressed in the myths are universal—they are Greek, they are Indian; everywhere we go there is this idea of life coming out of death, so to say, healing the world, healing nature after a period of sickness or cessation. What is redemption or the word *salvation*? It comes, as you all know, from the Latin root meaning "to be whole." Yet again, it is in the myth which from Tammuz moved a vast step forward to the suffering servant of the Lord of Deutero-Isaiah. It is important to observe that whether it was in Tammuz, or in the suffering servant of the Lord, or later in Christ, or in the prophet Muhammad and his intercessory role, or later on in the martyrdom of his grandson Husayn, redemption is not achieved by or through ideas or doctrines but through the lives and the sacrifices of human individuals. If I may be allowed a small digression here, our problem has been, to a large extent, that we have taken far too seriously doctrines and theological wranglings, and not seriously enough the lives and the models, the examples of the friends of God. The suffering servant of Deutero-Isaiah remained unidentified. Some said it was a prototypical character; others, that it referred to the entire Jewish people. Finally in the Church, beginning in the book of Acts and developing more clearly through the thought of Justin Martyr, the suffering servant was identified with Christ. The Gospels also refer to this somewhat briefly. The suffering servant must be all of these and none of them. In a way he is every one of us, both needing redemption and participating in a redemptive role for its achievement. I will come to this at some greater length later.

As we come to post-biblical Judaism and especially early Christianity, there are essentially two types or ideas of redemption. It may be observed here that the Swedish writer, Gustaf Aulén, is very right when he says there is no doctrine of redemption in

Christianity but only theories about it.[2] There was a redemptive act, but what was it? How can we express it in doctrinal form? It is good perhaps that there has not been agreement.

As I see them, there are two basic types of redemption in Christianity. The first is a death on the cross, where the cross becomes a prototype of the biblical or more specifically the Jewish temple altar. That sacrifice was the final sacrifice, all others before it being only a prelude to it. Hence, the Gospel of St. Matthew tells us that when Jesus died on the cross, the veil of the temple that separated the true place of sacrifice—the holy of holies—and the people was rent and the barrier, therefore, was removed. The idea of this type, i.e., redemption through death and the shedding of blood, is worked out in the New Testament most interestingly and clearly in the Epistle to the Hebrews.

The other type is one that characterizes the Eastern Church most notably. It is redemption not by death and suffering so much as by victory. Hence, the Easter hymn for the Greek Orthodox Church goes something like this: "Christ rose from the dead, trampling death and by death giving life to those who are in the graves." Here we have it in a nutshell, and to go into it in all its details and complexities is both beyond the time that I am allotted and also beyond my expertise.

The two basic ideas developed by medieval thinkers of Christ dying in order to appease either God or Satan or to set a trap for Satan have not been, in my view, as fruitful and creative or as poetic as the other idea which is also expressed in the thought of St. Paul, that Christ really conquered death by death. More interestingly, this idea was developed in the mystical theology of the Eastern Church, which had its beginnings in the Johannine corpus—both the Gospel and the Epistles. Christ, the second Adam, came not to abolish an original sin by dying for Adam, but rather he came in order to make us divine. He came in order to achieve victory over the demonia, the powers of evil. It was God visiting humanity in human disguise. Hence that Christianity which lived on strongly and converted numerous people in the Syro-Aramaic area or what we now mainly call the Arab world, was that Christianity which has been characterized by Christian writers as the faith of the merciful, i.e., *addīn arrahamānī*. It is that faith which Islām breeds, and I think we cannot understand Islām fully unless we see it in that Christian ritualistic context. It may be argued that even though the prophet of Islām lived in closer proximity to the Jewish community in Medina and interacted with it far more extensively on a daily basis, the overall influence of the spirituality of Eastern Christianity and its idea of redemption played a greater role in the formative period of Muslim piety.

To the two types of redemption discussed in Christianity, Islām added a third and a fourth. But before I talk about the Islamic idea of redemption it must be observed that the basic mystery which preoccupied humanity from its earliest beginning was that of suffering and death. Hence the idea or hope of redemption was born in suffering. In the West the suffering of Christ developed into an idea of a Christ contorted with pain. (The gory images that we see in much of Western medieval literature characterizing the suffering Christ were the products of the first type of redemption, that is, redemption as death.) In Eastern Christian piety, on the other hand, the cross is not really an altar of suffering and death, but a throne of glory. In many poems, notably that of Fortunatus,[3] and echoed even in Ireland in the "Dream of the Rood," we find the same notion of the universal cross as the throne of glory. Yet suffering was not forgotten, and the Christian Church, inasmuch as it itself participated in that redemptive role, did it through its witness. The greatest witness was that of martyrdom. The word *martyr* actually means witness. The point was vividly argued even early in the Church when Stephen, the first martyr, at the point of death declared that he saw the heavens opened and the Son of God seated on the right hand of God (Acts 7:55-56). However, that suffering had to be transferred from earth to heaven in order for it to be universal and eternal. Thus St. John Chrysostom (in a sermon sometimes wrongly attributed to St. Augustine) declares that Christ sits in heaven still bearing the marks of the nails and the wound of the lance in his side.[4] Therefore the emblems of suffering were not only to be embodied by the Church here on earth in its participatory role in the achievement of redemption, but they were also transferred to heaven, where they will be displayed before the angels until the final victory — the return of the Messiah, the Second Coming.

To understand the Islamic idea of redemption, in contrast, and the two types which I said Islām added to the Christian notion, is to look briefly at the Muslim view of man. For a long time Christian and Jewish orientalists in the West read the Qur'anic account of Adam as a gross distortion of the biblical account that, had he known better, Muhammad would have copied. It is only now, I think, that scholars are beginning to see the Qur'ān on its own terms. However different it may be from that of Genesis, the Qur'anic account of Adam must be seen on its own terms. What does it tell us? In some ways, the Adam of the Qur'ān closely resembles that of Genesis. Like the Adam of Genesis, Adam in the Qur'ān is declared to be made of clay and obtains the breath of life through the divine spirit that was breathed into him. Like the biblical Adam, the Adam of the Qur'ān sinned by disobeying the divine command. But here the comparison ends. The Qur'ān does not tell us that Adam ate of the fruit of the tree of knowledge, because knowledge was given to him even before his sin (Qur'ān 2:31-33). Knowledge was not the cause of his condemnation and damnation, but of his salvation. Adam was saved because he received words from his Lord. He was declared higher than the angels because he knew language which they did not know. So it is not knowledge that made Adam sin, but disobedience. While the biblical Adam becomes the first sinner for Christians, for Muslims Adam is not the first sinner but the first prophet, because with him the history of revelation begins.

In nine verses in the Qur'ān (2:30-39) we have a commentary on the story of Adam which was told several times in other Qur'anic verses. It is a commentary that goes beyond the creation of Adam. There God says to the angels, "Behold, I am about to place a vicegerent in the earth." The angels, knowing what we would do, said, "Would you place therein one who will spread corruption and shed blood, while we proclaim your praise and sanctify you?" He said, "I know what you do not know." Then Adam was taught the names of all creatures and the challenge was placed between knowing and choosing man and knowing and choosing the angels, who could only do that which is good. Satan, or Iblīs, in the Adam story plays a role not in spite of but by the permission of God. His sin was like that of Adam in essence. Both rebelled. But while Adam repented and turned to God, Iblīs persisted in his pride and would not accept that a creature of clay may be better than a creature of fire.

Redemption, then, in Islām begins with Adam, who was made for the earth. He descends to earth and the battle between good and evil begins on its true stage, the earth. Redemption is when this battle is finally concluded with the divine victory, with the victory of the Good.

The Qur'ān speaks not of ransom by sacrifice even though we do a commemorative sacrifice at the time of the *hajj* to commemorate the sacrifice of Abraham, but the Qur'ān insists that then neither the fat nor the blood of the animals reaches God. What reaches him is our piety or righteousness. So expiation or *takfīr* of sin must be done by the individual himself, and here, then, redemption is what men and women do with their own sin through repentance and through expiation through prayers, fasts, sharing their wealth with the poor, and so on. This is one type of redemption.

The other, and in a sense more important in that it has permeated Islamic life more deeply and is a type which may be considered as really the only legitimate type of Islamic redemption, is that of intercession—*shafāᶜah*. Contrary to what many Muslims say, intercession is not denied in the Qur'ān; rather, what is denied is that intercession will benefit those who are deep in sin. Any intercession must be a divine gift. The Qur'ān tells us, "Who shall intercede with him, save by his leave" (2:255). Furthermore, if we take the large number of *hadīths* known as *ahādīth ash-shafāᶜa*, or the traditions of intercession, we find so clearly the idea that it will be Muhammad who will intercede on behalf not only of the Muslims but the entire world. In a long and dramatic tradition related on the authority of Abu Hurayrah we are told that on the day of resurrection, people will be made to stand for seventy years. They will weep tears, and when their tears run out they will weep blood until the blood shall stop their mouths, and still they will not be judged. Then Muhammad will go and prostrate himself before God and intercede for people, not that they may be given paradise but at least that they must be heard—they must be judged—and hence the judgment begins.

While Muhammad, in popular Islām and in much of not-so-popular Islām, plays a very important intercessory role, intercession is not limited to him. Rather, in explanation of a very interesting verse in *Sūrat al-Baqara*, which comes after telling the story of David and Goliath and Saul, the text adds that had not God restrained or stopped some people by means of others, the earth would have been corrupted (2:251). Most people take that to mean that there must always exist in the earth people who pray, otherwise the earth will disappear. In a comment on that verse by the sixth Shīʿī imām, Jaʿfar al-Sādiq, we are told that God protects those who do not pray among the Muslims through those who do pray; those who do not fast through those who do fast; and those who do not go on pilgrimage through those who do go. Were they all to concur in neglecting the prayers, fasting, and pilgrimage, then they would all perish.

In another *hadīth* we are told that God blesses, that is, gives *baraka*, through the prayerful servant of God. He gives *baraka* not only to the person's own family but to his neighbors and neighbors' neighbors to the seventh neighbor. This notion of the earth being preserved, made whole, redeemed from evil through piety and prayers is most eloquently expressed in Islamic mysticism in Sufism, and systematically in the notion of the *qutb* or the perfect man. The *qutb* is he around whom the universe revolves, and every age must have a *qutb*, otherwise the earth could not stay in its place. Through his grace, the universe goes on running. This is put rather poetically by one Sufi writer, who says, *inna lillāhi ʿibādan idha arādū arād* ("There are those servants of God who, when they will something, God wills it as well"). So, then, wholeness or redemption, salvation, restoration can be achieved through personal expiation and through intercession widely considered.

Here again in Islām, as in Christianity and Judaism and even in Buddhism, there is the notion that the world is continuously evolving towards a state of perfection. In Buddhism this is expressed in the role of the future Buddha, Maitreya. It is an interesting notion which presents a reverse of Darwinian evolution. Darwin thinks that evolution is upward from the unicellular animal to the monkey to man and whatever. It appears that the religious concept is that the world evolves downward from a golden age to a silver age to an iron age to a clay age and then the whole thing will be dark until someone comes to restore things to their natural and earlier purity. This, in Islām, is the *Mahdi.*

In the *Mahdi* idea, Islām and Christianity again meet. I would like to argue here (and it is an argument that I am developing in an article to be published on the role of Jesus in Muslim eschatology in my Islamic Christology series—for the first articles in the series see *Muslim World,* vol. LXVI, No. 3, 1976; and vol. LXX, No. 2, 1980) that the first notion of the *Mahdi* was not that a person of the family of the prophet will be born, according to the Sunni Muslim view, or that he will appear at the end of time, according to the Shī‘ī Muslim view. Rather it will be Jesus who will return. If we are to find any Qur'anic basis for this eschatological event, it will not be for a future, so to say, Islamic *Mahdi,* but for Jesus, who is declared to be a sign for the Hour (Qur'ān 43:61). Muslim piety, in order to preserve itself and its own integrity, did not deny that Jesus will come to restore the world to its purity but affirmed that Jesus and the *Mahdi* will work together. Most of the hard work will be done by Jesus, who will kill ad-Dajjāl, the anti-Christ.

Here again, ad-Dajjāl is pictured as a human individual whose appearance is deformed, who is not human as he should be. To my knowledge, the best comment describing him is one that was made by the thirteenth-century Farīd Ud-Dīn ‘Attār, a Persian mystic who said that at the end of time there will come two Dajjāl, not one. (The Arabic word *dajjāl* means one who lies.) There will be one who has only his right eye and sees the world as all spirit. He will be a liar. There will be one who has only his left eye and will see the world as simply matter and material things. He will be a liar. The true vision of reality, then, is one that sees reality as a whole—both material and spiritual. The role of Jesus is that he will kill that liar, the anti-Christ, and restore the reality of the universe to its pristine purity. Symbolically it is said that Christ, when He comes, will break the cross and kill the swine (these two being the symbols that divide Muslims from Christians), and Islām in its essential aspects will prevail. This is redemption.

I could not end my talk without considering that ethos of redemptive suffering which the Shī‘ī community developed. In that ethos we see a continuity of history. It was on the spot where the women sat weeping for Tammuz that Husayn, the son of ʿAlī and grandson of the prophet, was killed on the tenth day of Muharram in the year 61 A.H. (A.D. 680). Very soon those who betrayed him formed an association, a group called at-Tawwābūn, the repenters. It was in that group that the seeds of a rich cult of Muharram were first sown and sprouted.

To be sure, the event was used and abused by many upstarts and pseudo-movements, but these failed as they were doomed to failure. What remains is the following: The world, according to the Shīʿī view and its history, must be read forward from creation to the *imāms* and backward from the day of resurrection to the *imāms*. In time the notion developed that the world was created for the sake of the pious, the prophet and his progeny. They were the lights of the world which, through a process of concretization, took on human form. All were doomed to be martyred. The idea again gradually arose, even though there is not full documentary evidence that every one of the eleven Shīʿī *imāms* were martyred. The Shīʿī community nonetheless insisted that that was the case. Those who were supposedly the noblest, supposedly the richest, had to undergo suffering in order to redeem humanity.

But how does humanity become redeemed? It is through the suffering of Husayn's mother, who is still weeping in paradise for his death, and that of his children after him. How is the world to be redeemed? It is by participation of the community every year in that suffering that the community redeems itself. So we are told in many traditions attributed to one or another of the *imāms* that whoever weeps even one drop of tears for the sufferings of the *imāms* will have the reward of paradise. But in the final analysis, redemption will be through intercession because the headless Husayn will stand before God to intercede for his people.

There is, finally, one important aspect of redemption, whether it be Christian or Islamic. Redemption is only one side of the divine judgment. Redemption must also imply judgment and condemnation. Christ will return on the clouds of heaven, as the book of Revelation declares (Revelation 1:7); and those who have stabbed him will mourn him. He will come not as the meek lamb of God but as the man who has a sword of fire coming out of his mouth with every word he utters. Before the new earth and the new heaven will appear, replacing the old earth and heaven, judgment must be executed on the wicked. Similarly, with Islām, the *Mahdi* when he comes will avenge the blood of Husayn before he fulfills his main mission; on this both Shi͑ī and Sunni traditionists agree. He must purify the earth of iniquity. Before he does that, he must avenge the blood of the martyrs.

The *Mahdi* will do his work and eventually die, but it will be Husayn who will return to rule the earth or the Muslim community for so long that his eyebrows shall fall upon his eyes from old age.[5] But the hope for a future restoration, for an eschatology of renewal, is best expressed in a Qur'anic verse and a comment by the sixth *imām* on that verse. The Qur'ān declares that on the last day when the trumpets shall sound and when judgment has been executed, the earth shall shine forth with the light of its Lord (Qur'ān 39:69). The sixth *imām* said, "When our *qā'im* (i.e. the one raised by God to renew human society and restore truth) shall come, the earth shall shine forth with the light of its Lord."[6]

Much of what I have been discussing may be regarded as poetic myth by people sitting here so many centuries removed from the events of Christ and Husayn and Tammuz. What does it say to us today? I have said that redemption in its widest sense is a corporate, not an individual, process. Whether it be the Church widely viewed or the Church of the Latter-day Saints or the Muslim community, for redemption to be meaningful and real for us today, we all have to take part in it as an ongoing process.

On the principles of the ideas that we can learn from the mythology of the past, we see that redemption means harmony between material and spiritual things. Redemption means sharing. The people who will be put on the right hand of Christ will be those who visit the sick, clothe the naked, visit the prisoner, and feed the hungry (Matthew 25:31-46). But, most of all, it remains for us to redeem the world from our own human folly—the folly that says that we will vie not with God but with the devil to make ourselves, as one Greek philosopher described us, the measure of all things. Hence, we make atom bombs and nuclear bombs, we make big sky-scrapers, but with all of this we forget the purpose of life, which is to be a life of righteousness—a bridge to eternity.

We who are in an academic position, who are average in society but who are committed, can yet also play a role. What we see today is the beginning of a new dialogue—to me, at least. I do not think, and I must tell you here and now, I do not think that you people will be any more successful in converting Muslims to Mormonism than any missionaries who were before you. But you could be successful in one important area; that is, to create an important dialogue that will lead to a fellowship of faith between you and us. I think that the truth is bigger than any concept of the truth held by any nation or religious community or individual. And to the truth there are many ways. We can all meet along the way and learn, but it is perhaps creative and quite suitable for each one of us to work his or her own way to God in the way he or she knows best. I myself was born in a Muslim community to a very devout family. But for fifteen years I was a fundamentalist Protestant; I was baptized and all of it, and I shouted more amens and hallelujahs than any of you. Why, then, did I return to Islām? Not because I feel that Christianity is not a redeeming process but because I felt that my roots are in that civilization, in that world, in that ethos, in that whole world view, and I think it is better for both Islām and Christianity that I did that.

In conclusion, I would like to say that Christ redeemed and continues to redeem us, not simply and only by his divine act, but by his humanity, a humanity that cared. Muhammad redeemed and continues to redeem us as we follow his life, his *sunna*, as a model for our lives. But in the end we must heed the words, "Work out your own salvation with fear and trembling." I pray that we will all be successful in that process and that we will strengthen each other as we traverse the weary way of this life into the life to come.

NOTES

1. See T. Jacobsen, *Towards an Image of Tammuz and Other Essays on Mesopotamian Religion and Culture*, ed. W. L. Moren (Cambridge, Mass.: Harvard University Press, 1970), pp. 73ff.

2. Gustaf Aulén, *Christus Victor*, trans. by A. G. Herbert (London: SPCK, 1965).

3. See the Hymn of Fortunatus quoted in Rev. Joseph Connelly, M.A., *Hymns of the Roman Liturgy* (Westminster, Maryland: Newman Press, 1954).

4. St. John Chrysostom, "The Lord's Passion" or "The Cross and the Good Thief," *Patrologia Latina* XXXIX, pp. 2047FF.

5. Mahmoud Ayoub, *Redemptive Suffering in Islam*, (New York: Mouton Publishers, 1978), p. 228.

6. Ayoub, *op. cit.*, p. 227.

12
Religious Practices of Egyptian Muslim Women

Jane I. Smith

Most writing about women in Muslim societies focuses on the roles assigned to them by the religious and social structure of Islām and on the opportunities afforded or denied to them in the present socio-political circumstance in various countries. I would like to discuss the activities of Egyptian Muslim women in the religious sphere, looking at what they do, and why, in the context of the familial and societal structure in which they must operate. Specifi-

---

Jane I. Smith is associate dean of academic affairs and lecturer in comparative religion at Harvard University. A graduate of Michigan State University in social science, she received a B.D. from the Hartford Seminary Foundation and her Ph.D. in the history of religions/Islamic studies from Harvard University. Professor Smith has published and lectured extensively on religious themes relating to Islām, and particularly on women in Islām.

cally, I will consider how, given the traditional ascription of authority to males and the continuing exercise of that authority, women
act to assure some degree of power in their own circumstances.

Just as it is extremely difficult to generalize about Islamic women
in the global context—although one notes frequent attempts to do
so—it is also difficult to treat women in any given country as a unit.
Egyptian Muslim women operate out of a variety of socio-economic
and cultural circumstances,[1] and represent very different modes of
response to the fact of being Muslim. As they differ, so do their
religious practices. Some of these practices are what one might call
borderline Muslim, on the fringes of what orthodoxy considers
acceptable, while others are centrally and totally religious. Still
others are only peripherally religious but are primarily social or
cultural. As a whole they constitute the variety of ways that these
women have found to be religious, to relate to that which is beyond
the ordinary, and to attempt to exercise some degree of control over
their own circumstances.

Egyptian religious practices as a whole—as can perhaps be said
about most of the Muslim world—are in many cases determined by
social and economic factors and thus are part of a class phenomenon in which both men and women participate. In other cases,
however, women's practices have developed precisely because
females to some extent have been excluded from the world of males
and therefore from *ʿibadāt* (acts of piety) which are part of the male
domain. It is only since 1971, for example, that Egyptian women
have been allowed to attend Friday prayers. Reasons for the earlier
exclusion are complex, and in general are part of the seclusion
which, while not Qur'anic, often has characterized the situation of
Muslim women.[2] Women are seldom seen at Friday prayers even
today, are normally forbidden from joining in the *zikr* ("remember-
ing," act of devotion) ceremonies, and in general are not part of the
formal religious structures in which men operate.

As a result of these restrictions, women not surprisingly have
emphasized those elements of formal Islām that have remained open
to them.[3] Within the five basic religious duties incumbent on all
Muslims, fasting is taken more seriously by women than prayer, the
latter being engaged in almost exclusively in the privacy of the
home. The structure of the month of fasting provides the occasion

for social interaction and a playing out of the feminine role in preparation of the meals which break the fast. Part of the social service aspect of Islām—traditionally provided for by the paying of the *zakāt* tax usually by males—middle- and upper-class women for some decades in Egypt have organized and participated in Muslim associations for social service and change.

In addition to these sorts of activities provided for by the structure of Islām, Muslim women have developed a range of religious practices that are more clearly characterized as their own. Because males by Qur'anic sanction are assigned authority over women,[4] women have had to develop a variety of ways to exercise power. Usually, these tactics relate to power over forces in the supernatural realm, but simultaneously they also provide the means whereby women exert some degree of control over their own circumstances and, in the process, over the men to whose authority they are Qur'anically entrusted. That which on the one hand represents a means of controlling forces in the world of the unseen, at the same time gives many women a means of coping with the material world and securing their own place in it.

Divination and healing, for example, are almost exclusively female activities. Egyptian sociologist Sayyid ʿUways[5] describes the practice in the Nile Valley in which certain women, usually of peasant stock, attempt to heal children suffering from problems of temperament. Securing a price from the mother, they tie up their long skirts, wade into the water, and immerse the child three times in the Nile. It is interesting to note that this is done for three consecutive weeks precisely at the time of the Friday prayer, the traditional male time to worship in the mosque. If the child is healed, his or her clothing is thrown into the Nile. It is mainly among women that one finds such practices as the wearing of sacred or magic rings supposed to contain certain kinds of occult powers. Common in Egypt as in most Middle Eastern cultures is the belief in the power of the evil eye, warded off by the wearing of charms and blue beads which women often tie on the necks or beds of their children. Again, it is most often women who engage in such Islamically suspect activities as palm reading and divination.[6]

One long-lived custom observed in Egypt primarily though not exclusively by women—again beyond the borderline of what ortho-

dox Islām finds acceptable—is that of the *zar* ceremony. *Zar* refers
both to the belief that one can be possessed by a spirit and to the
ceremony in which exorcism is believed to take place.[7] *Zar* ceremonies can be either public or private. In both instances the primary
actors are the women who believe themselves possessed by spirits or
ʿafrīts (believed to be male), the *shaykh,* who by means of dance
and trance induces the spirit to leave, and the friends and relatives
of the possessed woman, who encourage her in this process and
provide strong communal support and bonding.

In general, men disavow the efficacy of the *zar* ceremony and
even deny the possibility that their wives or female relatives might
thus be controlled by supernatural spirits or beings.[8] What is noteworthy, however, is that they seldom refuse to allow their women
to participate, either out of covert fear of the spirit or out of concern
that they will be publicly censured for refusing to allow their wives
help. It is also clear that the afflicted women derive a number of
benefits from this whole process. The symptoms are real and
include swelling of the legs or stomach, a high degree of nervous-
ness, and so forth; and the process of exorcism is often a traumatic
one, sending the women into a state of exhaustion. Nonetheless, the
benefits are real: a break in the monotony of a routine life, a way
for wealthy (and therefore more secluded) women to get out of the
house, a degree of control over the family finances, as the husband
must pay for participation in the *zar,* an opportunity to become the
center of attention among women friends and relatives, and even a
way to achieve a kind of status in the community.[9] While "cures"
are not uncommon, many women continue to be possessed for long
periods of time.

Another area of religious response in which women have been
primary participants is visiting the tombs of historical and contemporary saints. Many males also do this, of course, but women
certainly have found in the practices related to tomb visiting an
immediate and acceptable way to meet their social and psychological needs, as well as their devotional ones. Here again, it affords
them an opportunity to exert power over their own circumstances,
this time by appeal to an outside agency—the saint (*walī*).

While supplication of the *walī* has been historically condemned
as heretical and leading to the perversion of the faith, in general it

has remained part of the total fabric of Islamic religious response. Orthodox Islām admits the validity of praying through the saints to God, but not of praying to them; in common practice, however, this distinction often gets blurred. Today in Egypt the custom is widespread, and even has the sanction of the Azhar.[10] The *walīs* are seen as physically deceased but alive in their tombs, listening to the prayers and pleas of their visitors and responding to them. There are several aspects to the relationship with the saints (also called the *shaykhs*). In some of these, such as the *mūlid* (birthday observance) for the saint, men and women alike participate. Other elements of the *shaykh* cult are more particularly "female." The visit to the tomb, which may be located inside a larger mosque, on the grounds of a mosque, or by itself with some kind of protective structure, is called *ziyāra*. Often women use the *ziyāra* simply to sit in a peaceful place, enjoying a respite from the demands of husbands and family. It has been observed that while men generally come to the tomb and make a quick request of the *walī*, women often stay for long periods of time. Many times they will take parts of their garments and "clean" the railing of the tomb or dust off the ground around it as a way of honoring the saint and obtaining *baraka* (power, efficacy, blessing).

Another way of obtaining power is by asking the direct intervention of the saint in solving a personal problem. This generally entails making a *nadr* (vow) to somehow repay the *walī* should one's request be granted. Studies made both in Cairo and in Upper Egypt[11] indicate that the two requests most commonly made of *walīs* are to contract a successful marriage, either for oneself or for one's daughter, and to become pregnant.[12] Other popular petitions are requests for help in setting traps for one's enemies, specifically other wives or proposed wives of one's husband. It is not surprising that there is such strong emphasis on family and sexual matters. Not only do these roles constitute the total world of many women, but sexuality is the one area where women have final control over men, as it is they who are the source of reproduction. (This is undoubtedly one reason why birth control programs have met with great resistance, especially in rural Egypt.) When a difficult problem has found some resolution, the *nadr* is fulfilled. Fatima Mernissi, observing the similar phenomenon of women's visits to sanctuaries in Morocco, notes that the system of *nadr* is a satisfying one for women. If one goes to a doctor for an ointment, for example, one must pay whether or not relief is forthcoming. With the saint, payment (fulfilling of *nadr*) comes only with satisfaction. "Saints . . . embody the refusal to accept arrogant expertise," she says, "to submit blindly to authority, to be treated as subordinate."[13]

Often the relation to the saint, while "religious" in the implicit recognition that the *wali's* power comes only through his or her capacity to mediate the power of God, takes on a very different character from that of one's relationship to God himself. Respect and devotion are present, but the woman does not hesitate to rebuke her *wali* if she thinks that he or she is not listening or has been negligent in fulfilling a request. One woman, for example, is said to have rubbed a local saint's tomb with garlic (which she knew he disliked) to chastise him for apparent inattention. Here again a woman can assume a position of power and control over a male, even though he be a saint!

It is quite clear, then, that either consciously or subconsciously Egyptian Muslim women continue to turn to religious practices and customs that by definition set them apart from the more "orthodox" forms of religious response observed by the males in society. While some conservative male voices insist on assigning women an inferior status and excluding them from the male domain,[14] clearer and more obvious recognition is being given to the necessity of assuring increasing opportunity for women to participate in the religious structure. These several realities have led to an interesting situation with regard to Egyptian Muslim women. On the one hand we see the continuation of practices outside the male structure that assure women control over their circumstances, and which, in fact, give them a kind of power that equal participation would not. On the other hand, particularly in the urban educated middle and upper classes, many women reaffirm their role *within* the orthodox Islamic structure.

To understand the situation of women in Egypt, as in other parts of the Islamic world (and this is not even to speak of recent changes in legal circumstances for women), it is necessary to attempt to see things through Muslim as well as through Western eyes. What most Western observers of Islamic practices assume to be clear inequities in the circumstances of men and women—and therefore unjust if not immoral—are not necessarily viewed that way by Egyptian Muslim women. The various forms of liberation Muslim women see advocated in the West are often understood by them as even more insidious forms of bondage. They look at social and political circumstances in the West and see men and women in conflict, rather than functioning complementarily as in the Islamic system. They fear what they see as inevitable loss of male protection and support and reject isolated individualism.

Thus we find that certain traditional practices that were historically imposed on women are now being reinterpreted in forms that many Egyptian women not only accept but consciously choose as a means of affirming their allegiance to Islām. One interesting example of this is to be found in the adoption of new forms of dress. After centuries of enforced seclusion, many educated Egyptian women followed the example of the celebrated Huda Sha‘rāwī in the 1920s in discarding the veil and wearing Western dress as a sign of their newly realized liberation. As the century wore on, it became increasingly clear to Muslims in many parts of the Middle East that the wholesale adoption of Western ways would have undesirable consequences. The complex elements in increased Islamic consciousness of the last decade cannot be detailed here; but it is clear that many Muslim women have felt the need, with men, to affirm their identity as Muslims and to indicate in the process their disenchantment with many aspects of Western culture.

One manifestation of this attitude is the adoption by middle- and upper middle-class Muslim women of what is called "lawful dress" (*al-ziyy al-shar‘ī*), a conservative costume consisting of a long skirt or trousers, a long-sleeved tunic, and a headdress such as a scarf or wrapping that covers the hair but not the face.[15] Western observers may see the selection of this kind of dress as a step backwards, but for the Muslim woman it is very different from enforced veiling and seclusion. They choose this garb voluntarily as a sign of allegiance to Islām. It is not a coincidence that it began to appear a few years after the 1967 defeat of the Arabs at the hands of Israel, an event that engendered serious discussion about the need to return to strict Islām to be worthy of victory, which God guarantees his community in the Qur'ān.[16] Far from suggesting seclusion, the

lawful dress is seen by its advocates as ensuring that women will not
be subject to unwanted advances by male associates, thus per-
mitting them safe entry into a more active public life.

Not all of the educated women, of course, applaud this change
in dress. Many Egyptian women are Christians and repudiate the
costume's religious implications. Some feminists are outraged at
what they see as a return to *purdah*. Often more interested in
improving the status of women than in affirming the principles of
Islām, they nonetheless look to possibilities in their own culture
rather than to Western models for achieving the equality they
desire.

Contemporary Egypt, then, provides a cross section of women's
responses to their personal and social circumstances. Insofar as
these reflect the ways in which they are allowed to be Muslim—or
self-consciously attempt to identify themselves as Muslim—we can
call them religious. What is clear is that within the possibilities
afforded to them by their respective circumstances (social, educational, economic), they have developed an elaborate set of ways in
which to exert power in the face of designated male authority.
Struggling on many levels to achieve what they believe to be right
and fair, they also sagely recognize that the more viable option may
lie in maintaining—often through various kinds of manipula-
tion—a system that works for them. Conversing with a young
Muslim woman who is highly educated and well familiar with
Western culture, I pressed her on the Qur'ān verse which assigns
ultimate authority to men over women. "Doesn't it ever make you
angry?" I asked in a last attempt to arouse her female pride. "If I
viewed it out of context," she replied, "it might. But in context,
within the total Islamic system, it is the only viable way. I look at
your American system of liberation for women and I see families
falling apart and moral structures collapsing. If it is necessary for
my husband to have the last word—then let him. Frankly, it works.
And in the end, I can usually get my way by other means . . . ."

NOTES

1. Various categorical divisions of Egyptian women have been suggested by
anthropologists and sociologists; in general they may be viewed most easily as
falling into three main groups: rural, traditional urban, and educated urban.

2. One of the rationales offered for this exclusion is that a woman may be menstruating, therefore unclean.

3. It should be stressed that the prophet Muhammad did not place restrictions on women in the religious sphere but emphasized the divine message of the Qur'ān that women are fully responsible with men and fully accountable for their faith and actions.

4. "Men are in charge [or, are the protectors] of women, because God has given preference to the one over the other, and because men provide support for women from their means. Therefore righteous women are obedient." (Qur'ān 4:34.)

5. *Al-Khulūd fī Hayāt al-Misriyīn al-Muʿāsirīn* (Cairo), p. 42.

6. See Cynthia Nelson, "Public and Private Politics: Women in the Middle Eastern World," *American Ethnologist* 1 (1974): 556-61, for a discussion of power exerted by women over men in their roles as healers, magicians, etc. Nelson observes that the paucity of ethnographic descriptions of women's religious practices in relation to the supernatural is a very inaccurate measure of the extent of such activities.

7. These practices are not unique to Egypt. Generally felt to predate Islām, they are also found in Ethiopia, Sudan, and the Arabian peninsula.

8. There is a strong association between the *zar* ceremony and the wedding ceremony. In the private *zar*, the possessed woman dresses in her best clothing and is referred to as the bride. Many ceremonies even include the use of animal blood, possibly symbolizing the mandatory bleeding accompanying first intercourse on the wedding night.

9. For further detail on the variety of manifestations of the *zar* practices see such works as Hani Fakhouri, "The Zar Cult in an Egyptian Village," *Anthropology Quarterly* 41 (April 1968): 49-56; Lucie Wood Saunders, "Variants in Zar Experience in an Egyptian Village," eds. Vincent Crapazano and Vivien Garrison, *Case Studies in Spirit Possession* (New York: John Wiley and Sons, 1977), pp. 177-91.

10. See, for example, Farīd Māhir, *Karāmāt al-Awliyā* (Cairo), chapter 1.

11. See Sayyid ʿUways, *Min Malāmih al-Mujtamaʿ al-Misrī al-Muʿāsir* and Nawal el-Messiri, "Sheikh Cult in Dahmit" (M.A. thesis, University of Cairo, 1965).

12. Letters addressed to the *imām* Shāfiʿī in Cairo and sent through the public mail to the tomb are preponderantly from women.

13. "Women, Saints, and Sanctuaries," *Signs* 3, (Autumn 1977): 104.

14. See Yvonne Haddad, "Traditional Affirmations Concerning the Role of Women as Found in Contemporary Arab Islamic Literature," in J. I. Smith, ed., *Women in Contemporary Muslim Societies* (Brunswick, N.J.: Associated University Presses, Inc., 1980), pp. 61-86.

15. See John Alden Williams, "Veiling in Egypt as a Political and Social Phenomenon," in John Esposito, ed., *Islam and Development* (Syracuse, N.Y.: Syracuse University Press, 1980), pp. 71-85.

16. See Cynthia Nelson, "Social Change and Sexual Identity in Contemporary Egypt," in George A. DeVos, ed., *Responses to Change* (New York: D. Van Nostrand Co., 1967), p. 335.

Women and Worship
(Continued)

13
Muslim Women and Shrines in Shiraz

Anne H. Betteridge

Muslim women in Shiraz, Iran,[1] are more likely to enter upon local pilgrimage (*ziārat*) than are men. In writing about pilgrimage in Shiraz, I at first regarded this fact as rather unimportant, meriting only brief mention and cursory explanation. However, in the course of piecing together the relationship between women and *ziārat*, I

Anne H. Betteridge taught anthropology at Pahlavi University in Shiraz, Iran. She graduated magna cum laude from Mount Holyoke College, received her M.A. in anthropology from the University of Chicago, and is a Ph.D. candidate in anthropology at the University of Chicago with a dissertation topic on *ziārat* (pilgrimage) in an Iranian city. Professor Betteridge's research was conducted in Shiraz, Iran, with the objective of understanding the nature of the relationship between man and God in Shīʿī Islām.

began to realize that the relationship is significant and fundamental to understanding local pilgrimage as I observed it in Iran.

The nature of the association of women with pilgrimage is two-fold. First, on a social or behavioral level, women make pilgrimage to local shrines more often than men. Doing so enriches their lives both spiritually and socially. Second, women's local pilgrimages have a cultural aspect which touches the realm of belief and assumptions about the way the world is constituted. Because local pilgrimage is regarded as basically female in character, it is a ritual practice simultaneously suspect and beloved, not totally orthodox but to which many Iranians have a deep-rooted emotional attachment.

Shiraz is located in southwestern Iran; at the time of my residence there the population numbered just over 400,000. The character of religious observances in Shiraz, including local pilgrimage, is colored by the fact that most Iranians adhere to the Shī'ī sect of Islām[2] and revere the Shī'ī *imāms*, a series of men regarded as the rightful leaders of the Islamic community after the death of the prophet Muhammad. The majority of Shī'a recognize a succession of twelve *imāms*, and the people of Shiraz are no exception to this rule. Most of the shrines located in the city are the tombs of men and women supposed to be the descendants of the Shī'ī *imāms*. These descendants of the *imāms*, or *imāmzādehs*, are respected for their nearness to God by virtue of their descent and their great piety. On account of their privileged position, these saints are often appealed to by Shirazis who are in need of assistance, both material and spiritual. Men and women visit the shrines seeking cures, help with personal and family problems, and forgiveness of sins.

Men tend to frequent larger, more important shrines which are considered legitimate from a formal religious point of view. Women predominate at small, back-street shrines, often ramshackle sanctuaries of doubtful antecedents, mocked by men.

The extent of a woman's participation in and devotion to pilgrimage activity depends on a number of factors. The degree of her religious orthodoxy is important; those with strict backgrounds and orthodox education may regard the practice as a distortion of religion based on ignorance or misunderstanding. Others with a more strictly businesslike or scientific outlook may see it either as a diversion for women who don't know better or simply as a waste of time. A woman's age and stage of life also influence her ability to spend time visiting shrines. It is difficult for those with extensive responsibilities for young children or meal preparation to get away as often as they might like. Class membership alone appears to be less relevant; women tend to show fewer status-group differences in religious behavior than do men.[3] At the shrines one sees well-to-do women as well as those with tattered veils. The expense of their vows and the status of the shrines they visit may vary, but the women are differentiated more by dress and wealth than by the degree of their attachment to pilgrimage.

One of the attractions of visiting local shrines is that it is not a formal, highly structured religious activity. Muslim women's participation in formal religious activities is to some extent circumscribed by rules pertaining to their sex. A woman may not pray, enter a mosque, or touch a line of the Qur'ān while menstruating. For young mothers the care of children and household duties make attendance at the mosque difficult. Should women, usually older or childless, go to the mosque, it is often very hard for them to become deeply involved in the services. There women are physically separated from the men, who sit in the central part of the mosque in front of the speaker. The women may, for example, be on a high balcony at the rear of the hall or seated in a side section of the mosque, often marked off by a curtain. In either case, it is none too easy to see the speaker or hear clearly, especially if the sound is piped to the women's section by a faulty loudspeaker. The occasional presence of children in the women's area and the social atmosphere which may prevail can also affect the seriousness of women's attendance.

Interested in hearing a sermon, I went to the mosque one evening and was directed to a balcony over the courtyard where the men were gathered at the feet of the speaker, who was already seated on the *minbar* (stepped pulpit). The women around me were chatting, cracking the shells of seeds, and arranging themselves comfortably with a good view. I felt as though I were at a movie house rather than at a serious religious gathering. Needless to say, I was not able to attend to the sermon in detail. This is not to suggest

that I agree with the view men sometimes state that women are con-
stitutionally unable to involve themselves in the serious business of
Islām. It is simply that the formal, public setting of the mosque,
even when a woman is able to attend, works against her
involvement.

Rather than attempt to integrate themselves into the male
pattern of religious behavior, where they are often assigned the role
of spectators and kept on the ceremonial sidelines, women have
become very much involved in their own forms of religious activity
which give them greater scope for religious expression and allow
them full ritual participation. Among these activities are the preparation and serving of ritual meals, sermons recited by and for
women, classes conducted especially for women and girls, and
pilgrimage to local shrines. On these occasions women are not
relegated to peripheral positions and passive roles.

In contrast to the mosques, the structure of shrines and the way
in which they are used encourage informal religious activity and
allow women more freedom of movement. Particularly during
those times of day when men are at work, local shrines become
women's territory, popular places to gather and perform their
religious activities ranging from prayer to Qur'ān-reading classes.

Saturday evening is set aside as the time for visits to Qadamgāh,
a very popular shrine in Shiraz. At that time a great deal goes on
within the shrine building and in its courtyard. Inside women circumambulate the glass case which marks the footprint of 'Abbās,
half-brother of the third Shī'ī *imām*, Husayn. Off to the side a
group of women may be praying, while others are seated on the
floor playing with children and exchanging news. A few women
may prefer to sit alone and weep. Some listen to a sermon which
they have paid a blind man to recite for them. Outside in the courtyard people are seated on the ground eating, drinking tea, and
sharing a sweet, *halva*, which they have made in fulfillment of
vows.

On one Saturday night when I was seated inside the shrine, two
young men entered the building to pay their respects. As they went
straight to the glass case, and encircled it, they were the object of
intense and decidedly unfriendly scrutiny by the assembled women.
The young men soon became uncomfortable, no doubt aware that

they, apart from a blind man and the shrine employee, were the only men present. They left abruptly. I was later told by an old man who works at the shrine that men visit it on Fridays when they are not at work.

Even at those times when men are also present at a shrine, women are not cut off from participation in that which is taking place at the sanctuary. In larger shrines, separate rooms, alcoves, or large areas to one side of the entrance or tomb become women's areas as a result of popular usage. There they can enjoy nearness to the tomb and the company of other women without compromising themselves by coming too close to the men who are also paying their respects to the saint.

There is usually no formal central activity, such as a sermon, from which women can be excluded. Activities at a shrine are more a matter of personal choice than group involvement. Women freely circumambulate the tomb[4] and register their requests with the saints; they may also pray, sit a while with friends, or nap if they choose.

There are many reasons for women to be fond of visiting shrines. The opportunity to get out of the house is not least among them. An older woman, not able to get about as easily as she used to, envied me the time I spent visiting shrines in the city. As she put it, "You see something. You say something." In making local pilgrimages, women are able to escape their household tasks and domestic responsibilities for a time and come into contact with new people and situations. While men have varied experience of people in the course of their workday lives, women come into contact with such variety only on outings, such as shopping, visiting, and pilgrimage. Shopping is an end-oriented activity and one in which men often assume an important role. Too much visiting would compromise a woman's reputation, suggesting that she was not seeing to her duties at home, but visiting shrines is a praiseworthy religious act and one which the men of the house or other women would find hard to oppose.

Still, shrine visiting is not viewed uncritically by all men and women. The relative freedom with which women may visit shrines has led to their being viewed as places of assignation. Shrines may be the sites of innocent flirtations or more questionable encounters.

I was told, although I was unable to verify the report, that at major shrines such as the tomb of the eighth *imām*, Reza, in Masshad or that of his sister Ma'sumeh in Qum, a woman may indicate that she is available by wearing her veil (*chādor*) inside out. Author Ibrahim Golestan has described illicit goings-on at a shrine in his short story, *Sefar-e 'Esmat* (Esmat's Trip). In this story a destitute woman visits a shrine and is approached by a low-level clergyman, who as it turns out is actually a thinly veiled pimp recruiting women. It is sometimes said that the possibility of temporary marriage (*sigheh*) in Shī'ī Islām has been exploited to facilitate this kind of relationship. However, these doubts about pilgrimage tend to surface in jokes and offhand remarks. I never encountered a woman who had been prevented from frequenting a shrine because of suspicions regarding her motives.

Apart from the obvious opportunity to get out of the house, women go to shrines for a number of different types of activities — religious, social, and personal. Regularly scheduled events like Qur'ān-reading classes, prayer sessions, and particular visits are frequently arranged exclusively for women. Women and girls are welcome to take part in others. At these times, women know that programs of religious interest will occur and that a particular shrine will be crowded. The women gathered there are likely to include friends, all contributing to a convivial and supportive atmosphere. The women who visit the shrine share their faith and their sympathy. For example, on one visit to a small underground shrine I met an elderly woman who recounted to each woman at the shrine in turn the story of her son's automobile accident. Her son was at that moment in the hospital. In each instance, the women comforted her and assured her that her son would be fine, giving her the solace and encouragement she so much needed at the time.

Other pilgrimages occur as a woman chooses and not according to any specific schedule. A woman may prefer to avoid busy days and instead go to a shrine at a time when she knows it will be quiet, facilitating private prayer and communion with the saint. The immaterial benefits of pilgrimage were described to me in various ways. One woman told me that she enjoys *ziārat* because it is soothing, another described the experience as "heart-opening," and a third assured me that my heart would be enlightened by taking part in pilgrimage.

Anyone having a problem—emotional, spiritual or material—may take it to a saint in the hope of achieving some solution. The saints are felt to sympathize with men and women whose situations in some way parallel their own in life. Accordingly, women in Shiraz are able to find a sympathetic ear when appealing to female saints. Two shrines in Shiraz specialize in bringing about marriages, and at both the saint in residence was in life an unmarried woman. At another shrine it is said that the pregnant wife of its saint is also entombed there. Not surprisingly, the saint himself is inclined to assist women hoping for an easy childbirth and the birth of a son.

If a woman finds a particular *imāmzādeh* to be helpful, she may continue to seek help at his or her tomb. The relationship established between the woman and the saint may last a lifetime and prove very comforting to her in times of need. She knows that there will always be someone to whom she can appeal.

The relationship individuals have with the *imāmzādehs* is intensely personal, and one of its strengths lies in this quality. On one occasion I was surprised to find a woman shaking the grating around the tomb of Imāmzādeh-ye Ibrāhim, demanding his help. She threatened that if he failed, she would inform his father, the seventh *imām*. I subsequently learned that the pattern of alternately imploring and haranguing is very common and that people often have personal conversations with the saints and address letters to them.

Clearly one attractive element in local pilgrimage is the fact that pilgrims can make requests of the *imāmzādehs*. The way in which the process of asking for and potentially receiving favors proceeds is also important, which as Fatima Mernissi has pointed out, is particularly appealing to women.[5] In making vows at the shrines, women are able to take charge over some aspect of their lives and attempt to bring control into their own hands. A doctor must be paid for his services regardless of success, but a saint is recompensed only in the event that he or she proves to be of help. This is especially important to women who, for one reason or another, be it social, economic, or political, are unable to exert much control in their everyday lives. Even for those strong women who conduct their daily affairs as they wish, there are always discrete events which do not yield to conventional means of redress and on account of which women may seek divine aid. Difficult in-laws, barrenness, the desire for a son, or problems with a husband all may prompt visits to shrines.

The performance of local pilgrimage, then, has much to offer women. On a religious level, it allows them to play a central role in ritual; on a social level, it provides women with an opportunity to visit with one another in an approved setting; and on a personal level, it offers women a place in which to experience contact with divinity and attempt to control their lives in ways meaningful to them as individuals in their own right.

Discussions with men in Shiraz suggested a basic connection between beliefs about women and the character of local pilgrimage. In general, men tended to make disparaging remarks about women's participation in pilgrimage activity. They attributed the amount of time women were able to spend visiting shrines as due to women's leisure, unburdened by men's important tasks. This opinion is related to the general understanding of the nature of women I encountered in Shiraz. On numerous occasions I was told that women are emotional creatures, easily swayed by sentiment and inclined to be irrational. Men were described as serious, likely to reason clearly, immune to emotional concerns. In support of this stereotypical view, I was referred to passages in the Qur'ān concerning women (4:34) and reminded that a woman cannot act as a legal witness (2:282). Two women can serve as one witness, I was told, because two would correct the emotionally colored report provided by only one. I found that women generally accepted this view of their nature, some feeling that the weaknesses were inevitable, others regarding them as tendencies which could be surmounted.

These beliefs are related to views of women's religious behavior. Most men I consulted felt that women place too much emphasis on the social aspects of religious gatherings and are less well educated about Islām in general. Considering the pleasure women derive from the social atmosphere sometimes present at shrines and the fact that they find attendance at the mosque so problematic, these criticisms are not entirely without foundation. However, women's religious activities may be viewed in other, more flattering lights. Women who live opposite the shrine of Seyyed Fakhr al-Din in the south of Shiraz agreed that women make local pilgrimages oftener than men (although men could do it too) but felt that, since women have more time for these activities, they develop more faith by doing them.

A more penetrating explanation of women's involvement in pilgrimage was implied by a young man who worked at a local handicrafts shop. He had made a vow to a popular local saint but had not gone to the saint's tomb at a local shrine to do so. When I questioned further, he first voiced the same scorn as other men had: "Women everywhere devote more time to practices such as *ziārat* than men; women are more idle than men." Then he added a revealing example: If he has a request for a saint, he may send his wife to the shrine to make it for him. She has the time to go, but also "women are without pride." Men have pride and do not like to publicly display weakness or need.

It is in keeping with the view of women as more emotional and less rational than men that women perform *ziārat* to local shrines in behalf of their family members. In doing so they discharge part of their responsibility for the health and well-being of their relatives. This is not to suggest that men are not interested in local pilgrimage or in making vows, just that they express their religiousness in different ways.

The young man's remarks also suggest that much of the behavior that occurs at a shrine, such as expressing deep emotion and stating one's needs and perhaps shortcomings publicly, is not in keeping with notions of manliness. In effect, much of what takes place at a shrine involves a female mode of behavior, regardless of whether the pilgrim is a man or a woman. It is these "female" aspects of the pilgrimage which are often called into question. In the course of a discussion I had with men at a religious bookstore in Shiraz, the man behind the counter recommended a book to me: *Ziārat: Truth or Superstition?* The title indicates the crux of the problem. Men and some women formally educated in religion are ill at ease with the practice, while many other women are devoted to

it. There is no definite proscription of the practice, and some traditions (*hadīths*) support and encourage it. Paying one's respects at a
gravesite is laudable, but the way in which it is done during the performance of local pilgrimage is regarded by many as questionable.

In making pilgrimage to local shrines, men and women have the
opportunity to argue with their "betters" and, within limits, to
challenge the given order of things. They are also able to express
their feelings in ways that are otherwise inappropriate. In so doing
they are able to shape their ritual practice to their own require-
ments.

The pattern of challenge, harangue, expression of deep emotion,
and voluntarism in ritual is foreign to the mosque. The opposition
between the shrine and mosque is described by Brian Spooner in
connection with his descriptions of the religion of the shrine and the
official religion, which "contains rules of ritual prayers, fasting,
celebration, mourning and general conduct, which concern the will
rather than the heart."[6] He identifies the first of these two strains of
religion in Iran as unconscious, while the official religion is the
conscious religion.[7] I suggest that this opposition is at base a
description of the difference between female and male modes
elaborated in a religious context.

It is not surprising that funeral observances in which women are
involved are more likely to take place within the home or in a shrine
than in a mosque. It is not a time for dry observance of the passing
of a fellow human being and loved one but a time to rage and
lament, in so doing accentuating the sense of one's own life, and this
is inappropriate in the formal setting of a mosque.

The way in which shrine space is used at a funeral reflects differences in the styles of interaction between men and women, patterns
reflected in overall religious behavior. Men's style tends to be
restrained and formal. They sit on folding chairs in the shrine courtyard, facing the officiating priest. They look down, their hands held
over their eyes. At times they sob quietly or perhaps engage in
muted conversation with the men seated in adjacent chairs. Tea is
placed on small tables between the folding chairs. The atmosphere is
highly formal and subdued; and spaces are clearly defined in keeping with the nature of official religion as Spooner describes it.

In contrast, women in a shrine funeral sit on the floor inside the wall and perhaps around the central tomb. At one end of the room, backs against the wall, sit the grieving women of the deceased's family. Women attending the funeral first approach them, pay their respects and extend condolences, perhaps sitting with the bereaved women for a time and weeping with them. Then the women move back as others come to take their place in the "receiving line." As the guests move outward through the rows of seated women, the tone of the gathering becomes less somber until, in the outer circles, women are busily gossiping, catching up on the news of those more distant relatives and friends whom they see only on such formal occasions. All the while the seated women enjoy the tea and ice cream or sherbet that is served to the guests. The intimacy which prevails at women's gatherings is both physical, enforced by the pressure of bodies against one another as women plop down on the crowded floor, and social, as women exchange information and embraces and discuss their personal problems, aches, and pains. Just as the men's behavior suits the character of the "official religion," so do women behave in a way more consonant with the "religion of the shrine."

The fact that women are associated with local pilgrimage in Iran is neither accidental nor incidental. Men are associated with the mosque, religious texts, reasoned theological discussions, formal ritual assemblies—in short, with intellectual aspects of religion. Women's association with local pilgrimage points out that it is bound up with things of the heart, the troubling aspect of life which questions, unsettles, and answers obliquely. Women in Muslim Iran are regarded as frivolous, emotional, irrational, and at times dangerous; the things with which they are associated are consequently dismissed as either inconsequential or at times downright suspect. Even women's dreams are described in Persian as *chap* (unreliable, off the mark), literally, "left."[8]

Women are ritually polluted with the messy business of menstruation and childbirth, but these polluting elements are paradoxically life-giving. Similarly, local pilgrimage is disorderly and informal, but what goes on at the local shrines energizes religion. *Ziārat* gives scope to the personal and difficult aspects of life and allows both men and especially women to express their emotional sides—to grieve and wail in an approved setting and to celebrate joyously with others.

NOTES

1. The information on which this paper is based was gathered during four years in Shiraz, two years of full-time research and two subsequent years of residence in the city, from early 1975 into January of 1979.

2. For further information on Shi'í Islām see Seyyed Muhammad Hussein Tabataba'i, *Shi'ite Islam* (Albany: State University of New York Press, 1975).

3. See Mary-Jo Del Vecchio Good, "A Comparative Perspective on Women in Provincial Iran and Turkey," In L. Beck and N. Keddie, eds. *Women in the Muslim World* (Cambridge: Harvard University Press, 1978), pp. 482-500.

4. I was advised that, to avoid pressing against men performing the same action, women should hold back and not circumambulate the tomb when a shrine is crowded. In this instance, as so many others, ideal prescriptions and actual behavior often differ markedly.

5. Fatima Mernissi, "Women, Saints and Sanctuaries," *Signs*, 3 (Autumn 1977): 104.

6. Brian J. Spooner, "The Function of Religion in Persian Society," *Iran* 1 (1963): 93. See also his later article, "Religion and Society Today: An Anthropological Perspective," in E. Yar-Shater, ed. *Iran Faces the Seventies* (New York: Praeger, 1979), pp. 166-88.

7. Ibid, p. 94.

8. For further information on the negative meaning attached to the left in Islām, see J. M. Chelhod, "Pre-eminence of the Right, Based upon Arabic Evidence," in Rodney Needham, ed. *Right & Left: Essays on Dual Symbolic Classification* (Chicago: University of Chicago Press, 1973), pp. 239-62.

14
Moroccan Women's Integration of Family and Religion

Donna Lee Bowen

My view of Muslim women came as I sat with them, talked with them, and shared their generous hospitality and happy humor in the Middle East and North Africa. Specifically I have drawn my material from Morocco. I seek to make two points: First, that although the Muslim family system is somewhat different from that

Donna Lee Bowen is assistant professor in the Department of Government at Brigham Young University. A graduate of the University of Utah with a B.A. in political science, she received her M.A. and Ph.D. in Near Eastern languages and civilizations from the University of Chicago. Professor Bowen has conducted research in Morocco, Tunisia, Iran, and Egypt under the auspices of the Ford Foundation, a Fulbright-Hays Fellowship, Bourguiba Institute of Modern Languages, and NDFL Title VI Language Fellowships. Her research and publications have concentrated on aspects of women and family planning in Middle Eastern countries.

to which we are accustomed in the West, it is nevertheless a coherent system. Moreover, women work, are cared for, and are valued as an integral part of that system. Although the system may be discriminatory in parts, as all systems generally are, as a whole all pieces fit well together. Second, within the Muslim context, for most women the family is their working ground for the application of their religion. Therefore, what is beneficial for the family is of necessity good for Islām because Islām safeguards the welfare of the family and of its members. Women perceive their role in society as being ordained by Islām; they work within a Muslim context. Specifically they will define that which is Islamic as an action that benefits their relationship. An action which is not Islamic or opposed to Islām is an action that would harm their family.

It is important to realize that Islām is not simply a religion of prayer, but rather is a way of life wherein every aspect of life is part of worship. Islām applies to every action, to areas of faith, that which is unseen, and to action, that which is seen. Thus the way one prays or calls to God is Islām; also the manner in which one washes before prayer is Islām. Fasting for *Ramadān*, tithing for the welfare of the poor, making contracts in business, dividing booty after war, marriage, raising a family—all are done in accordance with Islām.

Marriage is the basic contract organizing interpersonal relationships, and the family which results from the contract is the basic unit of the community. The Islamic community is constituted to safeguard the welfare of the family and of the society which arises from the association of numerous families. Each part of the family has an outlined role. The father is to provide sustenance for the family; the mother is to bear, raise, and educate the children. The children are to be obedient to their parents and to care for them in their old age. Each part of the family fits together as in a mosaic, and each familial role is equally important in the community.

A contrast to this is found in Western theory. Elizabeth Cady Stanton, a thoughtful American feminist writing in the nineteenth century, took up the interests of women as separate from family interests. She examined marriage and family to determine why women in the United States were inherently unequal, why they did not have the right to vote, why they were not allowed to take their place in society beside men. She determined that the basic problem was that of the marriage relationship.

> We are in the midst of a social revolution to determine whether man and woman are equal ... or whether they were eternally ordained, one to be sovereign, the other slave .... John Stuart Mill says the generality of the male sex cannot yet tolerate the idea of living with an equal at the fireside; and here is the secret of the opposition to woman's equality in the state and the church—men are not ready to recognize it in the home.[1]

She also felt that organized religion was a prime instigator of the concept of man's "headship," and she worked to lessen the influence religion has on women. Close to the end of her life, in a speech entitled "The Solitude of the Self," she emphasized the need for female individualism and self-reliance, the culmination of all her thought over a long period of concern with feminist issues:

> The strongest reason for giving woman all the opportunities for higher education, for the full development of her faculties, her forces of mind and body ... is the solitude and personal responsibility of her own individual life. The strongest reason why we ask for woman a voice in the government under which she lives; in the religion she is asked to believe; equality in social life, where she is the chief factor; a place in the trades and professions, where she may earn her bread, is because of her birthright to self-sovereignty; because, as an individual she must rely upon herself, no matter how much women prefer to lean, to be protected and supported, nor how much men desire to have them do so. They must make the voyage of life alone. ... Seeing, then, that life must ever be a march and a battle, that each soldier must be equipped for his own protection, it is the height of cruelty to rob the individual of a single natural right.[2]

While many Muslim women would not argue with Mrs. Stanton's analysis, particularly with the fact that women are equal to men in the spheres outlined, they would phrase their own social and personal imperatives differently. Women need to be well-trained, educated, self-reliant, and able to take up places in public spheres as well as family spheres. However, women and family members share a relationship of mutual reciprocity whereby all share in a common cause, the well-being of their family. Thus, a family member sacrifices in one area to help someone else succeed in another. In fact, a common contemporary fear is that the Western

processes of industrialization, secularization, and unrestrained
capitalism assailing the Orient might corrupt their family life. They
feel no desire for the Western family life as they see it.

In Islamic countries, Stanton's phrase, "to make the voyage of
life alone," is not only unheard of but actually difficult to think of in
a Muslim system. Being Muslim, you are part of a community of
believers; and it is the purpose of the community, as set forth in the
Qur'ān, to make sure that every member of the community is
provided for. Whether someone is old or young, male or female, he
or she has a place within the system. To live separate from it is
unimaginable.

In the West, we view certain practices of Islām in regard to
women as discriminatory. For example, throughout the complicated
and detailed laws on inheritance, wives and daughters are consistently allocated less than husbands and brothers. If a woman dies
leaving children, the husband is entitled to one-fourth of her net
estate. (A woman in Islām has the total right to her property to be
held separately from the property of her husband.) If there are no
children, the husband obtains one-half of the net estate. On the
other hand, if the husband dies, the wife inherits one-eighth of the
estate and one-fourth if there are no children. In the case of plural
wives, they share one-eighth or one-fourth equally. If the parents
die, sisters generally receive half as much as brothers.[3]

In the West, this would be a clear case of discrimination. However, in Muslim countries the larger context of Islamic law is
designed to protect the woman's welfare. It guarantees a larger
share to her children or brothers, assuming that the sons or the
woman's family will continue to care for her. Thus within the
context of the family relationship, the woman will be well taken
care of. For example, to a Middle Easterner, the concept of a rest
home or retirement community is literally foreign. Putting one's
mother, grandmother, grandfather, or old uncle or aunt into an
institution far from the heart of the family is unheard of. It would
be punishment, a cruelty, to so repay the years spent raising the
younger generation.

Many parts of Islamic law are discriminatory. But when
examined within its total social context, or within the historical
context of legal development and social imperatives, much that
seemed inexplicable is explained. The system when followed

correctly ensures the welfare of both women and men by a series of elaborate checks, balances, and compromises. To pull pieces out of the system and examine them out of their context is both inaccurate and unfair.

Family law is a major concern of the larger body of Islamic law. Just as the method and times of prayer are discussed, marriage, divorce, and inheritance laws are all set out in the Islamic legal system comprised of the Qur'ān, *hadīth* literature, and the *fiqh* (jurisprudence) works. In the modern Middle East, personal status law or family law is the only *sharīʿa* (Islamic) law still in force, since adoption of Western codes and modifications has superseded other areas of traditional Islamic law. Family concerns are clearly discussed in legal theory. Accordingly, family matters are a legitimate area for theological and legal attention.

For women this point is especially pertinent. As the husband, children, and extended family constitute the major part of a woman's life, the welfare of her family constitutes a major expression of religion for her in everyday life. This point became clear as I researched a project on health and family size in the south of Morocco. I worked with three other researchers in two villages in Tafilalet, located in an oasis river valley far from the urban centers of Morocco. Our purpose was to check the validity of demographic data gathered earlier and also to develop some attitudinal information on the questions of health, the use of health services, and family size.[4] My personal interest was in the area of family planning. I had come to Morocco to study attitudes toward family and religion and had found that the best way to learn about any concept was to examine a force that attacked it. I had interviewed professors, lay religious men, and religious scholars. I saw this research project as a chance to determine how village women felt about the same ideas. So I went into the village prepared to ask women about their families, about the children, and whether or not Islām would permit family planning for them.

We were received very hospitably in the two villages. In the first place, we arrived between two weddings and were the only event of major interest in the village that week. In the second, our questions proved so fascinating that the village women followed us from house to house to help their friends answer questions and discuss the infinitely fascinating topics of children, health, and religion.

One of the first questions after we ascertained the woman's name and number of children was her age. Time is often relative in the Middle East, and the village women's ages proved to be relative as well. Most women would first giggle and indicate that that was an odd question of little import. Often the woman questioned would look at one of the observers and ask, "What did you tell her that you were?" The other would answer, "I told her that I was thirty-four." "Oh, well," the first would say, "if you're thirty-four, then I'm thirty-two." A third would then interject, "Oh, no, you're not. You're thirty-six, because you played with my sister, who is older than I am." They would remind each other of forgotten miscarriages, ascertain children's ages, and sometimes give us information on divorces and remarriages that the woman was too shy to give us. Soon the village information system opened wide and they told us anything that entered their minds as well as what we wanted to know.

After the questions on children, family size and occupation, health conditions, and usage of the local public health services, I would ask my questions about family planning. Some women understood the term *family planning*; others had never heard about it. Most felt that it was theoretically a good concept, apt to be useful someday although they doubted they'd ever use it. Others, a small percentage, were currently taking birth control pills. Some others had used contraceptive measures in the past.

My final question was whether their religion permitted use of family planning. The answers I received were so diverse that it took me two years to systematize the women's answers. Some women would answer, "Absolutely not. Islām has nothing to do with family planning. It is a threat to the family; it harms the family." Other women would say, "If you'll tell me what bus to take to the dispensary, I'll go there tomorrow for some birth control pills. It is the best idea I've heard of. It means that I can recover from my last pregnancy without fear of becoming pregnant again, that I can recover some of my health." For some people it meant hope; for others disaster. Some answered it in personal terms, others in religious.

I returned to the capital city, Rabat, and pored over the data. Finally I realized that the women who were against family planning and saw it as un-Islamic were women to whom any reduction of family size or the inability to have children threatened their position as wife and mother.

For example, one of the women that I interviewed was the wife of the religious leader of the village. Lalla Amira was a beautiful, healthy, vibrant woman thirty-four years old. She looked years younger and immeasurably healthier than her neighbors. She had been unable to have children. Although barrenness is accepted grounds for divorce, her husband had instead opened negotiations to take a younger wife. Evidently he was very close to Lalla Amira, because he was educating her himself. When asked about the religious permissibility of family planning, Lalla Amira answered that it was totally un-Islamic, that it is forbidden to take medicine not to give birth. Her husband, when interviewed, held that contraception was forbidden by the prophet Muhammad in the Qur'ān; Muslims must have many children.

Lalla Amira accompanied me to her neighbor, Hajja. Although slightly older than Lalla Amira, Hajja was small, thin, and sallow. Her six living children ranged in age from a twenty-year-old son to a two-year-old. Two children had died in infancy and she had miscarried once. She showed interest as I explained the concept of family planning, and told me that she had been quite ill—hospitalized once for twenty days and again for two months. She felt her health was a major concern and that childbearing was out of the question at this point, although she wouldn't mind having one more son. When I asked about the religious question she replied that if she were still strong it would be wrong to use contraceptives, but since she was weak, family planning was religiously justified.

Lalla Amira turned to Hajja and burst out, "Women should keep on having children as long as they are young enough, even if they are weak." Hajja remonstrated, saying that if health doesn't permit one to have more children, then using contraceptives shouldn't be forbidden. Lalla Amira paused confused, then retreated: "If the woman is weak, then she shouldn't have to bear more children, but if she is strong, then she should."

Neither woman hesitated to assert her understanding as to the Islamic position on family planning. Lalla Amira took a more conservative approach, due more to her childless state than to her

husband's answer. Almost all husbands gave the same answer, regardless of their wife's practice or opinion. Still she recognized the
validity of Hajja's position and finally agreed that a woman's
physical condition provided an Islamically valid reason for avoiding
childbirth.

Lalla Amira had no children; thus any limitation of what would
validate her existence as a woman and secure her position as a wife
was un-Islamic. For her, preventing birth was preventing a family
and endangering her role in the family and was therefore un-
Islamic.

For Hajja the question was entirely different. In order to preserve her health and life, to give her sufficient strength to nurture
her younger children, and to enable her to carry out the daily
housework, it was mandatory that she be healthy. For her it was
not then healthy to be pregnant. Pregnancies in these villages were
generally debilitating. Inadequate nutrition, rest, and medical care
all took a heavy toll on health. Lalla Amira's health was a startling
contrast to the other women her age. Frequently, for the woman
who had completed a good-sized family or who had health problems, another pregnancy was more dangerous to her ability to function as a capable wife and mother than use of contraceptives. In this
case, family planning was Islamically permissible because it helped
to preserve the family and the home.

In short, that which helped the family was considered Islamic;
that which harmed it was not. The women saw their lives and the
welfare of their families as a totality, with no separation of
husband's interests, children's interests, and their interests. Likewise, there was no separation of the religious and the secular.
Family planning as introduced to them was seen as being ambig-
uous—perhaps helpful. Its interpretation depended on what the
women needed. Contradictory practices were actually governed by
the same principle.

My comments generally describe the system as it should be, but
Islām includes an extensive backing system. Interrupting this type of
social organization is risky, just as judging certain practices out of
context is unfair. Interrupting traditional action can spell disaster if
one of the balances or checks is eliminated, leaving the individual
unprotected. Any system can be problematic. The point here is that

Muslim society is a total system, caring for individuals totally, but within its own context.

NOTES

1. Ellen Carol DuBois, ed., *Elizabeth Cady Stanton, Susan B. Anthony: Correspondence, Writings, Speeches* (New York: Schocken Books, 1981), pp. 131-32.

2. Ibid., pp. 247-48.

3. For a fuller discussion, see Asaf A. A. Fyzee, *Outlines of Muhammadan Law*, 4th ed. (London: Oxford University Press, 1974), pp. 405 ff.

4. My colleagues for this research were Sam and Wanda Notzon of the Centre Pour Les Etudes et Researche Economique Demographique, Bureau of Statistics, Rabat, Morocco, and Ellaia Mohammed, a graduate student in sociology. Two papers on the research have been presented: "Attitudes toward Family and Family Planning, in Pre-Saharan Morocco," Middle East Studies Association, New York, 1977; "Relation of Religions and Legal Attitudes toward Perception of Family Planning: A Moroccan Case Study," International Sociological Association, Uppsala, Sweden, 1978. A slightly different version of the research will be forthcoming in *The Maghreh Review*, London.

15
Another Islām:
Contemporary Indonesia

Frederick M. Denny

As Minister Almsjah has described Indonesia's vital new interpretation of Islām in our own century, I think it is equally impressive to recall that the tradition of making a vigorous hybrid of
Islām's religious principles and adaptation to local custom is an old
Indonesian tradition that goes back perhaps six centuries. There is a

Frederick M. Denny, associate professor and chairman of religious studies at the
University of Colorado in Boulder, is a graduate of the College of William and
Mary in philosophy. He received his B.D. at the Andover Newton Theological
School, his M.A. in the history of religions at the University of Chicago, and his
Ph.D. in Islamic studies and history of religions at the same university. Professor
Denny's research and publications have focused on interpretations of the Qur'ān.
This essay was extracted from a longer slide presentation on the role of women in
contemporary Indonesia.

great deal we can learn here about the interface of religion and culture.

Indonesia extends over a major part of the largest archipelago in the world, composed of approximately 13,700 islands—some of them very small—of which an estimated 6,000 are inhabited. The main islands are Java, Bali, Sumatra, Borneo (Kalimantan), Sulawesi (Celebes), and Irian Barat (West New Guinea). From east to west it occupies approximately the same range of latitude as the distance from Bermuda to San Francisco, and the population is currently estimated at something over 149 million.

Java and Bali comprise only 7.2 percent of the land area but contain 64.9 percent of the population. Java alone, approximately the size of North Carolina, contains more than eighty-five million people. Its economy is a continuation of a pattern centuries old that is based on its astoundingly productive peasant agriculture. It is also one of the older civilizations of Asia and, as Clifford Geertz pointed out in his *Islam Observed*, if anything, Java is an "overcivilized" part of the world.[1]

The modern republic of Indonesia, created after World War II, comprises about three hundred different ethnic groups speaking some 365 languages and dialects, of which some 250 are mutually unintelligible. A major development of nationalism was the creation of Bahasa Indonesian, a national language, developed from the Malay tongue.

The strong Islamic influence on Indonesian culture is comparatively recent, beginning perhaps in the fourteenth century and increasing in the fifteenth, sixteenth, and seventeenth centuries. However, the Hindu and Buddhist strains also add strong cultural elements and constitute significant minorities along with the Christians, among the approximately 90 percent of Indonesia that is Muslim. Java, for example, is characterized by the older aristocratic elites who are Muslim but who also pride themselves on being Javanese and do not completely repudiate the animism and mysticism of their Hindu-Buddhist past.

One of the most significant educational, social, and economic movements in Indonesia was the Muhammadiyah movement, founded early in the twentieth century as a development of the thinking of the modernist Muhammad Abdu of Cairo, and dedicated to religious reform and rethinking of Islamic principles. This movement has provided Indonesia with a sternly Islamic yet energetically progressive impetus toward improved education, health care, social work, and guild organizations. It is headquartered in Jogjakarta.

The National Islamic University — or college-level school system — has fourteen campuses in Indonesia and is a combination of coeducational colleges and theological seminaries. It focuses on Islamic subjects along with the more traditional modern curriculum. Students at these schools typically wear their regional costume rather than the more revealing Western dress for women, a subtle way of announcing simultaneously their Muslim and their national commitments.

Indonesia also has a system of institutes for children and youth of up to about eighteen years of age, where they learn to chant the Qur'ān but also learn exegesis and interpretation. In some cases they are coeducational. National contests in chanting the Qur'ān are also coeducational. Women are also included in classes for advanced study of the Qur'ān and will become regional teachers in other coeducational schools in chanting, recitation styles, and exegesis.

The west central region of Sumatra, a ruggedly mountainous island forming the western boundary of Indonesia, contains one of the world's most successful matrilineal and matrilocal societies, meaning that descent is traced through the mother and that the husband moves to the home of the wife. Assertive, proud, and strong, women are largely engaged in agriculture. Men spend a great deal of time traveling and, interestingly enough, operating restaurants which are renowned for their fiery *padang* cuisine.

In a typical traditional home, a long room in front is somewhat public. Guests are entertained and may even sleep there. The married women have separate rooms in the back of the house where husbands visit them at night. The sons of the household sleep in the mosque or bachelor's house from the age of seven or eight until they are married.

This matrilineal society seems at odds, in many ways, with traditional images of sequestered Arab women and a male-dominated culture. It's important, I think, to have these Sumatran images as a corrective, to remind us that Islām is a marvelously flexible religion that can accommodate a surprising range of local customs without jeopardizing the religious center of its doctrines.

NOTES

1. Clifford Geertz, *Islam Observed: Religious Development in Morocco and Indonesia* (New Haven: Yale University Press, 1960).

16
The Perceptible and the Unseen: The Qur'anic Conception of Man's Relationship to God and Realities Beyond Human Perception

Umar F. Abd-Allāh

Even in the modern age, in which the instruments of technology have magnified the powers of the human mind to a degree never before imagined, the modest radius of human perception and its inherent limitations remain primary epistemological facts of the human condition. Our perception of the present moment consti-

Umar F. Abd-Allāh, chairman of Islamic Studies at the University of Michigan, is a graduate of the University of Missouri in history and English. He received one Ph.D. in English literature from Cornell and another in Arabic and Islamic studies from the University of Chicago. Professor Abd-Allāh's interests include the language of the Qur'ān, comparative religion, and the origins of Islamic legal theory. He has traveled extensively in the Middle East and North Africa.

tutes only a small portion of the reality that envelops us; we stare myopically into the past and can only vaguely anticipate the future. The imperfection of human perception—the fact that the knowledge of man, however much he knows, is forever dwarfed by the vast domain of that which he does not and even cannot know—is one of the first foundations of religious speculation. That dimension which lies beyond the threshold of human perception—the world of God and supernatural beings, the infinite circumstances and particulars of the past, present, and future—is a natural focus of religious teaching. Although their answers sometimes differ, each religion addresses the reality of the unseen in human consciousness. What exists in that world? How can man acquire knowledge of it? What bearing does it have on his suffering and well-being in the material world? How is man's destiny and meaning of life connected to it?

Such questions were not asked only in another age, although for many today—given comforts of advanced technology and relative self-assurance that the material conditions and natural forces of our world are under adequate control—they may not have the urgency which they once had. Moreover, modern man, by virtue of his remarkable success in manipulating the material environment, is predisposed to look in the material world and not the dimension of the unseen for solutions to those problems which pertain directly to his material well-being or suffering. Furthermore, since the time of Kant, philosophical speculation in the West has gravitated from the metaphysical toward the more empirical and fundamentally epistemological dimensions of human consciousness. But for many, the realm of the unseen still holds the answer to fundamental philosophical questions about the nature and destiny of man and the world he lives in. Intermediaries between man and the unseen, those who claim to speak authoritatively about the world, remain an important part of human society. Somewhat peripheral figures today, in the past—especially in the pre-industrial societies of the medieval and ancient worlds—such intermediaries and their representatives (shamans, diviners, oracular speakers, prophets or their spokesmen) appear universally to have played a more central and conspicuous role in their societies and cultures.

Islām draws a conscious dichotomy between that dimension of reality which lies within the purview of man's perception and his five senses and that dimension which lies beyond. It calls the first of these the realm of the perceptible or of the visible (*ᶜālam ash-shahāda*) and calls the second of them the realm of the unseen (*ᶜālam al-ghaib*). To believe in the unseen, according to the Qur'ān, constitutes the first and most essential requirement of those who would seek guidance; such belief requires, in turn, acceptance of the three fundamentals: the absolute oneness of God (*at-tawhīd*), the institution of prophecy (*ar-risāla; an-nabūwa*), and the coming of the hereafter or return (*al-maᶜād*). But to believe in the unseen is not to know the unseen or even to desire knowledge of it beyond these fundamentals and the subsidiary beliefs connected to them. God alone, in the view of Islām, is the knower of the unseen and the visible, this being one of the unique attributes of Godhood (*ulūhīya*) and the Lordship (*rubūbīya*) which he shares with no created being. Man has the means to know and understand the perceptible, and the Qur'ān clearly directs him to make it the object of his speculation and investigation. But he has no means of delving into the unseen and knowing anything about it other than conjecture except through the vehicle of prophecy. Only by means of prophetic revelation, according to the Qur'ān, can man acquire that definitive knowledge (*ᶜilm*) of the important essentials of the unseen as they relate to his being which must be the foundation of his religious life. Like the religion of the biblical prophets, Islām declared other means of intermediation between man and the unseen to be illegitimate and invalid. It abolished the offices of the pre-Islamic shamans, oracular speakers, and diviners. Moreover, Islām emphasized in this process an approach to and a preoccupation with the unseen radically different from those of the pre-Islamic shamans and diviners. Their fundamental concern and that of the people who relied upon them had been with whatever good or evil the unseen held in store for particular persons or their tribes and clans in this world. Islām categorically rejected this emphasis and directed attention to those aspects of the unseen that emphasize God's omniscience and the ultimacy of the last judgment—in other words, to matters which have direct bearing on the spiritual and moral edification of man in this world and which focus his energies on positive action to fulfill the moral imperatives of the Islamic world view.

But in the Qur'anic view, although the realm of the unseen lies beyond the powers of perception of the human mind and cannot be known except through the medium of prophecy, the realm of the unseen does not constitute a single continuum which extends through the realms of the visible and the unseen together; the two worlds are not antithetical or diametrically opposed. Indeed, they constitute two different worlds only from the standpoint of human perception. From the standpoint of God the entire spectrum of reality, in the Qur'anic view, lies within the realm of the perceived and known. Moreover, because of the utter compatibility between the realm of the perceptible and the realm of the unseen, man's short existence within the realm of the perceptible should remain continually alive to the reality of God and those essential elements of the unseen which touch man's moral and spiritual life.

According to the Qur'ān, God created man with an instinctively believing nature (*fitra*), which has inherent knowledge of God and is oriented toward Him. Furthermore, the world of the perceptible which surrounds man is filled with the signs (*āyāt*) of God, which continually remind man of God's presence and his concern with the creation. Such signs of God are no longer to be viewed as omens or to be interpreted for purposes of divination. Rather, in the Qur'anic view, they are man's bridge of certainty linking him with the greater realities of the unseen—the oneness of God, the resurrection, and the last judgment—which have been taught by the prophets. In the Qur'anic view, the key to human dignity is man's ability to believe in God from the context of the perceptible world and without the ability to witness the unseen. Those who can live within the realm of the perceptible and yet believe in the greater realities of the unseen on the basis of the prophetic reports, confirmed by the implicit guidance of the *āyāt* of God in the world and the instinctive knowledge and spiritual aptitude of the *fitra* of the human soul, are those who, in the Qur'anic idiom, have eyes with which to see, ears with which to hear, and tongues with which to speak. Those who destroy this aptitude and who make the realm of the perceptible a barrier between them and the greater realities of the unseen are, in the Qur'anic view, blind, deaf, and dumb; more reprehensible than the beasts of the earth. They are the dead, while believers alone are the living.

PRE-ISLAMIC PARALLELS

Divine Intermediaries in the
Ancient Civilizations of Western Asia

Both the role of intermediaries—shamans, oracular speakers, and diviners—in the religious and cultural life of pre-Islamic Arabia and the prophecy of Muhammad in that context are to a remarkable extent similar to models in other parts of Western Asia in the ancient world. Clearly a strong element of continuity links religious practices of the pre-Islamic Arabs and those of the ancient Near East, just as fundamental parallels appear between Zarathustra, the biblical prophets, and Muhammad. Non-Muslims are frequently inclined to interpret such similarities as evidence of direct or indirect borrowing, of similar cultural legacies and backgrounds, or, occasionally, certain universally shared psychological and spiritual traits. Muslims, on the other hand, are inclined to interpret such parallels as evidence of the integrity of the Qur'anic claim that the prophetic message of Muhammad came as a confirmation and fulfillment of the original messages of the earlier prophets. One of the great prophetic and scriptural religions of the world, Islām regards itself as the primordial archetype of a universal monotheism which God revealed to the earth through numerous prophet-messengers (*rusul; mursalūn*) and prophets (*anbiyā'; nabīyūn*), both biblical and nonbiblical, Qur'anic and non-Qur'anic, whom he sent at different times to different places. The prophecy of Muhammad, who, according to Islamic belief, was the last of the prophets and prophet-messengers of God, marks only the end of the prophetic age and the culmination of revealed religion. Muhammad's teachings, according to the Qur'ān, confirmed and fulfilled the revelations of the prophets before him. His teachings were not new but old, the restoration of original prophetic teachings as old as man himself which had been lost, then renewed, then lost or rendered obscure again because of the disobedience and deviations of religious communities entrusted at various times with preserving the prophetic message. Islām (literally "peace through submission to the One God") was in its Arabian context the religion of Abraham restored, who himself, according to the Qur'ān, had with his son Ismāᶜīl (Ishmael) restored monotheism among the Arabs in his own time; and Islām, the religion of Abraham, was in direct continuity with the messages of Noah, Moses, Jesus, and the other major and minor prophets of history.[1]

The complex and varied religious practices of ancient Mesopotamia reflect a fundamental preoccupation with that aspect of the unseen which has direct bearing upon man's mortal well-being or suffering. Ancient Mesopotamian religion's interest in the unseen was pragmatic—chiefly concerned with discerning the future and predicting the probable success or failure of human undertakings. The gods and spirits of the ancient Mesopotamian world were seen as merciful to the extent that they would communicate the propitiousness of human undertakings through omens, warning signs, or, rarely, by speaking directly through oracles. If a particular undertaking seemed inauspicious, it could still be successfully undertaken by using ritual and cultic means for assuaging unfavorable gods and spirits.[2]

The oracular speakers, although a noteworthy part of the religious life of ancient Mesopotamia, were less important than the diviners, who throughout ancient Mesopotamian religious history stand at the center of upper-class social life and affairs of state. Less expensive divining techniques appear also to have been a fundamental part of the day-to-day life of the general people. The diviners were the "scientists" of the ancient Mesopotamian world, and the application of their art at the more sophisticated levels required extensive apprenticeship and study, close observation and recording of the natural world, the ability to read and research the studies and observations of the past, and the training to make inductive conclusions about the import of ominous phenomena. Analysis of the livers of sacrificial animals was probably one of the oldest techniques of Mesopotamian divining, but others included examining other entrails of sacrificed animals, observing astrological movements, augury (divination through the movements of birds), interpreting dreams, interpreting extraordinary events and occurrences, and so forth.[3] Oracular speakers—who in ecstatic states would speak directly in the names of particular gods or spirits—never appear to have received the social approval or encouragement of ancient Mesopotamian diviners. Records of events that include oracles have been found in the Old Babylonian city of Mari in the west of ancient Mesopotamia but simply confirm their apparently peripheral role. Their position appears to have been enhanced considerably in the later neo-Assyrian and Akkadian periods, but even here they remained secondary to the court diviners.[4]

Divination was also an important part of the religious life of ancient Egypt, although the ancient Egyptians did not develop such elaborate rituals. There is also evidence of oracular speakers in ancient Egypt, although oracular literature in Egypt constitutes a relatively rare genre. Moreover, much of the surviving oracular literature of ancient Egypt prophesies about the future without relying upon any intermediary but rather reflects the wisdom and acumen of the writer.[5] In ancient Syria and Palestine, the lands of the Fertile Crescent immediately west of Mesopotamia, both diviners and oracular speakers were apparently central to the religious and cultural life, although most of the evidence for the existence of such figures is biblical.[6] In contrast to ancient Mesopotamian and ancient Egyptian conventions, the oracular mode of intermediation was probably most prominent among the Amorites, the Western Semites, and their neighbors within Syria and Palestine, although techniques of divination coexisted alongside those of direct intermediation. The book of Deuteronomy (18:10-11) prohibits both types as "abominations" (*to⁽abōt*), rebukes "one who makes his son or his daughter pass through the fire" (presumably a reference to child sacrifice or a cultic practice of eliciting oracles from the deified dead), and bans the diviner (*qōsēm qēsamim*), the soothsayer (*me⁽onēn*), the augur (*menahēsh*), the sorcerer (*mekashshēp*), the charmer (*hōbēr hāber*), those who inquire of ghosts (*sho⁽el 'ob*), the wizard (*yidde⁽oni*), and those who seek oracles from the dead (*dōrēsh 'el-hamētim*).

Much of the history and teachings of the ancient Iranian prophetic figure Zarathustra may always remain in obscurity, but it is clear from what can be discerned about him that there are remarkable parallels between his life and teachings and those of the biblical prophets and the prophet Muhammad after them. Messenger of Ahura Mazdā (the wise lord), the supreme deity of Zoroastrianism, Zarathustra—who probably lived in Eastern Iran toward the end of the second or the beginning of the first millennium B.C.E.—preached a monotheism which militated against the paganism of pre-Zoroastrian Iran: a religious universe teeming with aggressive deities, the warlike ethics of its warrior bands, and cultic practices centered around sacrifice and priestly ritual. Zarathustra's message was emphatically antiritualistic and antisacrificial, emphasizing an inner religiousness of "good thoughts, good words, good deeds." It brought him—like the biblical prophets and the prophet Muhammad—into sharp conflict with the polytheistic religious hierarchy of his society. He condemned the religious beliefs and practices of his contemporaries as the fruit of ignorance and illusion and denounced their gods (the *daēvas*) as false. Zarathustra sought to end the intermediation and the ecstatic practices of the *kavis*, *karapans*, and *usijs*—priests, religious figures, and wise men of the old order—and their enmity toward him constituted his major source of opposition, resulting ultimately in his assassination, as an old man, by a *karapan* priest of the former religious hierarchy.[7]

The Hebrew tradition of Mosaic prophets shows unequivocal antagonism toward pagan techniques of intermediation. Such opposition between the prophetic and pagan modes of intermediation is epitomized in the biblical accounts of the monarchical prophets Elijah and Elisha in their struggle to destroy the cult of Baal with its oracular speakers, who held great power over the kings and large numbers of the people of Israel.[8] However, biblical accounts of the early prophets of Israel describe them as exhibiting ecstatic traits, and their record contains examples of clairvoyance, foreseeing and foretelling, wonder-working, and magical actions, although such traits are not common among the major prophets in the biblical tradition. The terms *hōzeh* and *rō'eh* (seer), which are occasionally used about the early prophets, suggest that they prophesied events to come in a manner analogous, in the view of some scholars, to that of the pagan diviners and oracular speakers. Use of the Greek *prophētēs* to translate the Hebrew *nābi'* (prophet) also seems to have contributed to such a conception of the early prophets, although other scholars argue that the Greek *prophētēs* served other functions in addition to foretelling the future and that the original sense of the word was probably more "forth-teller" (proclaimer) than "foreteller."[9]

The etymology of the Hebrew word *nābi'* has not been established. Some believe that it was borrowed from another ancient Semitic language; it appears, however, that the original sense of the word was "one who calls" or "one who is called."[10] The paradigm of prophecy in the Islamic religion is essentially the same as that of the Mosaic prophets of the biblical tradition. In both, the office of prophecy began with a call—often in the form of a vision—and was not an instinctive aptitude or disposition of one's personality, as appears generally to be the case with oracular speakers. The prophet received his message from God, occasionally through the intermediation of an angel (*mal'ak*). The prophets played a central role in the religious and cultural life of ancient Israel and were not simply monotheistic substitutes for the diviners and oracles of the ancient world, although they claimed the exclusive authority to speak to the people on behalf of God and the realities of the unseen world. They were bound to speak God's messages exactly as received and they could not filter or alter the content of their revelations. According to the Mosaic tradition, God would destroy any prophet who spoke false words or spoke on the behalf of other gods. But although the messages of the prophets would warn or make promises of things to come, their messages primarily contained commands from God and religious teachings which the people were morally obliged to hear and obey.[11]

The Pre-Islamic Arabian Background

Accurate understanding of the pre-Islamic background within which Islām arose is essential to the full understanding and the proper evaluation of the Islamic religion. For it was against this background that Islām articulated itself, and it was in this context that its first and most important religious and ideological struggles took place. Continuity characterizes a number of areas between the thought and practice of the earliest Muslims and the world view and culture in which they had been born; neither outwardly nor inwardly had the coming of Islām constituted an absolute transformation. The pre-Islamic Arab would, for all the minor and the radical transformations in the new society, still have noticed many things with which he was readily familiar. But these elements of continuity are not as important for understanding the dynamics and the historical accomplishments of Islām as the elements of discontinuity—those vestiges of an earlier religion and social order which, in many cases, were utterly obliterated except for literary and historical remnants. Islām's dramatic movement—vivid impressions of which form the most fundamental and abiding images and ideals of Muslim religious consciousness to this day—came in the wake of its uncompromising challenge to the religious hierarchy and the socio-political oligarchies of pre-Islamic Arabia. And Islām kept the religious and ideological "abominations" of its enemies in view, from its more imperious rhetorical statements to its seemingly inconsequential directives regarding mundane circumstances of day-to-day life, from the categorical declaration of the absolute Oneness of God to the every-day etiquette of invoking God's mercy upon one who sneezes.

There is sufficient literary evidence to show that the pre-Islamic Arabs used the words *al-ghaib* (the unseen) and *ash-shahāda* (the visible) in a manner similar to though apparently not identical with their usage in the Qur'ān. The two words constituted a semantic pair but appear to have been used in an essentially worldly sense; that is, *al-ghaib* referred to that dimension of material reality which lay outside immediate human perception, or the future, and *ash-shahāda* referred to the content of immediate perception. Still pre-Islamic Arabs may not have used them consciously to divide reality into the realm that lies beyond human perception and that which lies within.[12] Nevertheless, the world of the Unseen—the realm of God (*Allāh*),[13] the lesser gods, the angels (*al-malā'ika*), and the spirits (*al-jinn*)—had a deep effect and ubiquitous influence on the religious and cultural life of the pre-Islamic Arabs. The peoples of pre-Islamic Arabia included Jewish and Christian tribes, Zoro-astrians in the east along the Persian Gulf, indigenous Arab mono-theists (*al-Hunafā'*) who were neither Jew nor Christian, and—the majority—idolators (*mushrikūn*) who associated (*ashrakū*) lesser gods, angels, and spirits with God in their worship of him. In general, these tribes practiced animal sacrifice and intermediation with the spirit world to secure material benefit and avoid harm. Animal sacrifice was so closely tied to intermediation that it was essentially a part of it. The attempt to learn from the spirit world and to harness its forces through means of intermediation was the

major preoccupation of the religious life of the idolatrous pre-
Islamic Arabs. Drawing near to God, the gods, and the spirits (*at-
taqarrub*) and having means of access (*at-tawassul*) to their
knowledge and their powers to effect benefit or harm were the
objectives of various types of oracular speakers, shamans, diviners,
and other intermediaries and the objects of cultic rites and special
poems (*ashᶜār*) and prayers (*adᶜiya*), both oral and written.[14]

Although the pre-Islamic Arabs believed in *Allāh*, the supreme
God and Creator of the heavens and the earth, and a number of
lesser, intermediate gods, to whom they did not ascribe such attributes, the *jinn* (the unseen spirits of the earth) received greatest
attention in their religious life and practice. They deemed the *jinn* to
have an importance which they did not attribute even to the gods.
Intermediation with the spirit world—"drawing close" (*at-taqarrub*)
and "finding means of access" (*at-tawassul*)—characterized dealings
with the *jinn* more than intermediation with the gods; consequently
it appears valid to say that the pre-Islamic Arabs essentially
conceived of the *jinn* as an inferior order of terrestrial gods, even
though it was not their custom to refer to them as such. The Qur'ān
attacks sharply both worship of the *jinn* and the tribal belief that
connubial relations between Allāh and the daughters of the most
illustrious *jinn* had produced the angels, the daughters of God. (See,
for example, Qur'ān 6:100; 34:41; 37:158; JA 6:710, 738-39.) The
belief that angels were daughters of God had the practical effect of
elevating the status of the *jinn* in pre-Islamic religious practice; for,
according to the tribal thinking of that society, it meant that the
jinn—the closest of all created beings to man—had special access to
God himself through the good offices of his daughters, their own
maternal kinsmen.

Pre-Islamic Arabs divided spirits into two sorts: the evil and
unclean, and the clean and benign. Although intermediation was
directed at both types of spirits, cultic and ritual practices probably
centered on the evil *jinn* and the *shayāṭīn* (Satanic spirits) who
could inflict harm and bring chaos. Out of natural fear, they
devoted much attention to meeting the needs of and attempting to
appease the evil spirits (JA 6:706, 709).

Both evil and benign *jinn*, however, were analogous to the
human society and culture of pre-Islamic Arabia. Male and female,
the *jinn* procreated, ate, drank, slept, grew old, and eventually

died. Of all beings in the created world, they were the most like
man. They had genealogies; they formed families, clans, and tribes.
They had tribal leaders, tribal arbitrators (*hukkām*), and even kings
(*mulūk*). Their tribes, moreover, behaved like the Arab tribes themselves. They feuded with hostile tribes; they made alliances and
pacts with other tribes of *jinn* and, on occasion, with certain tribes
of human beings. They protected their allies, their clients, and their
protégés, and they would surely avenge the murder of any of their
tribal members or of those associated with their tribes. Like pre-
Islamic Arabs, there were sedentary *jinn* and nomadic *jinn*; there
were *jinn* who traveled by night and *jinn* who traveled by day (JA
6:711-14).

The powers of the *jinn* far exceeded those of man, although in
single combat it was conceivable that a man could kill a *jinn*, even
the invidious *ghūl* of the isolated deserts—as, on one occasion, the
famous poet Ta'abbata Sharran is reported to have done (JA
6:712-13). *Jinn*, with their prodigious strength, could travel swiftly
from region to region and into the heavens; indeed, it was by access
to the heavens that they were believed to have knowledge of future
events. Although the *jinn* usually remained in their invisible spirit
state, pre-Islamic Arabs believed that they could assume the shapes
of human beings and animals, especially snakes, dogs, and
scorpions. The *jinn* were most dangerous in their spirit state, simply
because they could attack without being seen. Renowned for their
eloquence, they were believed to inspire poetry; indeed, poet
Ta'abbata Sharran's name means "he carried an evil one under his
arm." Whereas the Arabs prided themselves on their fifteen
masterly poetic meters, the poetic meters of the *jinn* reportedly
numbered in the thousands. Close to the world of men and the
nature of men, *jinn*, more than other creatures, were capable of
feeling strong emotions of both love and hatred toward human
beings. The evil eye of the *jinn's* envy was more pernicious than the
evil eye of a human being; a hostile *jinn* could cause sickness,
plagues, fevers, epileptic seizures, demonic possession, and insanity
(*al-junūn*). One who was insane was said to be *majnūn*, that is,
possessed by a *jinn*. But *jinn* would also fall in love with human
beings and, by taking the form of a human being, have sexual intercourse with them. The genealogies of certain tribes were traced to

the children of such unions. Love, friendship, and other strong personal bonds between *jinn* and the pre-Islamic Arab intermediary were the reason for the *jinn's* assistance in providing information about the unseen (JA 6:711-14, 723-25).

There were also animistic elements in pre-Islamic Arab religion, such as the veneration of certain rocks, trees, wells, and caves that were believed to be imbued with spiritual efficacy and power. Such places and objects were the focus of pilgrimages, immolations, prayers, and special rituals which would harness the forces of such places for the spiritual and material benefit of the worshippers. Although not themselves part of the unseen world, these objects and places were deemed to possess a latent power which emanated from the spirits or the gods of the unseen (JA 6:706).

Shamans and Oracular Speakers

Pre-Islamic Arabia, like the lands of the Fertile Crescent, believed in both spirit intermediaries, who dwelt in the unseen world and would provide information about it, and diviners, who would discern the unseen through the interpretation of natural phenomena. Although shamans and oracular speakers—those who made direct contact with the spirit world—seem to have been more prestigious and influential in pre-Islamic Arabia, diviners, especially at lower social levels, were probably more common. Certainly there were a number of simple divining techniques which one could use with little or no expense. Use of oracular speakers and shamans, on the other hand—especially the famous ones—was often a costly matter, as were the more sophisticated divining techniques, which required the services of professional diviners.

The *kāhin* (shaman, soothsayer, oracular speaker—feminine *kāhina*) stood at the top of the religious hierarchy for idolatrous pre-Islamic Arabs. As a rule, the *kāhins* came from the most powerful clans within each tribe.

The *kāhin's* influence generally derived from his social standing within the tribe, his family and kinship relations, the comparative strength of his tribe, and his record in making successful predictions, giving sound counsel, and solving matters of arbitration. For in the absence of a central judiciary administration, a *kāhin's* judgment in arbitration depended on his personal prestige and the backing of his tribesmen, although they also sometimes secured ransom or hostages in advance.[15]

Both the *kāhin* and the *ʿarrāf* and the *sāhir* (sorcerer), a shaman-like figure who had direct contact with spirits, were closely, although not inseparably, connected with the religious and cultic life of pre-Islamic Arab idolatry. The idols of the gods, for example, would have *kāhins* who looked after their maintenance and spoke on their behalf. Frequently the *kāhin* would carry out his functions within the house or temple in which an idol was lodged. Many *kāhins* also worked in their own houses or would retire to secluded or partially secluded places to make contact with the spirits (JA 6:763-71).

Very little important business was conducted in the pre-Islamic Arab tribes without consulting one or more *kāhins*. The concluding of pacts and alliances, the making of war, the launching of attacks and raids, the discovery of criminals and murderers, the establishing of problematic genealogical connections, counseling marriage to a particular man or woman—all came under the aegis of the *kāhin*. He was, moreover, the chief guardian of Arab customary and tribal law; he solved difficult questions of inheritance, served as arbitrator (*hakam*) in disputes between individuals, clans, and tribes, called upon oracular powers to determine questions of guilt or innocence if disputed, and also ensured that judgment was in keeping with the precedents of tribal law. The revenge of unrequited wrongs—especially murders—was itself a quasi-religious practice in pre-Islamic Arabia, but the moral duty of revenge (*ath-thaʾr*) could not legitimately be assumed until one had sought redress through an arbitrator—generally a *kāhin*—and had failed.[16] The tribes also relied upon their *kāhins* to warn them of impending enemy raids or natural calamities, or to predict good times. *Kāhins* were sometimes called upon to find lost articles or strayed or stolen animals. (Finding of lost articles was more commonly the office of the *ʿarrāf*.) *Kāhins* would often accompany their tribes into battle or on raids to inspire the tribal warriors to fight bravely.

Although principally and invariably a spirit medium, the *kāhin* would sometimes also use divining techniques—conjuring by idols, examining the liver, entrails, or bones of sacrificial sheep, drawing omens from the movements and sounds of birds and other animals or from unusual natural phenomena, or interpreting dreams. By far the most common technique of the *kāhin*, however, was securing information from a spirit or from gods and spirits with which he was tied by close personal bonds. The familiar spirit of the *kāhin* was called most frequently his *tābi^c* (follower) or *ra'ī* (one who sees or is seen), although the expressions *sāhib* (companion), *mawlā*, or *walī* (close friend, patron, client), and *shaitān* (demonic spirit, no pejorative connotation) were also used. *Tābi^c* and the feminine *tābi^{c}a* were generally used for describing a *jinn*-lover (JA 6:711-14). Although some accounts tell of *kāhins* going into difficult and exhausting ecstatic states, the *kāhins* appear, in general, to have had much more natural relationships with their familiar *jinn*, whom they could see (hence, perhaps, *ra'ī*) although others could not. The *kāhin* is sometimes described as receiving information from his *tābi^c* by means of inspiration or revelation (*wahy*) and pronouncing them in the form of *saj^c*—that is, short, rhymed verses of varying meter, characterized by vague words and obscure references (JA 6:755-61).

Both the *kāhin* and the *sāhir* (sorcerer) required a payment in advance which was termed *al-hulwān* (from the root "to be sweet"). The *hulwān* was set by means of bargaining between the *kāhin* and his client. Technically, the *kāhin* shared it with his *tābi^c*; thus, the *tābi^c* also had to agree, a device that enabled the *kāhin* to profit even in cases in which his social relation to his clients might have dictated according to custom that he offer his services for less. Since the fees demanded could be substantial, pre-Islamic Arabs would often test the *kāhin's* effectiveness by hiding an object, which the *kāhin* was asked to find, or by asking obscure questions about the client, the answers to which the *kāhin* could not ordinarily be expected to know (JA 6:761-62).

Pre-Islamic Sorcerers

The pre-Islamic Arab *kāhin* and *sāhir* (sorcerer) both made some form of direct contact with spirits and both required the advance payment of a *hulwān*. But the *kāhin* contacted the spirit world chiefly for information, while the *sāhir* effected some harm or benefit through the medium of the spirits. Within the pre-Islamic world, therefore, the *sāhir* constituted one of the most important means of harnessing the latent powers of the unseen world. Unlike the *kāhins*, the sorcerers apparently had no cultic and ritualistic functions; nevertheless, the extent of their practice can be deduced from numerous references throughout the Qur'ān to *sihr* (sorcery) and related words. The familiar spirits of the *sāhir* were *jinn*, like those of the *kāhin*, and were also called by the same names: *tābic*, *ra'ī*, and *shayātīn*. The *sāhir* called upon their powers to produce love or hatred, sickness, distress, or visual hallucinations. But sorcery in pre-Islamic Arab society was associated with medicine, and the Arabic *tibb* (medicine) stood in its pre-Islamic context for the medicinal arts of the sorcerer, who in that capacity was referred to as *tābb* and sometimes *tabīb*, while one who was under the spell of a *tābb* was referred to as *matbūb* or *tābib*. In addition to curing a number of physical ailments and sicknesses through his spirit powers, the pre-Islamic *sāhir* was also deemed able to cure various types of insanity, which is not surprising, considering that the pre-Islamic Arabs associated insanity with spirit possession.

The pre-Islamic *rāqī* (charmer, sorcerer) held a position similar to that of the *sāhir*, although he primarily provided amulets, charms, and other devices and techniques to protect the client against sorcery, the evil eye, fever, and sickness. The most famous *sāhirs* of pre-Islamic Arabia were reportedly from Jewish tribes and were believed to derive their skills ultimately from Babylon. In general, however, Arab Jews and non-Jews practiced sorcery, while the office of the *kāhin* was essentially the exclusive reserve of Arabs (JA 6:739-45, 751-54, 762).

Diviners

Diviners and divining techniques were probably more common in pre-Islamic Arabia than direct spirit mediation through the *kāhins*, although spirit intermediaries—the *kāhins* and *sāhirs*—appear to have had higher status. The *carrāf* (one who knows; an emphatic noun) may have stood at the head of the hierarchy of diviners, although neither his profession nor his status is clear. Some pre-Islamic Arabs, for example, apparently drew no distinction between the *kāhin* and the *carrāf*. The prophet Muhammad explicitly prohibited both offices, implying a technical difference between the two. Unlike the *kāhins*, the *carrāfs* were not apparently associated with ritual and cultic practices; they did not function within the houses and temples of idol worship, nor did they rely upon *tābiᶜs* or *ra'īs*. One divining technique was *khatt*, rapidly drawing a number of straight lines in smooth sand or soil with a special instrument. The diviner would then slowly erase the lines. If a single line remained, the undertaking would be deemed inauspicious; a pair of lines denoted good fortune. The *ᶜarrāf* was also believed to have the ability to read one's destiny from the signs and markings of one's body. Children were often brought to *ᶜarrāfs* to have their futures foretold through such techniques. *ᶜArrāfs* also found stolen or lost items and animals. Interestingly, al-ᶜUkkāz, one of the most important annual fairs in pre-Islamic Arabia, was also a major center for *ᶜarrāfs* (JA 6:772-74).

Pre-Islamic Arabic idiom contained a number of other specialized titles for different types of diviners and their techniques. The *ᶜa'if*, for example, divined by studying the movements and the sounds of birds and animals and by reading the entrails of sacrificial animals. The *zājir's* office appears to have been restricted to augury and did not include animals other than birds (JA 6:774-75). *Munajjim* and *hazzā'* were applied to diviners who studied the movements of the stars and other celestial bodies. The *hāzī* (cf. Hebrew *hōzeh*) specialized in *al-khatt*, although he also interpreted the movements and sounds of birds, particularly the sounds of the raven (JA 6:775-76, 783). Special *kāhins* used divining arrows *azlām, aqdā* in the presence of their particular idols to determine the favor or disfavor of the god toward particular matters; but the common man also carried personal divining arrows which he could consult. Likewise, the common man would himself observe the flight and movements of the birds and animals that crossed his path at the beginning of an undertaking and drew omens from them. The everyday life of the pre-Islamic Arab was, indeed, filled with such omens—many of them as commonplace as yawning and sneezing—both, incidentally, viewed as evil omens presaging injury to others (JA 6:776-82, 786-800).

Islām systematically assailed reliance in oracular speakers, diviners, and the practices and superstitions associated with them. It declared such intermediaries and their practices to be *tāghūt* (gross transgression against God), the heavens sealed against the *kāhin* "mixed with a hundred lies." The offices of the *kāhin* and *ʿarrāf* and the practices of the *sāhir* were outlawed. The payment of a *hulwān* was prohibited as sin. Muhammad directed his followers to ignore evil omens and proceed with their undertakings if they were morally legitimate, by invoking the help of God. The prophet did not prohibit his followers from taking heart in auspicious signs, but he directed them all the same to "leave the birds perched in the trees." Divining arrows and the like were declared an abomination, their use tantamount to breaking one's covenant with God. Islamic etiquette directed Muslims simply to cover their mouths when they yawned and required that one praise God after sneezing, while others invoked God's mercy upon the sneezer. Neither sneezing nor yawning were considered evil omens (JA 6:756-59, 762, 772, 800). But Islām, in addition to these and many other specific prohibitions and alterations in pre-Islamic Arab custom, radically transformed the very conception of the realm of the unseen and man's relationship to it and to the material world around him.

THE ISLAMIC DEFINITION OF THE PERCEPTIBLE AND THE UNSEEN

Al-ghaib (the unseen) and *ash-shahāda* (visible) are, as we have mentioned, semantic pairs in classical Arabic. Izutsu refers to such words as "correlation words," each of which presupposes the other and derives its full significance from this integral correlation, even when used in isolation.[17] Classical Arabic affords many such correlation words, which are significant in understanding the structure of the Qur'anic world view. For example, *ad-dunyā* (the world at hand, or the life of this world) is such a correlation word in Qur'anic semantics as well as in general Arabic usage. Literally a feminine comparative adjective meaning "the nearer, closer, lower" life, *ad-dunyā* always points, even when used in isolation, to *al-ukhrā* or *al-ākhira* (the other world, the world to come, i.e., the hereafter), with which it is explicitly tied in Qur'anic usage.[18]

Al-ghaib and *ash-shahāda* have connotations which are not conveyed immediately by their English translations as the unseen and perceptible. *Ash-shahāda* in modern standard usage means either the act of bearing witness or the testimony which is given. In early Arabic, however, the primary meaning of *shahida*, the verb from which the noun *ash-shadāda* is derived, was "to be present," "to be on hand," and hence able to witness and bear witness to that which occurs in one's presence. The proper synonym of *shahida* in classical Arabic, therefore, is *hadara* (to be present, to be in the presence of something, to appear before someone or something). Its antonym in early and classical Arabic idiom is the verb *ghāba*, to go away, to go out of sight, from which is derived the noun *al-ghaib*. Thus, the verb continues to be used for the setting of the sun and other celestial bodies. *Ghāba* also was often used in a more restricted sense to stand for "going away on a distant journey" (i.e., *sāfara*), and in such contexts *shahida* still constituted its semantic pair, standing in that case for "remaining behind in the village or encampment" and, hence, being present and on hand.[19] In ancient Arabic usage, a married woman whose husband was away on a journey was referred to as *"imra'at mughīb,"* while a woman whose husband was present was *"imra'at mushhid,"* from the root *shahida*.[20]

Because of its semantic background, *al-ghaib* in its Qur'anic context refers to all things that stand without human perception — whether they stand outside of it by virtue of their nonmaterial nature as in the case of God and the angels or whether they have not been perceived or have not been retained in perception — as, for example, future events, forgotten things, or things of any period which are material but unknowable, as for example, the number of fish in the sea. The word, therefore, does not denote only supernatural realities.

In contrast, *ash-shahāda* primarily refers not only to things within the range of man's five senses but also, by virtue of their limited proximity to man in time and place, to things that are both perceived and retained in consciousness. God is called *ash-Shahīd* in the Qur'ān and extra-Qur'anic Islamic textual sources because he is proximate to all things — although also absolutely transcendent and distinct. He perceives and is knowledgeable of each detail. *Ash-Shahīd* as a name describes God simultaneously as omniscient and omnipresent. *Ash-shahīd* with reference to human beings means a religious martyr, from its passive participial meaning, "one who has been brought into the presence of another." For in Islamic belief, the sincere *shahīd* is alive, having been brought (*uhdira*) spiritually into the presence of God in Paradise.[21]

BELIEF IN THE UNSEEN AS OPPOSED TO DETAILED KNOWLEDGE OF THE UNSEEN

Belief in the unseen is identified toward the beginning of the Qur'anic text as an essential attribute of one who would seek divine guidance.[22]

> *Alif. Lām. Mim:*
> This is the book: In it there is no misgiving, a Guidance for those who are conscientious [toward God],
> Who believe in the Unseen, perform the daily prayer as it is meant to be performed, and who give generously of that which We [God] have bestowed upon them,
> And [for those] who believe in that which has been revealed unto you [O Prophet], and that which was revealed before you and Who have absolute certainty [of belief] in the Hereafter. (Qur'ān 2:1-4.)[23]

The direct object of the verb "to believe" (*āmana*) can be introduced by the preposition *bi* (in), as in this verse, or by the preposition *li* (to, for), as, for example, in Qur'ān 26:111. When *āmana* is used in conjunction with the preposition *bi*, however, that preposition adds greater meaning to the verb by virtue of its use as the element of transitivity in other verbs. This semantic enrichment is referred to by Arab grammarians as *tadmīn* (the assimilation of one meaning to another). In the case of *āmana*, use of *bi* lends it the associative meanings of "to recognize and acknowledge as valid" (*iᶜtarafa bi*), "to have fullest confidence in" (*wathaqa bi*), and "to submit to and recognize as valid" (*adhᶜana bi*).[24] As a consequence the Arabic expression, "they believe in the Unseen," is at once richer and more expressive than its English rendition. Moreover, because of the semantic pairing in Arabic of *al-ghaib* and *ash-shahāda*, some commentators contend that the original Arab receptors of the statement "they believe in the Unseen" would have heard the double entendre "they believe in the Unseen just as unequivocally as they believe in the perceived" (JA 1:115).

Generally speaking, traditional Qur'anic commentators did not understand this reference to belief in the unseen as belief about the existence of an unseen, spiritual dimension of reality. Some commentators interpret another Qur'anic passage, 45:24, as evidence that some Arabs had a materialistic view of the universe which denied the existence of greater nonmaterial realities; this interpretation is conjectural. In any case, Arabic and Islamic history shows that the overwhelming majority of pre-Islamic Arabs believed firmly in the existence of a highly consequential spiritual dimension. Thus, many commentators hold that "belief in the unseen" presumes belief in the spiritual dimension of reality and means in these opening verses of the second *sūra* belief in the fundamental articles of faith regarding the unseen as set forth in Islamic belief. It refers, then, to such things as belief in God, the physical resurrection of the dead, the last judgment, the hereafter, and so forth—things which Islām commands human beings to believe but which lie beyond the immediate confirmation of the five senses.[25] Belief in the unseen means therefore, according to the commentator at-Tabātabā'ī, belief in the three fundamentals: the absolute unity of God (*at-tawhīd*), the phenomenon of divine prophecy (*an-nabūwa*), and the hereafter (*al-maʿād*). Moreover, he continues, this definition of the unseen is either alluded to or specifically indicated within these first four verses of the *sūra*. Conscientiousness toward God (*at-taqwā*) necessarily implies in its Qur'anic and Islamic context belief in the Oneness of God and ethical behavior in accordance with that belief. Belief in prophecy is implied in the fourth-verse reference to belief in the revelation of Muhammad and the earlier prophets—divine revelation being, *par excellence*, that dimension of prophecy, according to Islamic belief, which pertains to the unseen. This same verse ends with an explicit reference to belief in the third fundamental, the hereafter (T 1:45-46).

But although the Qur'ān requires belief in these "great realities," it does not command the reader to seek detailed knowledge of the unseen. Indeed, it discourages the believer from excessive preoccupation with aspects of the unseen which have no direct practical importance to his spiritual and moral edification. The

Qur'ān states: "And they ask you about the Spirit [*ar-Rūh*]. Say: The Spirit is a matter among those pertaining [only] to [my Lord] and of which only He has knowledge, and you, [O people], have been given of knowledge but little." (Qur'ān 17:85.)

Ar-rūh (the spirit) has a number of meanings in the Qur'ān, as does its Hebrew counterpart *rūah* in the Bible. Sometimes it refers to angelic messengers, sometimes to spiritual aid, sometimes to divine revelation itself. In that context it would be similar to the biblical usage of *rūah* to indicate prophetic ecstasies. Although some commentators have held to this particular meaning of *ar-rūh* in this verse, many others have understood the verse as answering a question about the Spirit of God in the most general sense (A 15:155-64; T 13:198) and thus constituting a rhetorical and not a theological answer. For the purpose of the Qur'anic response is not to inform the people about the theological subtleties of the Spirit but rather to indicate that preoccupation with these kinds of questions is undesirable, for in the view of some commentators, the answer is beyond the capacity of most or all of the people (T 13:200; A 15:153; Q 4:224).

The commentator an-Nīsābūrī notes, however, that this verse should not be understood as a categorical prohibition against metaphysical speculation about realities of the unseen.[26] Although metaphysical understanding of the nature of the Spirit is difficult to attain, metaphysical understanding of the nature of God himself is much more difficult. Yet the Qur'ān abounds with verses which invite the human imagination to reflect on the wonders of God and his being (N 15:73). An-Nīsābūrī's point seems well taken, and one might consider as an example the parable of light (Qur'ān 24:35-42), a long and beautiful analogy between God, the light of the heavens and the earth, and a radiant crystal lamp of olive oil within a niche in a house of worship. A crucial difference between the Qur'anic response to questions about the Spirit and the numerous passages that allude to the wonders of the great realities of the unseen is the fact that the information about the Spirit was directly solicited, while these other passages are, as it were, freely given in token of God's bounty. The Qur'ān contains a number of solicited responses to questions that begin similarly, "They ask you about.... Say:...." ("*yas'alūnaka ʿan .... qul: ...*"). The Qur'anic responses to these questions vary considerably, depending on whether the question pertains to practical matters of *taklīf* (man's moral responsibility to obey revealed law) or to metaphysical and impractical questions. Such questions and their answers become, in the context of Qur'anic revelation, matters of immediate concern to the entire Muslim community and, consequently, establish religious and behavioral norms. Verses like the parable of light occur incidentally as embellishments to other discussions. Although such questions may have originated with a single person, they represent questions of the entire community to the prophet of God. In responding to them, the Qur'ān also evaluates the question, indicating whether it constitutes a legitimate concern for the community.

Examples of other questions addressed to Muhammad concern the phases of the moon (Qur'ān 2:189), which are used to determine the season of pilgrimage and other religious observances; what amount of their wealth inquirers should contribute to the cause of Islām (Qur'ān 2:215, 219); conducting war during the sacred months of Rajab, Dhū-l-Qiʿdah, Dhū-'lHijjah, and Muharram (Qur'ān 2:217); the legal status of wine and games of chance (Qur'ān 2:219); the treatment of orphans (Qur'ān 2:220); laws pertaining to women during their menstrual cycles (Qur'ān 2:222); the marital status of women (Qur'ān 4:127); laws of inheritance regarding those who die without ascendant or descendant surviving kinsmen (Qur'ān 4:176); what the law has made permissible (Qur'ān 5:4); and the division of booty in war (Qur'ān 8:1). All of these questions begin with the same wording as in the verse about the Spirit, but these are all matters of immediate importance to the practice of Islamic law and the Islamic code of behavior in the life of the community. As a consequence, the Qur'ān indicates that the questions represent valid communal concerns and it answers them in specific detail.

The eighteenth chapter of the Qur'ān, *Sūrat al-Kahf* (the cave), contains three stories which occur nowhere else in the Qur'ān. Each pertains to the *ghaib* of the historical past: 1) the story of the Sleepers of the Cave, 2) the story of Moses and his spiritual teacher, al-Khidr, and 3) the story of Dhū-'l-Qarnain (literally, "he whose headpiece has two horns").[27] Unlike the first two stories, the account of Dhū-'l-Qarnain begins with the formula: "And they ask you about Dhū-'l-Qarnain. Say:..." (Qur'ān 18:83). The Qur'ān

goes into surprising detail in presenting each story, even though
they seem to have no immediate value. Nevertheless, as traditional
and modern Qur'anic commentators have observed, the questions
about the Sleepers and Dhū-'l-Qarnain were presented to
Muhammad by his opponents to test the validity of his claim to
prophecy. Apparently no question was asked about Moses and al-
Khidr, so their story may be an unsolicited incidental. Moreover, as
commentators like at-Tabātabā'i demonstrate, the Qur'ān does not
present these stories as quaint or elaborately detailed accounts but
as prefigures of the eventual success of the Muslim community, then
young and vulnerable. Thus these tales are inspiring stories of
earlier believers whose examples early Muslims could emulate in
their own struggle (T 13:235-391; cf. Q 4:2255).

In *Sūrat Tāhā* (Qur'ān 20:105-106) another apparently
impractical question is asked: "And they ask you about the
mountains. Say: My Lord will reduce them utterly to dust and lay
them low like the valleys, leaving them barren and empty with no
living thing." The importance of this question and answer lies in the
cultural and religious context of pre-Islamic Arabs. They saw
mountains as the preeminent symbol of permanence and strength.
Doubters found it difficult to believe that God could obliterate the
mountains on the last day, as eschatological verses of the Qur'ān
promise. Thus, by entertaining this question about the mountains,
the Qur'ān at once vindicated the omnipotence of God and asserted
in the most vivid and profound terms the integrity of the Islamic
doctrine about the last day and the events that will accompany it.[28]

In contrast, the prophet Muhammad was frequently asked when
the hour of judgment would come; the Qur'anic response is essentially the same as the answer about the Spirit:

> They ask you concerning the Hour [of the coming of the judgment]:
> When will the time of its fulfillment be? Say: The knowledge of it is
> with my Lord alone; none will unveil it toward the time of its coming
> but He. It is a matter that weighs heavy in the heavens and the earth
> and will overtake you as a sudden and unexpected event. They ask you
> about it as if you had intimate knowledge of it and took pleasure in
> being asked. Say: The knowledge of it is with God alone. But the
> majority of mankind have no [true] knowledge. Say: I do not possess
> the power to cause benefit to my own soul or to ward off from it harm
> except to the extent that God wills, and, if I had knowledge of the

Unseen, my life would have been filled with abundance of good things, and trouble would have never afflicted me: I am only one who gives warning of a Divine punishment to come and good tidings of Paradise for a people bound together by belief. (Qur'ān 7:187-188.)

They ask you concerning the Hour [of the coming of the judgment]: When will the time of its fulfillment be?
On what basis could you [possibly] inform them of its time of coming?
The ultimate knowledge of it rests with your Lord alone. You are but a warner for those who stand in fear and awe of its coming:
It shall seem on the day when they [finally] behold it as if they had not lingered on this earth but a single evening or [a single night] and the following morn. (Qur'ān 79:42-46.)

While affirming that the prophet himself does not have access to the knowledge of all details of the unseen, these verses—like the verse about the Spirit—also support the Qur'anic principle that such knowledge is not essential to the community of believers. Indeed, some Islamic commentators observe that it is part of God's wisdom to hide the knowledge of the coming of the hour as well as the knowledge of the particulars of each individual's future and the time of one's death. The complete absence of such knowledge is intended as a source of spiritual and moral edification, since it requires the believer to prepare continually for the unexpected, for the end of his life, and for the moral consequences of judgment that come ultimately with death (A 21:109-111; N 9:98-100; T 8:371).

The first of these passages specifies that the prophet is not a "knower of the Unseen," does not have direct access to particular aspects of the unseen at will, and hence does not usurp a function that belongs to God alone. Muhammad's comment, "if I had knowledge of the Unseen, my life would have been filled with abundance of good [things], and trouble would have never afflicted me," is his renunciation of divination and foretelling. To the Arabs of his generation, preoccupied with predicting when prices would rise or fall, when and where the rains would come, which pasture lands would be best, the outcomes of wars, etc., the courageous redefinition of prophethood marks a clear break with pre-Islamic religiousness. In the words of some commentators, the verse proclaims the thorough *ʿubudīya* (lordship) of God. Delving into such aspects of the unseen is not the legitimate concern of the prophet or the community which follows him.

Moreover, the passage also implies that some among the pre-Islamic Arabs to whom the prophet preached did see him as a shaman-like *kāhin* figure: "They ask you about it as if you had intimate knowledge of it [and took pleasure in being asked]." (The semantically rich *hafiyun ʿanhā* carries both connotations of intimate knowledge and taking pleasure in being asked). Understood in this context, therefore, these verses also emphasize that not having such knowledge is not a defect or inadequacy in the prophet or any other human being (N 9:100; T 8:372).

God as Exclusive Knower of the Unseen

God is frequently described in the Qur'ān in terms of his knowledge of the unseen. He is, for example, *ʿālim al-ghaib wa-sh shahāda* (knower of the unseen and the perceptible, Qur'ān 6:73; 9:94, 105; 13:9; 23:92; 32:6; 39:46; 59:22; 62:8; 64:18). He is *ʿallām al-ghuyūb* (the supreme knower of [all] unseen things, Qur'ān 5:109, 116; 9:78; 34:48), and throughout the Qur'ān he is described repeatedly by adjectives indicating his exact knowledge of all particulars, be they hidden or manifest, future or past, exoteric or esoteric, exterior or interior: *al-hakīm al-khabīr* (the all-wise, having knowledge of all things, especially hidden things), *al-bātin* (knower of all things interior), *az-zāhir* (knower of all things exterior), and so forth. Such references to God, as the commentator at-Tabātabā'i observes, often occur in the context of references to the last judgment and the ultimate rewards of heaven and hell, where the justice of God's judgment depends on the fullness of his knowledge (T 7:146). Here again, we observe how the context of such Qur'anic references to God as knower of the unseen are—like other dimensions of the Islamic conception of the unseen—fundamentally linked to spiritual edification and the imperative of moral action.

God, according to Islamic belief, is absolutely unique. His uniqueness is one of the fundamental attributes of his oneness. He has no likeness and no opposite. Attributes such as eternal life, omniscience, omnipotence, and absolute transcendence with absolute proximity to all being are, as a consequence, attributes to his godhood (*ulūhīya*) and his lordship (*rubūbīya*). Knowledge of the unseen and the perceptible, which falls under the rubric of God's omniscience, is, according to Islamic belief, one such unique and essential attribute. "Say: None of the beings who dwell in the heavens or on the earth have knowledge of the Unseen but God, nor do they have any perception of when they will be resurrected from the dead. Nay, the knowledge which they [the disbelievers] have will come utterly to naught in the hereafter: Nay, they are in doubt about the hereafter itself: Nay, they are with regard to [the hereafter] completely blind." (Qur'ān 27:65-66.) God's exclusive knowledge of the unseen is absolute. No other creature in the heavens or on earth can have such knowledge and thus cannot be gods (T 15:385).

Those two verses occur within a broader discussion establishing the unique divinity of God. God's unique knowledge of the unseen, coupled with his power over the heavens and the earth, further indicate his godhood and absolute perfection (A 20:9; Q 6:2661). Moreover, the larger discussion also expresses the Qur'anic theme that religious belief must be based upon definitive knowledge (*ᶜilm*) and not upon conjecture (*zann*), which is the foundation, it argues, of the idolatrous religious conceptions of the pre-Islamic Arabs. Thus, by emphasizing that God alone has knowledge of the unseen, these verses—in addition to excluding other beings from divinity— also state quite clearly that God alone, as knower of the unseen, can be the only source of sound religion. In the Islamic context, this means that only prophetic religion—religion revealed to man by God through prophecy—can be authentic religion. Commentator an-Nīsābūrī adds that the reference in the second verse to doubts (*shakk*) about the hereafter established the conjectural nature of religious belief among Muhammad's opponents. For *shakk*, in the Qur'anic view, comes from lack of knowledge (*ᶜilm*), from ignorance and conjecture, and is thus different from negligence (*ghafla*), to which the Qur'ān also refers as a source of error. *Ghafla* springs from a lack of concern about the very subject matter of religious knowledge, irrespective of its content (N 20:9-11).

The Qur'ān also establishes the unseen as God's unique possession: "... Knower of the Unseen: Thus, He make manifest to no one the [unfathomable] Unseen, which is His, Except to that person with whom He is well-satisfied [to have elected] as a Prophet-Messenger. . . ." (Qur'ān 72:26-27.)

Knowledge of the unseen, this unique possession of God, is also portrayed in the Qur'ān as a matter of supreme value. It is precious knowledge. Hence, God's knowledge of the unseen and his sole possession of it are often described with the image of keys to the treasuries *khazā'in, mafātih*:

> Say: Behold, I [call you and take my stand] on the basis of a manifest proof from my Lord [which makes the Truth distinct from falsehood]; yet you have disbelieved in Him. I do not have in my presence [or my power] that [punishment] which you in your sarcasm wish for me to make come quickly:
> Ordination of judgment rests with God alone: He makes Truth stand out distinctly, and He is the best to judge between falsehood and Truth.
> Say: Were I to have in my power that [punishment] which you seek to hasten, the matter [of dispute] between me and you would have been decided. Yet [know that] God is the most knowledgeable of those who do wrong and are workers of oppression.
> In his possession [alone] are the keys to the treasuries of the Unseen: None has knowledge of them but He. He knows that which is on the land and in the sea. Not a leaf falls to the ground but that He has knowledge of it, nor is there a seed hidden within the dark recesses of the earth nor anything succulent or dry, [living or dead], but that [knowledge of] it is [recorded] in a [wondrous] Book that makes all things clear. (Qur'ān 6:57-59.)

The Arabic expression *mafātih al-ghaib* ("the keys to the treasuries of the unseen") affords this translation because *mafātih* is the plural of two words, *miftah* (key) and *maftah* (treasury; *makhzan*, that which is guarded under lock and key). Consequently, both meanings can be read into their common plural. The Qur'ān frequently uses the less equivocal word *khazā'in* (treasuries) in the same or similar contexts. (See, for example, Qur'ān 6:50; 11:31; 17:100; 38:9; 52:37; 63:7; 15:21.) Consequently, some commentators prefer to read *mafātih* also as "treasuries." It might also be noted that placing the prepositional phrase "in his possession" (*wa ʿindahu*) at the beginning of the sentence creates the semantic effect of what the Arab grammarians call *hasr* (restriction), implying that only God is characterized by this attribute, i.e., it is restricted to him (N 7:121; T 7:124-25).

The image of the unseen as treasuries implies the great value in knowledge of the unseen. All of the particulars of the unseen are, like precious jewels, locked away in a treasury to insure their preservation. This passage begins with an emphatic declaration of the absolute certainty (yaqīn) of the prophet Muhammad's call and his knowledge from God, who is characterized by this attribute of omniscience. One might also note the clear linkage in these verses — as elsewhere in the Qur'ān — between God's exclusive knowledge of the unseen and his ultimate judgment of mankind. In these verses, God is indeed the "best to judge between falsehood and Truth": and "the most knowledgeable about those who do wrong and work oppression" because he has the keys to the treasuries of the unseen. The verses begin with reference to God's knowledge of the unseen but end by reference to his comprehensive knowledge of all the details of the perceptible world: the "relative Unseen" (al-ghaib an-nisbī), which, although it lies within the scope of man's perceptive faculties, lies beyond his perception and retention because of the limitations of his senses. According to some commentators, these graphic illustrations are made in the concluding verse because few human beings are able to recognize on principle the astounding implications of saying that God has sole possession of the keys to the treasuries of the unseen. Thus, reference to his knowledge of each leaf which falls, each seed hidden within the dark recesses of the earth, and so on, helps to make this abstract principle more concrete.

It should also be added that this reference to God, who holds knowledge of the unseen under lock and key, would imply very clearly in the pre-Islamic Arabian context that the kāhins and their intermediary spirits are completely excluded from it. (See N 7:120-22; A 7:168-73; T 7:124-29.) Although the details of the unseen are very valuable, man does not need such knowledge for his welfare in this life. An-Nīsābūrī contends that the closing reference to God's knowledge of such seemingly insignificant particulars as the falling of a leaf from a tree or the presence of a seed in the earth is tied to the theme of moral and spiritual edifica-

tion which occurs generally in the Qur'ān in conjunction with
references to the unseen. If God has attached such value to these
things that he has recorded their occurrence in his wondrous book,
then how much more important—according to the logic of the
Qur'ān—must be the thoughts, words, and deeds of each human
being, which God also records in preparation for his judgment (N
7:121).

THE VITAL PROPHETIC LINK TO KNOWLEDGE OF THE UNSEEN

God, according to the Qur'anic commentators, knows the
unseen by virtue of his essence (dhāt). All other creatures may have
access to the unseen only when God imparts such knowledge
directly (ta'līm) (T 20:53) through that greatest of God's bounties to
mankind, prophecy. Such great realities of the unseen—the
Oneness of God, the hereafter—the core of religious truth—is
essential to man's prosperity in this life and the hereafter; thus, the
mercy of prophetic revelation makes it possible for mankind to
attain its greatest potential. Though the prophet has no independent
knowledge of the unseen, he has true knowledge from revelation
which he follows in obedience and submission. As a human being
different from other human beings, he has legitimate authority over
others because his revealed knowledge makes him "one who sees
clearly" in the midst of others who are blind (N 7:114; T 7:155-57):

> Say: I do not say unto you that I have in my possession the treasuries
> of God, nor do I know the Unseen, nor do I say unto you that I am an
> angel: I only follow that which has been revealed unto me. [But] say
> [unto them also]: Is he who is blind on a par with him who sees clearly
> [and perceives]? Do you not then reflect [on the error of your ways]?
> And give warning through [this revelation] to those who stand in fear
> [and expectation] of being gathered together into [the presence of] their
> Lord, having for themselves save Him no protector and no intercessor,
> that, perhaps, they be conscientious [toward their God]. (Qur'ān
> 6:50-51.)

Both verses, as at-Tabātabā'i observes, constitute an Islamic
definition of the nature of prophets and prophecy. The ʿubūdīya
(servanthood) of the prophet is very clear in terms of complete
subordination to God, from whom he receives his revelation and

whose dictates he must follow. He does not have direct access to the treasuries of God or knowledge of the unseen as a whole (T 7:97; cf. A 7:156). Nevertheless, although thoroughly human and subordinate to God, the prophet has greater stature than other human beings. By virtue of the revelation which he receives from God, he is *basīr* (having clear vision and perception), while those who lack such knowledge are *'a'mā* (blind). Thus the prophet has the authority to lead the community—just as those who have clear vision and understanding have the responsibility to guide the blind (T 7:97; cf. N 7:112). The authority of the prophet rests, therefore, in his definitive knowledge (*'ilm*) of the great realities of the unseen which he has received through revelation from God, the supreme knower of the unseen. Similarly, the authority of the *'ulamā'* (religious scholars) within the Islamic community, either clergy or sacerdotal class, rests in possessing this legacy of *'ilm* which they have received from their study of the Qur'ān and the prophetic traditions. In the Islamic view, the *'ulamā'*—the heirs of the prophets, according to *hadīth* (prophetic tradition)—have by virtue of their knowledge an authority analogous to that of the prophet himself.

In another passage, the Islamic paradigm of prophecy emphasizes the complete dependence of prophets upon God for their knowledge of the unseen and the high quality of knowledge of the unseen revealed to them. These verses, in the view of Qur'anic commentators, also embody the Islamic principle of the infallibility of the prophets and the corresponding implication that the diviners and the spirit intermediaries of pre-Islamic Arabia did not have access to the knowledge of the unseen *nor the divine protection accorded to prophets* (T 20:54-57; A 29:96-98; N 29:72):

> Say: I do not know whether that [ultimate punishment] of which you have been forewarned is at hand or whether my Lord shall allot for it a [longer] interval:
> Knower of the Unseen: Thus does He make manifest to no one the [unfathomable] Unseen which is His,
> Except to him whom He is well-satisfied [to have elected] as a Prophet-Messenger: And He sends forth [the angelic forces of heaven] to watch over him, from before him and from behind him,
> That He make manifest that [the Prophet-Messengers] have communi-

cated the messages of their Lord: Yet He has encompassing knowledge
of [all that they do and all that transpires about] them, and He takes
account of every thing, one by one, [which exists]. (Qur'ān 72:25-28.)

According to the Arabic semantics of the verse, God affords his
prophet-messengers *al-izhār ʿalā-l-ghaib*, that is, makes the revealed
truths "manifest" to them but also gives them power, as it were,
over *ʿalā*, their knowledge. (See A 29:98.) God imparts his message
after this fashion and then carefully protects his prophet-messenger
in the act of delivering the message so that his message, his revelation of the great realities of the unseen essential to human salvation,
reaches mankind exactly and without distortion or alteration. (See
T 20:54.)

Knowledge as Opposed to Conjecture

Prophetic revelation is man's only means of gaining explicit and
definitive knowledge of the great realities of the unseen that affect
his destiny. The Qur'ān repeatedly contrasts such definitive,
revealed knowledge (*ʿilm*) with the surmise and conjecture (*zann*) of
human beings who speculate about the unseen without the benefit
of revealed knowledge. Such verses emphasize that mere conjecture
(*zann*) about the unseen can never constitute a valid basis for
religious belief and practice. Traditional Islamic theologians, on the
basis of this position, articulated the corollary that the only essential
items of Islamic doctrine are those set forth unequivocally and
definitively with the revealed textual sources of Islām: the absolute
Oneness of God, the physical resurrection of the dead, the existence
of angels, the reality of the hereafter, and so forth. Other articles of
faith—particularly those containing ambiguities of textual
references, etc.—cannot be made central to Islamic doctrine, even if
they are deemed to be generally correct. Consequently, all Muslims
must accept the "definitively demonstrable" (*qatʿī*) articles of faith,
categorically set forth within the Qur'ān and the *sunna*, but a
Muslim's faith may not be termed unacceptable for differing on the
interpretation of a teaching whose textual sources afford,
semantically and otherwise, a plurality of legitimate interpretations—as long as the interpretation he follows is among those
which can be supported by one of these interpretations.

The opposition between revealed knowledge about the unseen (*ᶜilm*) and conjecture is summarized in the Qur'ān 6:115-16:

> And the words of your Lord are perfected in Truth and Justice, in precept and command: There is nothing which can alter His words, for He it is Who hears and knows all things.
> And if you should obey most of those who are upon the earth, they would lead you astray from the path of God: Behold, they follow only conjecture and do naught but surmise.

Another passage is:

> Those who have associated [false objects of worship with God] will say: "Had God not willed, we would not have associated [anything with Him] nor would our fathers before us nor would we have declared anything to have been prohibited [which we have declared unlawful]." In like fashion did those who were before them disbelieve until [ultimately] they tasted the severity of Our [wrath]. Say [unto them]: "Do you have in your possession any definitive knowledge (*ᶜilm*), which you might bring forth to show us? Indeed, you follow only conjecture (*zann*), and you do naught but surmise." Say: [Know], then, that the ultimate truth and the manifest proof rest with God alone. Indeed, had He willed, He would surely have guided you, all of you together. (Qur'ān 6:148-149.)

By denouncing adherence to conjecture (*zann*) and surmise (*khars*) in matters of religious belief, both verses require that Qur'anic revelation be followed instead. The perfect and unalterable "words of my Lord" in the first verse portray graphically the lofty status Islām associates with the revealed message. These words are "perfected in Truth and Justice," which, in the view of some commentators, means that they are complete and perfect sources for all dimensions of the religious message. For the prophetic message, in the Islamic view, consists primarily of teachings or precepts of truth and codes of behavior and law. Truth and justice are predicates of each of these aspects of the prophetic message respectively (N 8:9; cf. A 8:10; T 7:328-29; Q 3:1195). The first and second verses also indicated that the conjecture under condemnation pertains to religious belief. In the first verse, for example, it is conjecture about the path of God which, if followed, would lead one away from the path. The second verse specifically condemns conjecture about doctrinal matters and religious law; for the verse

condemns the theological position of *shirk* (associating false objects
of worship with God) and the religious taboos of the pre-Islamic
Arabs of declaring, on the basis of conjecture, certain types of
camels and the like to be unlawful for food (see F 2:175).

An-Nīsābūrī notes with regard to the first of these verses that the
statement that most of the people of the earth would lead one
astray, if they were obeyed and followed, also implies without
saying that most of the people of the earth—in the absence of
prophetic revelation—are in fact astray. It is, of course, because
they have already gone astray that following them would lead one
astray (N 8:10). The second verse implies that the idolators
(*mushrikūn*) referred to have invoked a theological argument of
absolute determinism (*jabr*) to justify their idolatry: "Had God not
willed, we would not have associated anything with Him nor would
our fathers before us nor would we have declared anything to have
been prohibited which we have declared unlawful." It should be
noted that the closing verse, after having rejected the validity of
their appeal to absolute determinism, ironically inverts their claim
by asserting that God in his omnipotence, had he willed, could have
constrained them to receive guidance despite their recalcitrance:
"Indeed, had He willed, He would surely have guided you, all of
you together." Although these verses affirm free will against the
argument of absolute determinism, it is also important, as some
commentators observe, that these verses indicate that the nature of
the will of God—the very question of free will and the like—is a
question pertaining to the unseen. Ultimately, therefore, it must be
answered by reference to *ʿilm*—prophetic, revealed knowledge—and cannot be answered on the basis of conjecture and
surmise. The Qurʾān challenges the idolators, therefore, to produce
their *ʿilm*, yet as commentators observe, the question itself is
rhetorical, sarcastically pointing out the fact that they have no *ʿilm*
at all which they can produce. (See Q 3:1227; N 8:50.)

A frequently cited summary of the Qurʾanic doctrine that *ʿilm*
alone must be followed in matters that pertain to religious belief in
the unseen is:

> Divine not that of which you have no definitive knowledge [*ʿilm*]:
> [Your] hearing, [your] sight, [your] heart—for each of these are you
> responsible [and regarding each of them will you be questioned].
> (Qurʾān 17:36.)

Most commentators understand the Arabic *la taqfu* (divine not) to mean something more like "do not pursue" or "do not preoccupy yourself with." The primary sense of the verb *qafā, yaqfū,* from which this negative command comes, is to track or to follow after, although it has a number of other connotations as well. (See Mj 2:758; F 3:227; N 15:34; A 15:72; T 13:92; Q 4:2227.) I prefer the rendition of ar-Rāghib al-Isfahānī—the great Qur'anic semanticist—who takes *lā taqfu* to mean "judge not on the basis of divination (*al-qiyāfah*) or conjecture (*zann*)." Although the verb *qafā* comes from the root QFW, while *quyāfah* from the root QYF/QWF, the two roots often merge with each other and occasionally share identical meanings.

Qur'anic commentators generally agree that this verse refers to conjecture in matters of religious belief and cognate concerns that pertain to the unseen (see A 15:73) where revealed knowledge alone is acceptable. The faculties of hearing and sight are, as at-Tabātabā'ī observes, the chief faculties by which knowledge is acquired; the heart (*al-fu'ād*), in its Qur'anic context, is the seat of feeling, reason, and understanding—therefore that faculty by means of which knowledge comes to its fruition in human beings. It should be noted that the Qur'ān uses the demonstrative pronoun *ulā'ika* to refer to these faculties—an especially meaningful reference in this connection, for in standard Arabic usage it refers to rational beings. The Qur'ān therefore speaks as if each of these faculties had a life and identity of its own and were an independent locus of reason. Moreover, the demonstrative pronoun *ulā'ika* refers to things far away from the speaker; thus, in addition to emphasizing the important status of these faculties themselves in the sight of God, using this particular demonstrative pronoun (*hā'ulā'i* would be used for rational things at hand) sets them on a lofty and distant pedestal. (See T 13:95; A 15:74-75.) In characteristically Qur'anic fashion, this verse, while incisively establishing the greatness of man's faculties of perception and knowledge, concludes by referring to the moral responsibility which necessarily comes with man's possession of these God-given gifts. They are to be used for discovering the dictates of truth and justice and living in accordance with them. Possessing such attributes confers that responsibility, and man will ultimately be questioned on his obedience to that requirement. (Cf. T 13:92-93, 95.) Sayyid Qutb notes that the verse establishes an

appropriate modern criterion for human thought; unlike the amoral
scientific method, it emphasizes joining the spiritual and moral
capacities of the human heart with reason in the search for truth and
progress (Q 4:2227).

BELIEF IN THE UNSEEN WITHIN THE LIMITS
OF THE PERCEPTIBLE WORLD

The Inherent Nobility of Mankind

In the Islamic view, human beings—the children of Adam—
have been created, like Adam, their father, in the very best of
molds. They possess the potential—not exceeded by even the angels
of God—to be among the best of all created beings. These gifts of
potential greatness are also coupled with a negative potential to be,
like man's adversary, Satan, among the most evil of created beings.
Indeed, man's negative potential is so great that he can violate his
nature and cease to be human, cease to be himself. Man is,
however, basically good, in the Islamic view; he inherited no
original sin from others. Consequently, when man is evil, he contra-
dicts his own soul; when man is great, he is then truly man, fulfilling
the dictates of his noble soul. Man's inherent goodness bespeaks the
dignity which God has bestowed upon him among all creatures:

> Behold, We, [God], have conferred great dignity upon the children of
> Adam and have borne them over the land and the sea, providing them
> sustenance of the good things of the earth, wholesome and pleasing,
> and We have favored them far above many beings whom We have
> created. (Qur'ān 17:70.)

All of God's creations have been formed in an excellent fashion
(Qur'ān 32:7); yet, of all created things, man has been fashioned in
the most excellent manner:

> Verily, We have created man in the best of conformations; then We
> reduce him to the lowest of the lowly, except for those who believe [in
> God] and perform deeds of righteousness: For theirs shall be a great
> reward without end. (Qur'ān 95:406.)

The Arabic *taqwīm* conformation would appear here to refer to
man's outward form; certainly other verses in the Qur'ān draw
attention to the beauty and nobility of the human form. *Taqwīm*,
however, also refers to both the inner and the outer properties of

man which buttress his dignity.[29] It should also be noted that the verbal noun *taqwīm*, having the primary etymological sense of making a thing stand firm and upright, emphasizes the inherent uprightness and goodness of the human soul. *Taqwīm* is a synonym of *taswiya* (making a thing sound: giving it due proportion; making it stand upright), which the Qur'ān also uses for describing the manner in which God has created the human soul:

> [Consider] the human soul and that Power Who gave it due proportion and then endowed it with [knowledge of] the evil and the good [of which it is capable]: Indeed, he who purifies it shall have attained the ultimate success [after which there is no failure], while he who pollutes it shall have deprived [himself of all happiness]. (Qur'ān 91:7-10.)

The excellence of the human form, man's upright stature, the types of foods which man eats, the sustenance with which he has been provided, the shelters within which he lives, the clothing he wears to beautify his appearance and to protect him from the elements, his ability to travel with relative ease across the land and over the seas—all of these indicate, in the Qur'anic view, the great bounty God has bestowed upon man and the special mercy and providential care (*ᶜināya*) that characterizes God's lordship relationship with man, his merciful intervention into man's life. Thus, man himself becomes a sign (*āya*) of God's manifest and merciful presence in the world; indeed, in the view of the Muslim mystics man is a microcosm of the macrocosm in which he has been created: "And there are on the earth manifest signs of God's presence for those endowed with certainty of faith, and so likewise are there such signs within your very selves: Can you not see, then, and perceive?" (Qur'ān 51:20-21.) Among these signs, according to Qur'anic commentators, is the conspicuous individuation of the human species, itself indicative of the fact that man is a species of highest status—for the more individuated a species, the greater it is by comparison with less individuated species (see T 1:116-18; Q 1:57, 355-56; 14:401-2; Qr 1:281-82). Each human being is distinctly and conspicuously different from other human beings—they have different faces, different voices, different accents, and so forth. This in the view of a number of commentators is the meaning of the verse: "And among His signs to you of His greatness are the creation of the heavens and the earth and the variations in your tongues and your colors: There are in this, of a certainty, signs for those who have true knowledge" (Qur'ān 30:22). In Arabic, "tongues" (*alsina*) includes all modes of human speech and not just distinctive languages—languages, dialects, accents, and even different tones of the voice (A 21:21; Qr 14:17; Q 4:2241).

The hallmark of human excellence in the Qur'anic view is human intelligence and those faculties directly associated with it, most notably the ability to speak and to write. As a result, man can have insight into himself, his world, and God; hence, man's possession of these faculties is also the basis of his moral responsibility toward God, his creator. (See T 13:155-56; Qr 10:293-94; Q 4:2241). *Ar-Rahmān* (the most merciful God), *sūra* 55, enumerates God's blessings to man. Many commentators hold that the *sūra* lists them in order of their greatness, beginning with the gift of language (Qr 20:119; T 1:116-18: "God, the most-Merciful, imparted the knowledge of the Qur'ān, created man and imparted unto him the knowledge of clear and lucid speech" (Qur'ān 55:1-4).

The Excellence of Man and the Burden of Moral Responsibility

The dignity of man is not a gift carelessly or freely given. In the Qur'anic view, it implies a weight of moral responsibility comparable to the gifts and potential which man has received. This weight of moral responsibility (*taklīf*) is the standard for man's earthly life by which he will be judged in the resurrection and given eternal life—reward or punishment—in the hereafter. Indeed, the conspicuous individuation of the human species, in the view of Qur'anic commentators, is not merely an indication of human excellence with regard to other species but a manifest sign (*āya*) of the unique moral responsibility which each human being bears and by which each will be judged. It is, therefore, both the distinct honor and burden of man to have been designated, in view of his excellence, God's vicegerent (*khalīfa*) in the earth. Adam was meant to be God's *khalīfa* on the earth before the Fall, and the Fall, as al-Qurtubī observes, did not result in the depravity of Adam's soul. In Islamic belief, God forgave Adam for his fall. Rather it was Satan in his disobedience who became depraved and fundamentally evil through the Fall (Qr 1:321, 281-82). The following verses treat vicegerency of man and allude clearly to his inherent excellence (he instructs the angels and God orders them to prostrate themselves before Adam) and his moral burden:

> And [call to mind] when your Lord said unto the angels: "Behold, I am about to establish a vicegerent (*khalifa*) on the earth." They replied: "Will You establish on [earth] one who will spread corruption in it and shed blood, while it is we who exalt your glory and praise, affirm Your perfection, and hallow Your [name]?" He answered: I know that which you do not know.
> And he imparted [unto Adam] the knowledge of all the words [for all things] and then presented the things named before the angels and said: "Tell Me the words for these [things], if what you say is true." They responded "Glory be to You [in Your perfection], we possess no knowledge save that which You have imparted to us: You, in truth, are the all-Knowing and the all-Wise."
> [God] said: "Adam, inform them of the words for [all] these [things]." And once he had informed them of the words for them, [God] said unto the angels: "Did I not say unto you that I possess the knowledge of the Unseen in the heavens and the earth and that I know [all] that you do outwardly and all that you [inwardly] conceal?"
> And [call to mind also] when We, [God], said unto the angels: "Prostrate yourselves before Adam." They then prostrated themselves before him except for Iblīs [Satan]: He refused and gloried in his arrogance and thus became of those who [knowingly] reject [God] and deny his favor. (Qur'ān 2:31-34.)

> It is He, [God], Who has established you as the vicegerents (*khalifa*) of the earth and has raised some of you in degrees of excellence above others in order that He might test you regarding that which He has bestowed upon you: Verily, your Lord is swift in retribution; yet, behold, He is indeed most forgiving, most merciful. (Qur'ān 6:165.)

> It is He, [God], Who has established you as vicegerents (*khalifa*) upon the earth: Thus, [know] that whoever [willfully] rejects [God in disbelief and ingratitude] shall bear the burden of his disbelief, and the disbelief of the disbelievers increases them in their Lord's sight only in loathsomeness, and the disbelief of the disbelievers increases them only in [greater and greater] loss. (Qur'ān 35:39.)

As God's vicegerent upon the earth, man carries the moral responsibility to establish order, justice, and prosperity throughout the world. Consequently, man is accountable if he fails to meet these objectives as a result of negligence and irresponsibility. However, his reward hereafter will be the greatest of honors if he has sincerely tried to attain these goals. In the Qur'anic view, man's inability to perceive the realities of the unseen directly without the mediation of prophets and prophet-messengers is not a defect in the excellent nature with which he has been created. On the contrary, the moral test which man undergoes on the earth, his attempt to live up to the standard of God's vicegerency, his greatest moral, ethical, and spiritual achievements, are meaningful only because they take place within the realm of the perceptible, the great truths and the impending realities of the unseen. As the Qur'ān emphatically and repeatedly teaches, when the veil of the unseen is removed at the time of the resurrection and men witness the realities of the unseen, all human beings will believe, all will loathe evil, all will desire to do good, but only those will be justified who had believed, worked righteousness, and withstood evil before knowing the consequences of such acts.

At the same time, however, the boundary between the perceived and the unseen is never a barrier between man and God in this world. For the excellence of the human soul, according to Islamic belief, also consists in the fact that God in his providential care (*ᶜināya*) and justice has endowed each soul with an instinctive pre-disposition (*al-istiᶜdād al-fitrī*) to know God and the realities of the unseen within the limitations of the perceptible world. Moreover, God has given creation the power to reflect his majesty, presence, and power, and to prefigure the impending realities of the unseen; thus, the material world becomes for the believer an objective correlative confirming what the prophets have taught and what the soul unconsciously knows. Such implicit guidance, which in Islamic belief encompasses all aspects of man's being and environment, reflects God's desire to guide man and be both merciful and just in requiring heavy responsibilities from him. Consequently, it is man's ability to believe in the unseen, to serve and worship a God whom he cannot see, touch, or hear, and his ability to attain full moral and spiritual edification under such circumstances which constitute the roots of human dignity. It is those characteristics of the human soul which, according to Islamic belief, release man's positive potential. When God commanded the angels, who initially perceived only the negative potential of the human spirit, to bow down before Adam, he was providing evidence of that positive potential.

The Nature of Man's Soul

The inherent nature of the human soul is, as we have seen, excellent, endowed with dignity and innate moral sense, untainted by the depravity of original sin, yet capable of great evil as well as great good. This inherent nature (*fitra*) is essentially the same in all human beings in all times and places, regardless of sex, ethnic group, or situation. Moreover, Islām, according to the Qur'ān, is the universal religion of the human *fitra*: "And so set your face steadfastly toward the one, true faith in sincerity and devotion, turning away from all that is false, in accordance with the inborn nature (*fitra*) with which God has created mankind. There is nothing that will alter the nature of that which God has created." (Qur'ān 30:30.) The universality of the human *fitra* alluded to in this verse is made quite explicit in the following *hadīth*, ascribed to the prophet Muhammad: "No child is born but that it is born following the *fitra*. It is the child's parents who make it become a Jew, a Christian, or a Magian. Likewise livestock give birth to offspring that are sound and completely whole: Do you find in their offspring any marks of branding or other inflicted blemish?" (Qr 14:27.) A similar *hadīth* states that each child's *fitra* remains intact until it is able to express itself in speech; then its parents are able to alter the child's inherent religious predisposition.[30]

Traditional Islamic scholars interpret passages like these to characterize the *fitra* as having an instinctive knowledge of God, his oneness, and the Lordship relationship between God and man:

> And [call to mind] when your Lord brought forth from the loins of the children of Adam [all of] their progeny and called them to bear witness regarding themselves, saying [to them]: Am not I your Lord? They replied: Indeed You are, and [to this] have we borne witness. [Of this We remind you] lest on the Day of Resurrection you say: It is something of which we were completely unaware. (Qur'ān 7:172.)

> Behold, We [God], offered the trust (*al-amāna*) of moral responsibility to the heavens and the earth and the mountains, but they refused to take it and had great fear of it. Yet man took it upon himself, and, lo, he has become a great doer of injustice, exceedingly ignorant.
> [And so it is] that God will punish the hypocrites, both men and women, and the men and women who associate [false objects of worship] with God. And so also is it that God will turn in forgiveness

and mercy to the believing men and the believing women: For God is, indeed, most forgiving, most merciful. (Qur'ān 33:72.)

From these and similar texts, Muslim scholars hold that God made with all human beings in the premortal existence a universal primordial covenant, the basis for all the later prophetic covenants established between God and particular religious communities in history. As part of the legacy of this covenant, the *fitra* imprints each soul as it begins its secondary existence with immediate (*darūrī*), intuitive knowledge of God and the great realities of the unseen that pertain directly to human destiny. (See Q 3:1391-94; T 8:322; K 3:245-49; Qr 7:314-16.)

Thus, though man is charged with the moral obligation to believe in God and the great realities of the unseen even though they lie beyond his immediate perception, God provides intuitive knowledge linking man with the world beyond. The Qur'ān repeatedly refers to its message and those of earlier prophets as a "remembrance" (*dhikr, dhikrā*) or "that which causes one to remember" (*tadhkira, tadhkīr*), while it calls upon the recipient of the Qur'anic message to "make himself remember," to "call to mind" (*tadhakkara, idhdhakkara,* etc.). The revealed message is neither foreign nor new, even though it pertains to realities which lie beyond man's mortal experience; on the contrary, it reminds him of primordial knowledge and of a primal experience deeply imprinted upon his soul: "And, therefore, continue to remind (*dhakkir*) [them], for this remembrance (*adh-dhikrā*) greatly benefits those who believe. I have not created the [hidden] spirits of mankind but that they serve and worship Me." (Qur'ān 51:55-56.)

The Created World as Mirror of God's Presence

One of the most dominant themes in the Qur'ān is that the creation is filled with *āyāt*, with signs and portents of God's presence and of his continual and merciful intervention in the world. It is, moreover, one of the most fundamental capacities of *fitra* that it senses and understands these *āyāt*; they constitute, as Izutsu has pointed out, one of the most profound communications—albeit nonverbal—between God and man, reflecting God's desire that man receive guidance in this world and that man's faith in God, even though it is faith in the unseen, lead him to absolute certainty and conviction.[31] Although each finite thing is an *āya* (sign) of the infinite, it is the Qur'ān's custom to draw attention to the symbolism of everyday *āyāt:* the rhythm of the seasons, day and night, weather, birth, life and death, and so forth. The pre-Islamic Arab searched the physical world for omens—the rare, even freakish accidents of nature. No doubt the Qur'anic emphasis upon normative, day-to-day *āyāt* which continually encompass man's life is deliberate, aimed at fundamentally altering the pre-Islamic attitude toward the unseen. The Muslim cannot see the world as a place for omens; instead he sees the fabric of material reality both in its day-to-day events and in its rarest manifestations as dyed with the glorious presence of God whose creative act accounts for it all. Moreover, by focusing man's attention on the miraculous and marvelous in the mundane, the Qur'ān seeks to wake him from his stupor of negligence (*ghafla*), to make him see the world anew as the wonder which it is—a wonder which cannot account for itself. Furthermore, while the pre-Islamic Arabs sought omens to discern the propitiousness of their undertakings, the Qur'ān directs man to look at the *āyāt* of the world to buttress the truth of the unseen realities set forth in prophetic guidance, to see reflected the oneness of God, his great power in creation, his omnipresent hand, his bounty and mercy. The creation of life within the womb of the mother, the coming of the rains and the revival of the dead earth, and similar natural events are signs that prefigure the resurrection of the dead and new life in the hereafter.

This theme, closely linked to concepts discussed earlier, is illuminated in these verses about the *āyāt* of God in the created world and the implicit guidance they provide the believer:

> Behold, in the creation of the heavens and the earth; the alteration of the night and the day; in the ships that move swiftly over the sea bearing things beneficial to man; in the waters—dew, rain, and ice—which God sends down from the sky, giving thereby life to the earth after it was dead and causing to multiply thereon all manner of living creatures; and in the change of the winds and the clouds running their appointed courses between the heavens and the earth: In all of these there are signs (*āyāt*), indeed, for a people who use their reason. (Qur'ān 2:164.)

> And among His signs (*āyāt*) [to you of His greatness] are the creation of the heavens and the earth and the variations in your tongues and

your colors: There are in this, of a certainty, signs for those who have
[true] knowledge. (Qur'ān 30:22.)

And We, [God], shall show them Our signs (*āyāt*) upon the distant
horizons and within their very selves until it shall become manifest to
them that this revelation is, indeed, the truth (Qur'ān 41:53).

And there are on the earth [manifest] signs (*āyāt*) [of God's presence]
for those endowed with certainty of faith,
And so likewise are there [signs] within your [very] selves: Can you
not see, then, and perceive? (Qur'ān 51:20-21.)

The World as Ornament or Symbol

To clarify the Qur'anic conception of the *āyāt* of God, Izutsu
draws upon Karl Jaspers, who makes the symbolic nature of the
world one of the roots of his philosophical system. Seen on the level
of common understanding, for example, a tree is simply a tree.
However, perceived on a higher level of true existence or true
existential reality, a tree becomes something new, something
wondrously unfamiliar. In Qur'anic parlance, this second level is
that of perceiving the things of the world as *āyāt*; it is the level of
perception of those who use their "intellect" or "reason" (*ʿaql*),
those who "reflect" (*tadabbarū*) and "think deeply" (*tafakkarū*),
those who have "(true) knowledge" (*ʿilm*), and so forth. One who
perceives the world on this level, as Izutsu points out, "suddenly
finds himself in a strange world, standing in front of God." The
world, having taken on symbolic power to mirror the infinite,
becomes, according to Jasper's image, a *chiffreschrift*, a vast code of
ciphers, a code, however, which only those can read who perceive
the world at the level of true existence.[32]

It would probably be correct, in terms of Qur'anic semantics, to
refer to the level of commonplace understanding as perception of
the world as ornamentation (*zīna*), while the higher level would be
that of perceiving the ornamentation of the world as *āyāt*. The
theme of the beautiful ornamentation of the world runs throughout
the Qur'ān; it is especially central, however, to the message of *Sūrat
al-Kahf* (the mountain cave), *sūra* 18, as at-Tabātabā'ī demonstrates
in his commentary:

"Behold, [We], God, have made that which is upon the earth to be a
[beautiful] ornamentation for the earth in order that We may test

[human beings] as to which of them is the best in conduct and deed. Yet, verily, We will reduce [ultimately] all that which is upon its [surface] to barren dust, a bleak and desolate plain." (Qur'ān 18:7-8.)

Although the English word *ornamentation* often conveys a sense of superficiality, perhaps gaudy or trivial, the Arabic *zīna* of the world is not evil, according to the Qur'ān. It is man's incorrect attachment to it which is evil; if man takes a correct attitude toward it, it becomes a source of good for him and his society. Man is to enjoy the *zīna* of the world in the spirit of justice and judicious moderation, realizing that it has no inherent value, cannot itself fulfill his soul or bring happiness, and that love for it must always be secondary to the moral responsibility inherent in man's dignity. Man can properly enjoy the *zīna* of the world in understanding that the world's beauty and goodness originate in the same source of its symbolic power to mirror God—it is the handiwork of a unique, merciful, and omnipotent Creator, who in his wisdom has created in the most excellent fashion all that he has created and who has created each thing for a purpose and nothing in vain.

Vision and Blindness, the Living and the Dead

Prophetic revelation, be it that of the prophet Muhammad or of earlier prophets, is described in the Qur'ān as light (*nūr*). (See, for example, Qur'ān 4:174; 5:15, 44, 46; 7:157; 42:52; 6:8; 64:8.) It illuminates man's soul, calls forth the power of the material world to evoke the remembrance and awareness of God, imparts to man true vision, and gives life to his soul by linking it with the great realities of the unseen. In the following verses the Qur'ān is referred to by a similar image as *basā'iru min Rabbikum* (manifest proofs from your Lord which make you see and understand). *Basā'ir*, the plural of *basīra*, comes from the root BSR, which connotes having clear vision and, consequently, clear understanding:

Such is God, your Lord: There is no god [no object of worship], but He, Creator of every thing [which exists]. Therefore, worship and serve Him; for He it is Who has everything under His care. Human vision (*al-absār*) cannot see Him; yet He encompasses [in His sight] all human vision: He is infinitely subtle and unfathomable (*al-latīf*), Knower of all things [hidden and manifest] (*al-khabīr*).
Manifest proofs (*basā'ir*) have now come to you [all] from your Lord,

enabling you to see and to understand: Whoever, therefore, chooses to see and perceive (*fa-man absara*), does so for his own benefit, and whoever chooses to remain blind (*fa-man ʿamiya*), does so to his own detriment. And [say to them, O Prophet]: I am not a keeper over you. (Qur'ān 6:102-4.)

These verses categorically describe God as unseen: "Human vision cannot see Him." Yet revelation has enabled man to perceive and to understand him; it has given the believer eyes with which to see, while those who turn away from it have chosen spiritual blindness.

This theme of blindness and vision, death and life, occurs frequently in the Qur'ān:

... Behold, it is not [their] eyes which become blind, but blind have become the hearts which are in [their] breasts (Qur'ān 22:46).

Verily, you cannot make the dead to hear, nor can you make the deaf hear your call, once they have turned their backs and gone away.
You cannot guide the blind out of their error: None can you make hear [your call] except those who believe in Our signs and willingly submit themselves to Us. (Qur'ān 30:52-53; cf. 27:80-81.)

... It is but a remembrance (*dhikr*) and a divine discourse (*qur'ān*), making all things clear,
In order that he give warning to those who are alive and that the Word [of God] be fulfilled against those who [knowingly] reject [God] and disbelieve. (Qur'ān 36:69-70.)

CONCLUSION

Islām fundamentally reoriented the attitude of the pre-Islamic Arabs to the unseen. It abolished all types of mediation between man and the unseen except that of prophetic revelation, a position analogous to that of the great biblical prophets and, apparently, to the ancient Persian prophetic figure Zarathustra before them. Islām directed man to reflect on the world perceived by his five senses, the realm of the perceptible, yet emphasized that limiting man's senses to the realm of the perceptible did not constitute a barrier between him and the great realities of the unseen. On the contrary, although man had no direct access to the unseen save through the mediation of prophets, his soul and the created world were filled with signs of God, confirming the prophetic message and providing a path to certainty about the unseen within the context of the perceptible.

Thus, in the Islamic view, the inherent knowledge of man's soul (*fitra*) and the signs of God (*āyāt*) in creation constitute a primal communicative link between God and man, nonlinguistic, intuitive, and unconscious. Together the *fitra* and the *āyāt* of God form a network of implicit guidance throughout the realm of the perceptible, an implicit guidance which buttresses the explicit guidance in the messages of prophetic revelation. The *āyāt* of God are not omens. They do not foretell the success of undertakings, forewarn of failure or misfortune, or mirror the pleasure or the displeasure of God's will. Neither through direct contact or divination from omens in the realm of the perceptible can man, according to Islamic belief, discern his destiny or the immediate future. Moreover, Islām deemed such a preoccupation with the unseen to be morally reprehensible, detrimental to man's moral and ethical edification. To fulfill the purpose of life and attain fullest moral and spiritual development, man needed to believe in only the major realities of the unseen: the oneness of God, prophetic revelation, the judgment, the hereafter, and so forth. The inability of man's *fitra* to sense the realities of the unseen through the *āyāt* of God lay at the root of human dignity and facilitated man's spiritual and moral perfection within the realm of the perceptible.

The dichotomy between the realm of the perceptible and the realm of the unseen is meaningful only from man's finite consciousness. In the omniscience of God, all reality constitutes a single continuum, eternally known and perceived. The duality between the perceptible and the unseen is, from the viewpoint of man, epistemologically but not existentially real. Existentially, reality constitutes a single continuum; thus, the realms of the perceptible and the unseen do not constitute antithetical and contradictory worlds. Despite qualitative differences (lower and higher, less and more perfect), they are not mutually exclusive orders of existence. Thus, man's earthly life, although bound to the realm of the perceptible, stands forever upon the threshold of the unseen. Symbolic and emblematic continuity links his experience within the perceived world and the great realities of the unseen, which yet are native to his soul and explicitly described in prophetic revelation. Far from being a defect in his constitution, man's inability to directly witness the unseen is necessary so that man's life in the world constitutes a valid moral test. It is only in such a context that his spiritual and moral accomplishments are meaningful.

The apparent duality between the world as *zīna* (beautiful ornament) and the world as *āya* (sign of God) is also an epistemological and not an existential fact. A function of man's perception and the inclination of his heart, this dichotomy is necessary, according to Islamic belief, so that existence in this world constitutes an appropriate test for man's soul. The world in itself, however, constitutes a single reality. Because it exists as the flawless handiwork of God, man can perceive it as beautiful and attractive ornamentation in itself and also as a sign of God's perfection and relation to the world. Although the material world is sufficiently beautiful and rewarding to tempt man's high soul, it is not sufficient to fulfill his soul. Preoccupation with the world for its own sake, therefore, will necessarily lead to injustice, unhappiness, and evil. When man can see the world only as ornamentation, only as an object in itself, he becomes, in Qur'anic parlance, blind and deaf, dead in life, even though he has physical sight, physical hearing, and biological life. For when the world of the perceptible has become for man an object in itself, he lives in contradiction to his own being. On the other hand, when man lives justly and judiciously with the *zīna* of his material world, its beauty taking on the emblematic power to mirror the world of reality beyond—when it ceases to be only *zīna* and becomes also *āya*—then man is truly man, his existence is linked through the perceptible to the unseen. Worthy of the dignity God has bestowed upon him, he is alive and awake; he has eyes with which to see and ears with which to hear; he is then capable of being God's vicegerent (*khalīfa*) on the earth and of fulfilling the purpose for which he was created.

NOTES

1. See, for example, Fazlur Rahman, *Major Themes in the Qur'an* (Minneapolis and Chicago: Bibliotheca Islamica, 1980), pp. 80-87. This work can also be consulted as an introduction to other fundamental paradigms of the Qur'anic world view.

2. See A. Leo Oppenheim, *Ancient Mesopotamia: Portrait of a Dead Civilization* (Chicago and London: University of Chicago Press, 1964), pp. 171-83, 206-23; and his "Perspectives on Mesopotamian Divination," in *La divination en Mesopotamie ancienne et dans les regions voisines,* 14th Recontre Assyriologique

Internationale (Strasbourg, 2-6 juillet 1965), Travaux du Centre d'Etudes Superieures Specialises d'Histoire des Religions de Strasbourg (Paris: Presse Universitaires de France, 1966), pp. 36-40.

3. See Oppenheim, *Ancient Mesopotamia,* pp. 206-27; his "Perspectives," pp. 37-38; Robert R. Wilson, *Prophecy and Society in Ancient Israel* (Oxford: Basil Blackwell, 1973), pp. 29-31. I would like to note, without attempting to detract from the overall quality of Lindblom's work, which I am not qualified to judge, that his short discussion on Islamic parallels and especially on the prophecy of Muhammad is misleading and reflects, unfortunately, misconceptions and inaccuracies which are still too frequent in Western scholarship pertaining to Islām.

4. See Wilson, *Prophecy and Society,* pp. 90-111, 118-28; Oppenheim, *Ancient Mesopotamia,* pp. 221-22. Translations of the oracular records of Mari are available with discussions and analysis in Friedrich Ellermeier, *Prophetie in Mari and Israel,* Theologische und Orientalistische Arbeiten, Band 1 (Herzberg am Harz: Verlga Erwin Jungfrau, 1968), pp. 76-165.

5. Wilson, *Prophecy and Society,* pp. 124, 128.

6. Ibid., p. 129.

7. See Mary Boyce, *A History of Zoroastrianism,* vol. 1: *The Early Period; Handbuch der Orientalistik,* ed. B. Spuler *et al,* Erste Abteilung: Der Nahe und der Mittlere Osten, Bank 8: Religion (Leiden/Cologne: E. J. Brill, 1975), pp. 11-12, 186-91, 279-80; Gherardo Gnoli, *Zoroaster's Time and Homeland: A Study on the Origins of Mazdeism and Related Problems,* Instituto Universitario Orientale: Seminario di Studi Asiatici; Series Minor 7 (Naples: Tipografia Don Bosco, 1980), pp. 181-93, 227-28; Lindblom, *Prophecy,* pp. 31-32.

8. Wilson, *Prophecy and Society,* pp. 194-212.

9. See Lindblom, *Prophecy,* pp. 49-56, 61, 217; Wilson, *Prophecy and Society,* pp. 130, 139. In Lindblom's view the terms *hōzeh* and *rō'eh* indicate that the revelatory experiences of the early Hebrew seers were partly visual and partly auditory (pp. 55-56). Regarding prophets, see Lindblom, p. 1; cf. H. W. Parke, *Greek Oracles* (London: Hutchinson University Library, 1967), pp. 13-16.

10. Wilson, *Prophecy and Society,* p. 137; cf. Lindblom, *Prophecy,* p. 100.

11. See Wilson, *Prophecy and Society,* pp. 156, 162-64, n. 54, pp. 211, 251; Lindblom, *Prophecy,* pp. 54-56, 61-65; 217-18.

12. See Toshihiko Izutsu, *God and Man in the Koran: Semantics of the Koranic Weltanschauung* (Tokyo: Keio Institute of Cultural and Linguistic Studies, 1964), pp. 82-85.

13. To remove common Western misconceptions, it should be noted that Allāh, even in its pre-Islamic context, denoted the supreme deity, who had no equal and was deemed the creator of the heavens and the earth. Derived from the Arabic root *'LH,* from which comes *ilāh* (a god, cf. Hebrew elōh, god, from which the biblical elōhim, God). *Allāh* probably comes from *al-ilāh* (the God). Pre-Islamic Arab Jews and Christians used *Allāh* to stand for the Abrahamic God of the Bible, and, like Muslims, Arabic-speaking Jews and Christians use the word *Allāh* in that sense today.

14. See Jawād ᶜAlī, *Al-Mufassal fī Tārīkh al-ᶜArab qabl al-Islām* (The Topical Study of the History of the Arabs before Islam) 10 vols. (Beirut: Dār al-ᶜIlm

li-'l-Malāyīn; Baghdad: Maktabat an-Nahdah, 1968-1973), 6:705-6; hereafter cited parenthetically as JA.

15. See Emile Tyan, *Histoire de l'organisation judiciare en pays d'Islam* (Leiden: E. J. Brill, 1960), pp. 41-43; JA 6:763-77.

16. Tyan, *Organisation judiciare*, pp. 29-33, 51; JA 6:763-71.

17. Izutsu, *God and Man*, p. 85. Izutsu's subsequent work, *Ethico-Religious Concepts in the Qur'an* (Montreal: McGill University Press, 1966), which grew out of his *God and Man* and other earlier works, is a valuable study of a number of such correlation words that make up the core of Qur'anic ethical semantics. The academic and scholarly quality of *Ethico-Religious Concepts* is superior to that of *God and Man*; both books, however—especially in light of the fact that their subject matters do not completely overlap—are among the best works currently available in English for the investigation of the language and the fundamental conceptions of the Qur'ān. Regarding Izutsu's views on the nature of Qur'anic semantics, see *Ethico-Religious Concepts*, pp. 3-15.

18. See Izutsu, *God and Man*, pp. 84-89. Izutsu suggests that the frequent occurrence of *ad-dunyā* in pre-Islamic Arabic poetry implies that the concept of the hereafter—*al-ukhrā*, *al-ākhira*, the natural semantic counterpart of the word—must have also been present in pre-Islamic Arab society, even if not as pronounced. M. M. Bravmann, in his *The Spiritual Background of Early Islam: Studies in Ancient Arab Concepts* (Leiden: E. J. Brill, 1972), pp. 32-38, has also discussed the frequent occurrence of *ad-dunyā* in pre-Islamic Arab poetry. While also holding that *ad-dunyā* is a correlation word, Bravmann contends that its pre-Islamic semantic partner was not *al-ākhira* but *al-bu^cad* or *al-ba^cad* (the distant lands and territories of the horizon), as opposed to the immediate encampment or tribal area at hand. *Ad-dunyā* is often referred to negatively in such poetry, not because the life of this world is viewed negatively, but because the *dunyā* in this territorial sense was the realm of women, children, the aged, the timid, and the sick; it was that relatively safe world in which heroic attainments were unlikely—unlike the distant *bu^cd* of the horizon, which was fraught with danger but which also afforded adventures and acts of manliness (*murū^ca*) and heroism. *Ad-dunyā* was the retreat of the meek, while *al-bu^cd* was the realm of the dauntless and heroic Bedouin traveller.

19. *Shahida* is used in this sense, for example, in the Qur'anic verse pertaining to the Fast of Ramadān (Qur'ān 2:185), "*fa-man shahida minkumu-sh-shahr* (then whoever among you 'witnesses' the month)...." Many traditional commentators understood *shahida* to mean in this context, "whoever among you is not on a journey (*ghā'ib*) but at home in his village or encampment." Note also Qur'ān 74:13, *banūn shuhūd* (sons by his side), referring to sons who because of their father's prodigious wealth are not constrained to go on long and dangerous journeys in search of a livelihood. See Muhammad ibn Mansūr, *Lisān al-^cArab* (The Language of the Arabs), 15 vols. (Beirut: Dār Bairūt, Dār Sādir, 1388/1968), 1:654-57, 3:238-42; al-Husain ibn Muhammad ar-Rāghib al-Isfahānī, *Al-Mufradāt fī Gharīb al-Qur'ān* (Unusual Qur'anic Expressions), ed. Muhammad Sayyid Kīlānī (Cairo: Matba^cat al-Halabī, n.d..), pp. 267-68, 366-67; *Al-Mu^cjam al-Wasīt* (The Intermediate Lexicon), Majma^c al-Lugha al-^cArabīya, 2 vols. (Tehran: Al-Maktaba al-^cIlmīya, n.d.), 1:499, 2:673-74.

20. The feminine form of the adjective was not used, since like a number of other adjectives of this type, it was never applied to men.

21. See *Lisān al-ʿArab*, 3:238-39, 242; *Al-Mufradāt*, pp. 267-68; *Al-Muʿjam*, 1:499-500.

22. It must be noted, however, that the expression in this verse, "those who believe in the Unseen" (*al-ladhina yuʾminūna bi-l-ghaib*) also affords another reading as "those who believe in God while they are in the unseen," i.e., when they are alone and not seen by others or when—as a necessary condition of earthly life—they cannot witness God witnessing them. This ambiguity arises out of the semantic possibilities of the preposition *bi* (in), which, when used with the verb *āmana* (to believe) designates the object of belief when the verb has a transitive sense. But this preposition is also used to designate the place in which something occurs, and this would be its use in this verse if *āmana* is read in its nontransitive, complete (*tāmm*) sense as meaning "to have belief." A number of traditional commentators—although hardly all of them—prefer this second rendition, probably in view of the numerous Qurʾanic verses in which the expression "*bi-l-ghaib*" (in the unseen) is clearly used in a locative sense. See Qurʾān 5:94; 21:49; 35:18; 36:11; 50:33; 57:25; 67:12. These other verses do not use *bi-l-ghaib* in conjunction with the verb *āmana*, however, but with transitive verbs like *khāfa* (to fear), *khashiya* (to fear; to hold in great awe), and *nasara* (to come to another's aid; to champion), which take direct objects and do not use the preposition *bi* to express their transitivity. These verbs do not have the ambiguity implicit in *āmana*; moreover, their direct objects are explicitly mentioned—e.g., to fear God in the unseen—whereas *āmana*, in the verse above, would have to be read either as *tāmm* (nontransitive; abstract) or as having an elided object, if *bi-l-ghaib* is to have a locative sense.

23. Translations from the Qurʾān are my own; I have, however, often consulted *The Message of the Qurʾan*, trans. Muhammad Asad, (Gibraltar: Dar al-Andalus, 1980), which, to my knowledge, is the best English translation currently available.

24. See al-Hasan ibn Muhammad ibn al-Husain, *Gharāʾib al-Qurʾān wa Raghāʾib al-Furqān* (The Marvel of the Qurʾān and the Desired Elucidations of the Furqān [the Criterion, another name for the Qurʾān]), ed. Ibrāhīm ʿAtūwah ʿIwad, 30 vols. (Egypt: Matbaʿat al-Halabī, 1390/1970), 1:145, 149; hereafter cited parenthetically in the text as N by volume and page. Shihāb-ad-Dīn Mahmūd, *Rūh al-Maʿānī fī Tafsīr al-Qurʾān al-ʿAzīm wa-s-Sabʿ al-Mathānī* (The Spirit of the Meanings in the Interpretation of the Most Illustrious Qurʾān and the Seven Oft-Repeated verses), 30 vols. (Beirut: Dār Ihyāʾ at-Turāth al-ʿArabī, 1970), 1:110; hereafter cited parenthetically in the text as A by volume and page.

25. N 1:149; A 1:45-46; ʿAlī ibn Muhammad ibn Ibrāhīm, *Tafsīr al-Qurʾān al-Jalīl* (The Commentary of the Illustrious Qurʾān), 4 vols. (Beirut: Dār al-Maʿ-rifah, 1970), 1:23; Sayyid *Fī Zilāl al-Qurʾān* (In the Shades of the Qurʾān), 6 vols. (Beirut: Dār ash-Shurūq, 1393/1973), 1:39-40, hereafter cited parenthetically in the text as Q by volume and page; Muhammad ibn ʿAlī, *Fath al-Qadīr: Al-Jāmiʿ baina Fanni-r-Riwāya wa-d-Dirāya min ʿIlm at-Tafsīr* (The Enlightenment of the Omnipotent God: A Work Combining the Disciplines of Tradition and Intellect with Regard to the Science of Commentary), 5 vols. (Egypt: Matbaʿat al-Halabī, 1383/1964), 1:34,

hereafter cited parenthetically in the text as F by volume and page; Muhammad Husain at-Tabātabā'ī, *Al-Mīzān fī Tafsīr al-Qur'ān* (The Scales of Balance in the Commentary of the Qur'ān), 20 vols. (Beirut: Al-Matbaᶜa at-Tijārīya, 1390/1970), 1:45-46, hereafter cited parenthetically in the text as T by volume and page.

26. Cf. Lindblom, *Prophecy*, pp. 57-58.

27. A number of modern commentators note the great similarity between Dhū-'l-Qarnain in the Qur'ān and the ancient Persian king Koresh (Cyrus), who released the Jews from the Babylonian captivity and helped them rebuild the temple in Jerusalem, as described in the books of Daniel, Isaiah, and Ezra and in the writing of Herodotus. They also note archeological discoveries that depict Koresh wearing a helmet with two long horns. (See T 13:382, 391-92.)

28. See Q 4:2352-53 and Muhammad ibn Ahmad, *Al-Jāmiᶜ li-Ahkām al-Qur'ān* (The Summa of the Legal Rulings of the Qur'ān), 20 vols. (Cairo: Dār al-Kitāb al-ᶜArabi, 1387/1967), 11:246, hereafter cited parenthetically in the text as Qr by volume and page.

29. See Muhammad al-Amīn ibn Muhammad al-Mukhtār, *Adwā' al-Bayān fī Īdāh al-Qur'ān* (The Radiant Lights of the Clear Discourse [i.e., the Qur'ān] for Illuminating the Meaning of the Qur'ān through the Qur'ān), 9 vols. (Saudi Arabia: Muhammad ibn ᶜIwad ibn Lādin, 1400/1980), 9:330.

30. Imād-ad-Dīn Ismāᶜīl *Tafsīr al-Qur'ān al-ᶜAzīm* (The Commentary of the Magnificent Qur'ān), 7 vols. (Beirut: Dār al-Andalus, 1386/1966), 5:359-60, hereafter cited parenthetically in the text as K by volume and page.

31. Izutsu, *God and Man*, pp. 133-39.

32. Ibid., pp. 134-35.

17
God's Love
for Mankind

Elder Carlos E. Asay

A few years ago my wife and I purchased in Beirut a gold plaque with the Arabic inscription, *Marhaba biikum*, meaning "Welcome." Upon our return to the United States, we placed the plaque on the front door of our home, and it has been there ever

---

Elder Carlos E. Asay is a member of the Presidency of the First Quorum of the Seventy of The Church of Jesus Christ of Latter-day Saints. A graduate of the University of Utah in social science, he received his M.A. from Long Beach State College and his Ed.D. from the University of Utah in educational administration. Elder Asay has served as an administrator in the Granite School District and the Jordan School District of Utah, was professor of education at Brigham Young University, and was chairman of its Secondary Education Department in 1969. He also served on the BYU-Hawaii faculty. Elder Asay by training and experience has maintained a close interest and involvement in Middle Eastern affairs, initiated by his missionary service for the Church in Syria from 1947-1950.

since. We love this work of art for many reasons: it is very beautiful; it provokes many inquiries and produces many interesting conversations; it reminds us of some marvelous memories gleaned through travels in the Middle East; but, most important, it inspires us to extend welcome to all who grace our premises after the inimitable manner of the Islamic people.

Added to all the other greetings which have been given you in this conference, I add one more, *Marhaba biikum.* I do so in behalf of the leadership of the LDS Church.

I also desire to express to those from countries abroad a very special *shukran.* This thanks is extended through you to all who have befriended members of our faith as they have traveled, lived, and worked among you and your peoples over the years.

The word *thanks* seems most anemic as I acknowledge all of the goodnesses shared with me by members of the Islamic faith during the time I lived in Lebanon and Syria. I served a mission for my church in that part of the world from the fall of 1947 to the spring of 1950. I choose to refer to that experience in the Middle East as my two-and-one-half-year *hajj.* I use this expression with deep respect, even reverence. For my Church pilgrimage into a part of the Islamic world had a sanctifying influence upon my life, and I regard it as something most sacred. Though I cannot claim the real honors of a real *hajj,* I feel that I completed in the Arab world a journey of faith, love, and sacrifice. And in the process of that journey, I experienced a spiritual renewal which has directed the course of my life and made all the difference.

During my stay in Lebanon, I was invited to participate as a member of the National Lebanese Basketball Team. I wore proudly the colors of that nation in international competition. (If I weren't so modest, I would add that we won more than our share of the victories.) My final games with the Lebanese team were played in a tournament in Istanbul. When the tournament was over and the day before I was scheduled to leave Istanbul, the leader of the Sports Federation requested that I go with him to the *sūq* (an underground marketplace) to purchase a Persian rug for his wife. While shopping for this rug, my friend casually and cleverly solicited my advice on color, design, size, etc., as dozens of pieces were displayed before us. I singled out one that was especially beautiful. I was certain that that carpet would please my friend's wife. The next day as I boarded my plane for Athens, the first leg of my travel home, my friends—my Muslim friends—presented to me a baggage claim slip. This slip informed me that the beautiful Persian rug—the one of my own selection—had been checked in my name.

I assure you that the rug given me is one of my most treasured possessions. Each time I look at it, sweet memories flood into my mind. The rug symbolizes the generosity and gift-giving tendency found among Muslim people. As the rug seems to take on added vividness of color through wear, my feelings of gratitude and thanks toward my friends become deeper and keener with each passing year. The word *shukran* or thanks falls short in conveying the love I feel for those who shared with me a special *hajj*.

I commend all of you for choosing to participate in this symposium. Whether you learn through speaking or listening or both, I am certain that much has and will yet be gained from this exchange of ideas.

In 1855, in an address delivered in the Bowery at Salt Lake City, Elder Parley P. Pratt, an early leader of The Church of Jesus Christ of Latter-day Saints, said: "We would do well to look into the bearings of the history of nations, and the dealings of God with them, as impartially as we can, at all times, and cull out all the good there has been, is, or may be, and acknowledge the hand of God in all things, in His dealings with the nations as well as in other things." (*Journal of Discourses* 3:42.)

Elder Pratt's thoughts echo the teachings of some ancient American prophets. Permit me to quote from the Book of Mormon:

> And the Lord God hath sent his *holy prophets among all the children of men*, to declare these things to every kindred, nation, and tongue (Mosiah 3:13; italics added).

> For behold, the Lord doth grant unto *all nations*, of their own nation and tongue, to teach his word, yea, in wisdom, all that he seeth fit that they should have (Alma 29:8; italics added).

> Thus saith the Lord God: I will give unto the children of men line upon line, precept upon precept, here a little and there a little . . . . I bring forth my word unto the children of men, yea, even upon *all the*

nations of the earth.... For I command all men...that they shall write the words which I speak unto them.... *I shall also speak unto all nations of the earth* and they shall write it. (2 Nephi 28:30; 29:7, 11, 12; italics added.)

How very fortunate for mankind that God's word was given in diverse ways to the people of India, of Persia, of Babylon, of Arabia, of China, of Greece, of Rome, and of America. Each spark of inspiration, each revealed law, and each guideline for living was an expression of God's limitless love for the family of Adam. It mattered not whether the word came in high or low places or whether it was conveyed in loud or in muted voices. Some of God's light was reflected through a religious leader in ancient Arabia; additional light was received by an American religious leader in the nineteenth century. What mattered was that saving truth was received by man from God—the divine fountain of eternal truth. And what mattered even more was whether those who received such truths had sufficient reciprocating love and faith to live accordingly.

On 15 February 1978, the First Presidency of the LDS Church issued a statement to the world regarding God's love for all mankind. I desire to read portions of that statement. As I do so, you will note that thoughts previously mentioned are amplified.

> Based upon ancient and modern revelation, The Church of Jesus Christ of Latter-day Saints gladly teaches and declares the Christian doctrine that all men and women are brothers and sisters, not only by blood relationship from common mortal progenitors but also as literal spirit children of an Eternal Father.
>
> The great religious leaders of the world such as Muhammad, Confucius, and the Reformers, as well as philosophers including Socrates, Plato, and others, received a portion of God's light. Moral truths were given to them by God to enlighten whole nations and to bring a higher level of understanding to individuals....
>
> Consistent with these truths, we believe that God has given and will give to all peoples sufficient knowledge to help them on their way to eternal salvation, either in this life or in the life to come....
>
> Our message therefore is one of special love and concern for the eternal welfare of all men and women, regardless of religious belief, race, or nationality, knowing that we are truly brothers and sisters because we are sons and daughters of the same Eternal Father.

This profound and inspired statement is pregnant with eternal truths. It speaks of the fatherhood of God, the brotherhood of man, revelation, prophets, knowledge, salvation, love, and other concepts worthy of our study. As one studies these concepts in the LDS public notice and compares them with concepts found in Islām, a number of similarities emerge. Though you have already reviewed some of these similarities, I would like to mention again two or three which I feel are most significant:

1. *Prophets and Revelation.* We read in the Qur'ān: "We believe in Allāh and that which is revealed unto us and that which was revealed to Abraham, and Ishmael, and Isaac, and Jacob, and the tribes, and that which Moses and Jesus received, and that which the prophets received from their Lord. We make no distinction between any of them, and unto him we have surrendered." (Qur'ān 2:136.) I do not know how much meaning is lost in translating these words from the Arabic language to the English tongue. Nonetheless, it is a beautiful and very profound statement.

In the Mormon or LDS faith, a comparable message about revelation is found: "We believe all that God has revealed, all that He does now reveal, and we believe that He will yet reveal many great and important things pertaining to the Kingdom of God." (Ninth article of faith.)

2. *Golden Rule.* Another similarity from the Qur'ān is: "Offer to men what thou desirest should be offered to thee; avoid doing to men what thou dost not wish to be done to thee." Our LDS version of the Golden Rule from the Book of Mormon reads: "Therefore, all things whatsoever ye would that men should do to you, do ye even so to them, for this is the law and the prophets." (3 Nephi 14:12.)

3. *Obedience and Works.* One of my favorite teachings taken from the Qur'ān deals with obedience and works:

Righteousness does not consist in whether you face towards the east or the west. The righteous man is he who believes in Allāh and the last day, in the angels and the scriptures and the prophets; who for the love of Allāh gives his wealth to his kinsfolk, to the orphans, to the needy, to the wayfarers and to the beggars, and for the redemption of captives; who attends to his prayers and pays the alms-tax; who is true to his promises and steadfast in trial and adversity and in times of war. Such are the true believers; such are the God-fearing." (Qur'ān 2:177.)

This teaching is similar in intent and content to two of the LDS Articles of Faith:

> We believe that . . . all mankind may be saved, by obedience to the laws and ordinances of the Gospel. . . .

> We believe in being honest, true, chaste, benevolent, virtuous, and in doing good to all men; indeed, we may say that we follow the admonition of Paul—We believe all things, we hope all things, we have endured many things, and hope to be able to endure all things. If there is anything virtuous, lovely, or of good report or praiseworthy, we seek after these things. (Third and thirteenth articles of faith.)

I need not say more about the similarities between the LDS-Christian beliefs and Islām. Most of you are far more knowledgeable on this subject than I. It is apparent, however, that Muslims and Mormons have much in common as their basic tenets of faith are compared. Quite obviously, God's love for both peoples has been expressed abundantly through the revealed word. Both peoples have been blessed to drink living waters from the divine fountain of eternal truth.

In my view, and my view may be somewhat limited, one of the greatest services extended by Muhammad was to purge his world of idolatry and center worship in one God. Perhaps the greatest service extended by the Prophet Joseph Smith was to reveal the nature of that true and living God. Together, the followers of Muhammad and those who accept Joseph Smith as the prophet of another restoration are expected to fulfill certain services for mankind. Is it not written that where much is given, much is expected? Is it not reasonable to expect those who have been blessed with light and knowledge to share it with others? Do not those who have been designated as receivers of truth have guardian responsibilities?

Permit me to suggest three duties to perform or challenges to be met by those who are standard-bearers for the true and living God. These selected challenges are not presented as being all-inclusive; yet I feel that they carry a sense of urgency and apply to both Islamic and Mormon peoples.

1. *Look to God—the fountain of truth.* We who are privileged to know God are obligated to introduce him to others so that they, too, might worship him in spirit and in truth. We must declare him to the world and invite men and women everywhere to look to him.

Materialism abounds in this modern world; and materialism, with all its evils, seems to breed false worship or no worship at all. In the Book of Mormon we read of a people who were not watchful in their worship. Consequently, they were led by evil influences to pervert their worship. (See Alma 31:8-36.)

The New Testament includes reference to a people who worshipped an unknown God. This misdirected worship, we are told, was done in ignorance and "God winked at" it. The account concludes: "But now [God] commandeth all men every where to repent." (Acts 17:30.) Not only must we engage in true worship, but we must assist others to do the same. We must help our brothers and sisters look to God and live.

2. *Share living waters.* As with the first, the second challenge applies to both the Muslim and Mormon peoples. It has to do with sharing the living waters or living truths which flow from the fountain of truth—God. Such sharing should be attended to with great earnestness or urgency.

I can best illustrate the urgency of sharing by telling you of an incident which occurred in Tasmania. Until recently, Hobart, a large, beautiful city in Tasmania, was divided. Half of the city's population was located on one side of a river channel and the other half of the population lived on the opposite side of the river. A few years ago, the city fathers determined that they had to do something to unite people. At great expense, they constructed a bridge which spanned the river and provided citizens with ready access to businesses and homes situated on both sides. All was fine with the bridge in place and the people were happy with the arrangement. However, late one night a ship much too large for the channel sailed up the river and collided with the bridge. This collision came without warning. The bridge was severed, traffic was interrupted, and many people were drowned. The following report of this terrible accident appeared in a local newspaper the next day:

> *Hobart.*—A man and his wife told today of their seconds of terror in a car hanging half over the collapsed span of the Tasman Bridge with a 50-metre drop to the water below.
> Mr. Frank Manley, 44, of Cambridge, his wife Sylvia, daughter Sharon, 16, and brother-in-law John Fitzgerald, 33, were driving along the mile-long bridge last night when suddenly there was no more roadway.

Today, Mr. Manley, still shaking, told how his wife screamed: "Quick, there's no bridge."

Mr. Manley said: "That was it. It was too late. We were partly over the bridge—almost half the car was hanging.

"Sylvia scrambled out and told Sharon and John in the back seat to get out quickly.

"It's a two-door car and when I opened my door there was nothing—just a sheer drop.

"I scrambled out with my back pressed hard against the pillar of the car and eased myself back on to the crumbling roadway," Mr. Manley said.

Mrs. Manley said: "As soon as I got out I ran down the road to tell people to stop.

"I just ran. I didn't look back. I tried to stop this bloke in a yellow car. He was going too fast. He nearly ran me down.

"I screamed at him and he slammed into the back of a car beside us and pushed him over the edge so that car was hanging like ours.

"Then came a bus. I waved. He turned his wheel and just missed a car."

The man in the other car left teetering over the brink is Mr. Murray Ling, of Bellerive.

He, his wife and two children were crossing the bridge when the lights went out.

"I stopped three feet from the gap—I think.

"I got out and started waving and a car came through fast in another lane.

"He thumped into another car, flew past and dropped over the edge."

I ask the question: What prompts women like Mrs. Manley and men like Mr. Ling to throw all caution aside and place their lives in the balance in situations like this? Were not their actions prompted by the feelings of brotherhood which seem to reside within all of us? Instinctively, it seems, men and women display a kinship of spirit when extreme crises arise and lives hang in the balance.

We occupy positions in this modern life much like those occupied by Mrs. Manley and Mr. Ling on a broken bridge. We too possess knowledge that will save. We too are in a position to warn and to share precious knowledge. For you see, we are familiar with the fountain of truth and we have tasted of living waters. We know what fate awaits those who race forward in life without faith, without purpose, and without morality. Unless we step forward and sound the signal, many will travel on dangerous paths, persist in reckless living, miss turns and bridges, and place their souls in jeopardy.

Much of Muhammad's and Christ's and Joseph Smith's teachings were in the form of warnings. Their warnings, particularly to the unbelievers, need continued voicing, perhaps more so today than at any time in history. Let us not forget that our lives are intertwined with the lives of others, and we can do few things of greater import than to share truth, even living waters, with others.

3. *Keep the waters pure.* We are guardians of truth and caretakers of the waters of life. Allow me to share with you another Mideast experience which gives insight into the task of keeping the waters of life pure.

While serving in the Middle East, I established a choice friendship with a prominent Arab official. He offered my companion and me the courtesies of his home and more. That is, he shared with us his profound wisdom and insights about religion gathered over a lifetime of living and serving. On one occasion, he expressed high regard for LDS teachings and practices. Among other things, he complimented the Church for its simplicity, the apparent purity of its doctrine, its service orientation, and the extreme devotion shown by its members. Then he questioned, "Can your faith survive the test of time?" He explained, "I would like to be around in another generation to observe your Church when it is established worldwide and broadly recognized, it is less persecuted and generally accepted, it can boast of meetingplaces and other evidence of affluence, and it has members of mixed backgrounds and races. If under conditions of public acceptance and prosperity you can preserve your purity of doctrine and integrity," he added, "the truthfulness of your claims will be verified."

I have pondered the words of my Muslim friend many times over the years. A generation has come and gone since he made his profound observation, and conditions have changed. I feel that my faith has weathered the storm and passed successfully the test of time. Yet I'm concerned about the continuing need to exercise care and to keep the waters pure. As the standards of men in the world deteriorate, we must be watchful in making certain that our attention to the standards of God does not lessen. While man's tendency to flaunt commandments seems to increase, our allegiance to holy laws must become stronger. When men seek to pervert or contaminate the wells of living water, we must guard the springs and guarantee their purity.

In conclusion, may I cite one more similarity between the Islamic and LDS faiths. First, I shall read from the Qur'ān: "Have you thought of him that denies the Last Judgment? . . . It is he who turns away the orphan and does not urge others to feed the poor. Woe to those who pray but are heedless in their prayer; who make a show of piety and give no alms to the destitute." (Qur'ān 107:1, 7.) What a pointed statement pertaining to the need for works to support admissions of faith!

Now, let us turn to some modern scriptures and receive corresponding instructions:

> If ye turn away the needy, and the naked, and visit not the sick and afflicted, and impart of your substance, if ye have, to those who stand in need—I say unto you, if ye do not any of these things, behold, your prayer is vain, and availeth you nothing, and ye are as hypocrites who do deny the faith.
>
> Therefore, if ye do not remember to be charitable, ye are as dross, which the refiners do cast out, (it being of no worth) and is trodden under foot of men." (Alma 34:28-29.)

These two sacred statements remind us all of the need to not only hear and believe, but *to do*. What good is achieved if we fail to translate instructions received in churches and mosques into righteous living? Why pray if the words spoken while on our knees are betrayed by the actions taken while on our feet? Of what value is a symposium like this if the added understanding between Muslims and Mormons does not strengthen intercultural and interfaith relationships?

It is my humble and sincere prayer that through this sharing experience the relationships between members of the Islamic and LDS faiths will be strengthened. I pray that what I have said and what other speakers have said will foster respect, correct misunderstandings, bridge differences, and heal divisions (if there are any) between both religions. I also pray that the proceedings of the conference will intensify the faith of all concerned.

Above all else, I hope you return home with a greater under-standing and appreciation of God's love for all mankind—a love that has been demonstrated throughout the ages as honest men have sought divine direction. May we bask in that holy love and invite others to do the same. Let us do all that is within our power to cause others to look to God so that they might live a fullness of life. May we share liberally the living waters and living truths, and may we strive individually and collectively to safeguard truth and keep the waters pure. This I ask in his holy name, amen.

Index